MISS JULI
AND OTHER PLAYS

JOHAN AUGUST STRINDBERG was born in Stockholm in 1849, the son of a shipping agent and a local serving-maid. After desultory studies in Uppsala, he wrote his first major play, *Master Olof*, in 1872. It was not performed until 1881, and supporting himself as a journalist, teacher, and librarian he eventually made his breakthrough in 1879 with *The Red Room*, a novel which owes much to Balzac and Dickens. He married his first wife, Siri von Essen, an actress, in 1877 and between 1883 and 1889 they lived abroad, in France, Switzerland, Germany, and Denmark. In 1884 he was tried for blasphemy over a collection of short stories, *Getting Married*. His international breakthrough came with the major naturalist plays of the 1880s, *The Father*, *Miss Julie*, and *Creditors*, but in 1892 he turned his back on Sweden and on the theatre and spent several more years abroad, devoting himself to the natural sciences and to alchemy. When he resumed writing plays in 1898 he produced twenty-two in four years. Several of these, including *To Damascus* (1898) and *A Dream Play* (1901), helped revolutionize the European theatre. He divorced Siri in 1891 but was married again, to the Austrian journalist Frida Uhl (1893–7) and the Norwegian actress Harriet Bosse (1901–4). Although best known for his plays, Strindberg was also a painter and a photographer as well as a prolific writer of novels, autobiographies, short stories, poetry, essays, and works of history, sociology, and linguistics. He was always a controversial figure in Swedish public life, and contributed, through his writing, to the discussion of a wide range of issues. On his sixty-third birthday he was honoured by a torchlight procession of workers and students, and awarded an 'Anti-Nobel Prize', raised by a national subscription. He died in Stockholm in 1912.

MICHAEL ROBINSON is Professor of Scandinavian Studies at the University of East Anglia. Formerly Professor of Drama and Theatre Arts at the University of Birmingham, he has published studies of Beckett and Strindberg and written widely on modern drama and theatre practice. He has also edited and translated a two-volume selection of Strindberg's Letters (1992) and an anthology of Strindberg's Essays (1996) for which he was awarded the Bernard Shaw Translation Prize in 1997.

OXFORD WORLD'S CLASSICS

*For over 100 years Oxford World's Classics have brought
readers closer to the world's great literature. Now with over 700
titles—from the 4,000-year-old myths of Mesopotamia to the
twentieth century's greatest novels—the series makes available
lesser-known as well as celebrated writing.*

*The pocket-sized hardbacks of the early years contained
introductions by Virginia Woolf, T. S. Eliot, Graham Greene,
and other literary figures which enriched the experience of reading.
Today the series is recognized for its fine scholarship and
reliability in texts that span world literature, drama and poetry,
religion, philosophy and politics. Each edition includes perceptive
commentary and essential background information to meet the
changing needs of readers.*

OXFORD WORLD'S CLASSICS

——

AUGUST STRINDBERG

Miss Julie
and Other Plays

——

Translated with an Introduction and Notes by
MICHAEL ROBINSON

OXFORD
UNIVERSITY PRESS

OXFORD

UNIVERSITY PRESS

Great Clarendon Street, Oxford OX2 6DP

Oxford University Press is a department of the University of Oxford.
It furthers the University's objective of excellence in research, scholarship,
and education by publishing worldwide in

Oxford New York

Athens Auckland Bangkok Bogotá Buenos Aires Calcutta
Cape Town Chennai Dar es Salaam Delhi Florence Hong Kong Istanbul
Karachi Kuala Lumpur Madrid Melbourne Mexico City Mumbai
Nairobi Paris São Paulo Singapore Taipei Tokyo Toronto Warsaw

with associated companies in Berlin Ibadan

Oxford is a registered trade mark of Oxford University Press
in the UK and in certain other countries

Published in the United States
by Oxford University Press Inc., New York

All enquiries regarding performance of these translations should be
directed to the Rights Department, Oxford University Press
at the address above

The moral rights of the author have been asserted

Database right Oxford University Press (maker)

First published as an Oxford World's Classics paperback 1998
Reissued 2008

British Library Cataloguing in Publication Data

Data available

Library of Congress Cataloging in Publication Data

Strindberg, August, 1849–1912.
[Plays. English. Selections]
Miss Julie and other plays / August Strindberg; translated with
an introduction by Michael Robinson.
(Oxford world's classics)
Contents: The father—Miss Julie—The dance of death—A
dream play—The ghost sonata.
1. Strindberg, August, 1849–1912—Translations into English.
I. Robinson, Michael, 1944– . II. Title. III. Series: Oxford
world's classics (Oxford University Press)
PT9811.A3R63 1998   839.72'6—dc21   98–15458

ISBN 978-0-19-953804-1

1

Typeset by Pure Tech India Ltd, India
Printed in Great Britain by
Clays Ltd, St Ives plc

CONTENTS

ABBREVIATIONS

The following abbreviations are used throughout this volume:

ASB   *August Strindbergs brev*, 20 volumes to date, edited by Torsten Eklund and Björn Meidal (Stockholm, 1948–).

SgNM   refers to the collection of Strindberg's drafts, notes, and manuscripts deposited in the Royal Library in Stockholm. Thus SgNM 15: 4, 7 refers to File 15, folder 4, page (or item) 7.

SE   August Strindberg, *Selected Essays*, edited and translated by Michael Robinson (Cambridge, 1996).

SL   August Strindberg, *Selected Letters*, selected, edited, and translated by Michael Robinson, 2 vols. (London and Chicago, 1992).

SS   Strindberg's *Samlade Skrifter*, edited by John Landquist (Stockholm, 1912–20).

SV   denotes a volume in the ongoing edition of Strindberg's *Samlade Verk*. The five plays translated here have all been edited by Gunnar Ollén except for *The Dance of Death*, for which Hans Lindström has been responsible.

INTRODUCTION

In Sweden, Strindberg's literary breakthrough came not with a play, but with *The Red Room*, a satirical novel, published in 1879. This often amusing Dickensian narrative was remarkable at the time for the immediacy of its language, its impressionist cityscapes of Stockholm on the cusp of modernity, and the candour with which it portrayed different aspects of late-nineteenth-century Swedish society. But while it is still widely regarded as the first authentically modern work in Swedish literature, it remains largely unknown outside Scandinavia. This is unfortunate since, in being both amusing and prose fiction, it challenges the received image of Strindberg as the self-obsessed and self-dramatizing author of a few bleak plays which sometimes make for effective theatre, but which are otherwise flawed by their author's pathological misogyny, his abiding failure to distinguish himself and the often mundane events of his life from his writing and thus achieve the balance necessary to successful art, and by an unstable temperament that all too often degenerates into real mental illness. In fact this is an alarmingly partial view which, ironically, fails to distinguish between the writer and his work, and assumes that because the protagonist of a play like *The Father* or the narrator of an autobiographical fiction like *Inferno* is arguably deranged, their author must be too.

Alongside the plays, a comprehensive introduction to Strindberg's work would therefore need to assess his achievements in many other fields—as a novelist, short-story writer, historian, poet, autobiographer, essayist—and to recognize that in every one of these genres he demonstrates an artistry that goes far beyond what is often regarded as merely the direct transposition of his lived experience into words. It would need, too, to consider his work as a painter, which not only contributed much to the development of his new writing style in the mid-1890s but also commands attention in its own right for the way in which it foreshadowed developments in modern art.

Nevertheless, Strindberg's international reputation undoubtedly rests upon his plays, especially the five translated here. Like most nineteenth-century Scandinavian dramatists, including Ibsen, he began by writing plays on historical subjects, and his early masterpiece, *Master Olof* (1872), was the first of what was to become, by 1909, a sequence of twelve dramas on Swedish history which remain the most important contribution to the genre since Schiller. Also like Ibsen, he turned to the realistic treatment of contemporary subjects in prose only in middle age (*Marauders*, which preceded *The Father* by a year, was written in 1886). Unlike Ibsen, however, who spent the remainder of his career exploring the possibilities of the theatrical form that he had evolved in a play like *A Doll's House* with almost metronomic regularity, Strindberg produced his dramas in fits and starts, and after writing several of the key works of psychological naturalism during the 1880s he abandoned the theatre for several years, only to confound his critics by re-emerging in 1898 with the first part of *To Damascus*, in which he employed what was, for the period, a radically new and innovatory dramaturgy which seemed to mark a decisive break with his earlier achievement in *The Father* and *Miss Julie*.

The Father

The Father was in fact the first of Strindberg's plays to be performed outside Scandinavia, by Otto Brahm's Berlin Freie Bühne in 1890. He wrote it in February 1887 while living in Bavaria, in the fourth year of a self-imposed exile from Sweden following the animosity aroused there by a volume of satires on the contemporary Swedish establishment, *The New Kingdom* (1882), and the negative criticism provoked by his two-volume history, *The Swedish People* (1880–2), in which he sought to write the history not of Sweden's kings, but of the common people. He had subsequently become still further estranged from his native country by the trial he faced for blasphemy in 1884. This arose from some comments on the sacrament of 'that rabble rouser' Jesus Christ in his collection of stories *Getting Married* (1884); although he was acquitted, the trial confirmed his reputation as a dangerous writer, and he now found it difficult to publish his books in Sweden. Of greater significance, so far as the direction of his future work is concerned, was his conviction that the whole affair had been a conspiracy by the movement for women's emancipation. He therefore remained abroad, mostly in France and Switzerland, and made a precarious living during the middle years of the decade, during which he wrote the four-volume autobiographical fiction

The Son of a Servant, whose title stresses his identification with his mother, a former serving-maid, and a sociological study of the French provinces, *Among French Peasants*.

The Father therefore represents a change of direction on Strindberg's part, a move away from what he later described as 'ephemeral political and social so-called questions' towards 'artistic-psychological writing' (ASB VI, 335). For more than a decade what is called the Modern Breakthrough in Scandinavian literature had been dominated by writing that sought to 'subject problems to debate', according to a formulation of the Danish critic Georg Brandes in 1871. Strindberg himself could regard the 'theatre as a weapon' with which to combat 'the bluestockings' (ASB VI, 137), and in some respects *The Father*, like *Miss Julie*, is associated with the ongoing discussion of the woman question, sexual morality, and marriage which was widespread in Scandinavia—Ibsen's *A Doll's House* and *Ghosts* are obvious examples of this trend. In Strindberg's case, though, the debating of such problems, to which he readily devoted a collection of stories like *Getting Married*, is rarely the overriding concern of his best plays; there, his immediate interest is rather in the shifting psychological states of his principal characters.

Nor is *The Father* the complete naturalist drama it is often claimed to be. Strindberg had Zola's manifesto *La Naturalisme au théâtre* (1880) in mind when writing the play, and was certainly attracted by the experimental method of Flaubert, Zola, and the Goncourt brothers, with its pretensions to scientific rigour and its claim to objectivity and impartiality. During the 1880s he argued that literature 'ought to emancipate itself from art entirely and become a science' (SL 1, 202), and in *The Son of a Servant* he had sought 'to emancipate literature from art' by taking 'the corpse of the person I have known best and learnt anatomy, physiology, psychology, and history from the carcass' (ASB V, 344). But *The Father* demonstrates an impatience with the detailed accumulation of information about a character's heredity and environment that naturalism, as defined by Zola, required. The density of circumstantial detail in which Ibsen immerses his characters in *Rosmersholm* or *Ghosts* makes the few stage properties specified by Strindberg at the start of his play seem perfunctory, while the majority of his characters are identified merely in terms of their profession (The Captain, The Doctor, The Parson) or by charactonyms (Nöjd and Svärd—see notes to pp. 2 and 23).

Consequently, the milieu in which events unfold has little of the determining significance normally expected of naturalism; nor is the audience given much information about the characters' pasts, apart from a few passing remarks on the Captain's difficult upbringing and on Laura's behaviour as a child. Indeed, observing as it does the three unities of time, place, and action, *The Father* is in many respects a very traditionally structured, Aristotelian play. In raising the question of paternity, the Nöjd episode with which it opens prefigures the principal action and functions as a conventional expository prologue. Even the way that the text is printed, with a new scene for each entry or exit, recalls the conventions of the classical theatre.

In fact Strindberg was interested in what he called 'the greater Naturalism which seeks out those points where the great battles take place', rather than the objective treatment of 'the much-longed-for ordinary case . . . which is so banal, so meaningless . . . [and] which is so beloved by those devoid of personality, who lack temperament' (SE 78). For him the scientific approach entailed a conception of the writer as a vivisector engaged in anatomizing his characters and consequently, since he believed that 'A writer is only a reporter of what he has lived' (SL I, 38) and generally took his material from life, this also meant the ruthless and frequently painful analysis of those among whom he lived, as well as of himself. Thus, in *The Father* he created a kind of laboratory situation in which he explored certain possibilities inherent in his own deteriorating marriage to his first wife, Siri von Essen, whom he had married in 1876, and whose career as an actress foundered after the births of their children and the years spent abroad with the demanding and hypersensitive Strindberg. He is not the play's protagonist, and nor is Laura Siri, but the play stages a conflict between two figures in which their private dilemma was recognizable, even though he did not really doubt the parentage of his own (three) children or really believe that Siri was seeking to have him declared insane. Nevertheless, as frequently happened where his literary works are concerned, the intense experience of writing the play and taking on the Captain's role led him to question the borderline between fact and fiction. As he wrote, in a frequently quoted letter addressed as a kind of testament to the young Swedish writer, Axel Lundegård:

It seems to me as if I'm walking in my sleep; as if my life and writing have got all jumbled up. I don't know if *The Father* is a work of literature or if my life has been; but I feel as if, probably quite soon, at a given moment, it will suddenly break upon me, and then I shall collapse either into madness and remorse, or suicide. Through much writing, my life has become a shadow life; I no longer feel as if I am walking the earth but floating weightless in an atmosphere not of air but darkness. (SL 1, 255).

This is the danger of Strindberg's method—as of any actor who loses himself too deeply in a role—and shortly afterwards he demonstrated the way in which life could draw its inspiration from literature as readily as literature might draw upon life by consulting a specialist about his mental health: apparently he was now convinced that Siri really had assumed Laura's role, and was trying to have him certified.

Strindberg's 'greater naturalism' is therefore not a slice of life nor even the carefully crafted expository method of Ibsen, in which the long reach of the past is uncovered in a present crisis; but instead the intense, immediate drama associated with what he called 'the battle of the brains' (*hjärnornas kamp*). This is fought, not with theatrical swords or daggers, but with the equally lethal mental cut and thrust of two implacably hostile minds, bound to each other by desire and hatred. It is a battle in which one of them ultimately destroys the other's will and commits what Strindberg, in writing about Ibsen's *Rosmersholm*, called 'soul murder' (*själamord*), by which he meant the kind of semi-conscious, self-preserving destruction of the hated other: the way that Laura penetrates beneath the skin and destroys the Captain, or in *Miss Julie*, the way that Jean first seduces Julie and then reduces her to suicide by way of suggestion.

What is also new is the savagery of this predominantly psychological conflict and the complexity of its motivation, especially when internalized in an individual. Through his self-analysis in *The Son of a Servant*, Strindberg had come to see identity as continually shifting and discontinuous, both where an individual's relationship to the various people encountered in society is concerned (hence the way in which the Captain is depicted in a series of scenes with different antagonists) and in terms of the physiological and psychological forces that have contributed to its making. In describing the kind of 'characterless character', or *multiplicité du moi*, that is consequently required of the new drama, he drew heavily on the contemporary French and English psychologists whom he read with enthusiasm during the 1880s. In particular, he found 'a complete diagnosis of myself' (ASB V, 333) in Henry Maudsley's *The Pathology of Mind* (1879), and confirmation for his sense of the self as an aggregate of atoms or ensemble of instincts in Théodule Ribot's *Les Maladies de la volunté* (1883) and *Les Maladies de la personnalité* (1885). Accounts of Jean Martin Charcot's use of hypnosis in the treatment of hysterics, and his subsequent reading of Hippolyte Bernheim's *De la suggestion et de ses applications à la thérapeutique* (1886—see note to p. 60), which emphasized the suggestive influence that one mind can have upon another, led Strindberg to apply these ideas in the naturalist plays, for example, in the representation of the Captain's supposed abulia or the way in which Laura gains an ascendancy over him by means of suggestion.

Again, unlike the meticulously observed characters of naturalism, the two central characters here can be seen simply as representatives of male and female principles. While performances of the play frequently undermine such crude sexual politics, the Captain as a military man and a scientist represents masculinity, with its codes of the heroic and the rational while Laura, with her deviousness, corresponds to what nineteenth-century misogyny considered 'the instinctive villainy' of woman. This contributes in turn to the way in which the contemporary Darwinian imagery of the play concerning a perpetual struggle and the survival of the strongest or fittest ('If we really are descended from the apes, it must have been from two different species', the Captain remarks at one point) resonates well beyond a purely naturalistic framework, engendering the many references throughout the play to classic models of heroic masculinity and feminine deceit: the Captain, for example, is compared to Agamemnon, Hercules, and Samson, which casts Laura as Clytemnestra, Omphale, and Delilah.

Miss Julie

Miss Julie, like *The Father*, is remarkable for the rapidity with which the action unfolds within a concentrated formal structure. The opening words, 'Miss Julie's quite crazy tonight; absolutely crazy!', precipitate the audience directly into the action, which develops with virtually no exposition, and then holds and intensifies their attention as the protagonist is caught in an elaborately motivated trap which hinges on her offstage coupling with her servant Jean, then tightens its grip until the release of her suicide and the final line: 'It's horrible! But there is no other way! Go!' According to Strindberg, this form of play, which lasts approximately ninety minutes and is performed without an interval, 'make[s] the pain brief, [and] lets the action spend itself in a single movement' (SL 1, 291). He would employ it again to great effect in his next play, *Creditors*, and the four Chamber Plays of 1907.

Miss Julie was written in about two weeks during late July and early August 1888. A letter to his publisher, Bonnier, proudly claims for it the honour of being 'the first Naturalistic Tragedy in Swedish Drama' (SL 1, 280), and it represents Strindberg's major achievement as a naturalist writer for the theatre—so 'naturalistic', indeed, where its language is concerned that Bonnier considered the play too 'risky' and refused to publish it. It had to wait eighteen years for its first professional production in Sweden and an unexpurgated text was not published or performed there until well into the following century.

The naturalist credentials of *Miss Julie* are outlined in the Preface, which remains the single most important manifesto of naturalism in the theatre. There Strindberg discusses both his choice of subject—a case from life documented in great detail, which illustrates the way an individual behaves under the influence of inherited, environmental, and historical forces—and its treatment, since he recognizes that to realize the impact of these forces on the characters entails a revolution in staging (the stage properties, for example, must be substantial and real), and consequently in the kind of acting required to render the play plausible and effective.

As well as proclaiming a new theatre and helping Strindberg to rationalize what he had achieved in a play that nevertheless ultimately eludes the formulas he uses to describe it, the Preface was partly written to convince Zola of his naturalist credentials. Strindberg had sent him a copy of his own French translation of *The Father*, in the hope that he would promote it, but Zola's response was lukewarm. Although he praised the play in general terms for its 'daring' idea, which is presented to 'powerful and disquieting effect', he found the characterization abstract. According to Zola, Strindberg's figures lacked 'a complete social setting' (*un état civil complet*). Hence the insistence here, in both the Preface and the play, on the multiplicity of motives that drive Julie. Unlike the Captain in *The Father*, whose fate is only loosely attributed to his impoverished childhood and his experience of women, what happens to her is very fully explained by the combination of environmental and inherited circumstances that Strindberg catalogues in the Preface (thirteen in all, see p. 58), and on which he expanded in a letter to Georg Brandes, who was not the last to find the ending problematic: 'The suicide is properly motivated: her dislike of life, the longing for a family to die out in its last defective individual, the aristocratic feeling of shame at intercourse with a lower species; more immediately: the suggestions from the blood of the bird, the presence of the razor, the fear of the theft's discovery, and the command by the stronger will (primarily the servant, more remotely the Count's bell). Note that left to herself, Miss Julie would have lacked the strength, but now she is driven and led on by the numerous motives' (SL 1, 295–6). Given these circumstances, Julie is lost from the moment she steps down both literally and metaphorically into the unfamiliar habitat of the kitchen where the prosaic Kristin holds sway (it is her terrain, and she even outfaces Jean there). But the inevitability of her end, which leaves her to take the responsibility for what has happened even though she never willed it, does not belie the complexity of Strindberg's attitude to Julie. The hostility with which he discusses her case in the Preface is at odds with the benediction of the sunlight that engulfs her at the end of the play, and even in the Preface he is unsure whether an audience ought to respond to her fate with the pity and fear that Aristotle attributed to tragedy or the indifference of the natural scientist. Similarly, Jean is described as a sexual aristocrat on the one hand, and depicted as a slave in thrall to his master on the other. However, any ambiguity enhances rather than endangers the play's impact, and for all its documentary importance the Preface, which was of course written after the play, is in any case a simplification of the text it introduces.

In *Miss Julie* the 'battle of the brains' is fought not only in the sphere of sexual politics but also in terms of class, and the way in which Strindberg explains this conflict changes significantly even as he is writing. As usual, the play is a snapshot of Strindberg's intellectual life at the time of its creation. The final scene, for example, demonstrates his continued belief in the power of waking suggestion that he derived from Bernheim, while his debt to Darwin shows in the simplified scientism of his references to 'the process of differentiation' or to Jean as the founder of a 'species', who survives because he can adapt and change whereas Julie, bound by the rigid conventions of her upbringing and moribund class, has to die. But the Preface also betrays the recent, not yet wholly assimilated impact on Strindberg of the philosophy of Nietzsche, which he had been introduced to by Georg Brandes. When Brandes loaned Strindberg *Beyond Good and Evil*, the response was prompt and ecstatic. 'The uterus of my mental world has received a tremendous ejaculation of sperm from Friedrich Nietzsche, so that I feel like a bitch with a full belly,' Strindberg exclaimed in September 1888. 'He's the man for me!' (SL 1, 283). Brandes also drew Strindberg to Nietzsche's attention and the misogynistic philosopher was greatly impressed by *The Father* and *Getting Married*. Strindberg went on to read *The Wagner Case* (1888), and Nietzsche subsequently sent him *The Genealogy of Morals* (1887) and *Twilight of the Idols* (1888), which seemed to endorse his own developing ideas about the repressive nature of Christianity, the relativity of truth, and the relationship between conscious and unconscious and instinct and intellect. They also confirmed him in his present demand for a 'transvaluation of all values', and supported the arguments he had already advanced in the *Vivisections* of 1887 concerning the decisive battle of the brains currently being fought between the exceptional individual and the mundane representatives of everyday mediocrity. And like Strindberg, Nietzsche was also an acute psychologist. Their mutual enthusiasm resulted in a brief correspondence that was only cut short by Nietzsche's descent into the insanity that already manifests itself in his last brief letter to Strindberg, signed 'The Crucified'. But notwithstanding his references to the nobility of the 'Aryan' in the Preface, and to the emphasis he places on Jean as the masculine aristocrat, Strindberg's play ultimately transcends the limitations of these terms as well.

This is no doubt due, in part, to the complexity of the personal experience which he brought to the writing of the play, a complexity which illuminates his employment of autobiographical elements in the plays generally. According to the Preface, the text is properly naturalistic because it is based on a 'real incident'. Numerous real-life sources have been suggested, both by Strindberg and others. To his contemporaries and the majority of his critics, the immediate inspiration for the calamitous coupling between Julie and Jean would seem to have been his own relationship as the self-styled 'Son of a Servant' with Siri von Essen, who came from an old Finland-Swedish family of landed gentry and had been a baroness, married to a Swedish aristocrat, when Strindberg first met her. In *A Madman's Defence*, the autobiographical fiction in which he had only recently portrayed their relationship, Strindberg describes the sexual conquest of the aristocratic Maria by his alter ego, Axel, in terms and imagery similar to those applied to Jean and Julie in the play: 'the son of the people had conquered the white skin, the commoner had won the love of a girl of breeding, the swineherd had mixed his blood with that of a princess.' And Siri, by playing the role of Julie in the play's Copenhagen première, seemed to compound an identification which, twenty years later and in appropriately biblical terms, Strindberg would reaffirm when he thanked Manda Björling, the actress who created the role at the Intimate Theatre, for her 'beautiful portrait of a poor person, to whom I was perhaps too hard in my own hard days, when everyone's hand was raised against me, and mine against everyone' (SL 2, 794).

But another impetus for the play came from the bizarre relation-ship that Strindberg witnessed between an eccentric Danish woman, who called herself the Countess Frankenau, and her steward, Ludvig Hansen, who were living at Skovlyst, the half-ruined manor house at Holte, some twenty kilometres north of Copenhagen, where *Miss Julie* was written. Strindberg assumed that Hansen was having an affair with the Countess, when in fact he was her illegitimate half-brother, a relationship they sought to conceal out of respect for their dead father's memory. Hansen also had an interest in hypnotism in common with Strindberg, but the friendship they struck up was soon complicated by Strindberg's brief sexual entanglement with Hansen's young sister, Martha Magdalene, and it ended in mutual recrim-inations. Strindberg took to carrying a revolver in self-defence and accused Hansen of being a gypsy, a degenerate Nietzschean pariah, and a thief, while Hansen tried to blackmail Strindberg and charged him with corrupting a minor. Both the disgust which Julie feels after she has coupled with Jean (she regards it as an act of bestiality) and the recognition throughout the play of the irresistible power of instinct-ual sexual feelings may in part be traced to these events.

For the manner of Julie's death, however, Strindberg found a precedent in the suicide of the eminent Swedish novelist Victoria

Benedictsson. On the night of 21 July 1888 she had cut her throat with a razor at the Hotel Leopold in Copenhagen, following a previous attempt that January which Strindberg had witnessed. Like Julie, Benedictsson had been dressed as a boy as a child, in her case by a father who also taught her to ride and shoot, and in Strindberg's eyes her pseudonym, 'Ernst Ahlgren', only confirmed that she was what the Preface terms a 'half-woman'.

But identifications do not stop there. He also claimed in two letters 'about the real Miss Julie', that 'Miss Julie . . . is about how [a general's daughter] Miss Rudbeck seduced her stable-boy' (ASB VII, 142), and ended up not dead, but 'a barmaid' in Stockholm (ASB VII, 126). There are also literary sources, including the novels of the Goncourt brothers that Strindberg singles out in the Preface as having attracted him 'more than anything else in contemporary literature', as well as Jens Peter Jacobsen's novel *Fru Marie Grubbe* (1876), the story (also taken from life) of a seventeenth-century Danish noblewoman and her relationship with a coarse and brutal groom. Strindberg so admired Jacobsen's novel that in the early 1880s he considered turning it into a play (ASB II, 272, 328, 370).

Finally, there is a deep affinity between Strindberg himself and Julie, whose character accords with his recent self-analysis in *The Son of a Servant*, where Johan, his pseudonymous self, is, like Julie, 'an ensemble of reflexes, a complex of urges, drives, and instincts, [which are] alternately suppressed and unleashed' (SV 20, 166–7). Both Johan and Julie are presented as 'characterless characters', or what the Preface, in one of the first attempts to account for the *bricolage* of the modern self, calls 'conglomerates of past and present stages of culture, bits out of books and newspapers, scraps of humanity, torn shreds of once fine clothing now turned to rags, exactly as the human soul is patched together'.

Nevertheless, as Strindberg urged one of his translators, it is important to 'read my . . . dramas only as that; they are mosaic work . . . from my own and other people's lives, but please don't take them as autobiography or confessions. Whatever doesn't correspond with the facts is poetry, not lies' (SL 2, 736–7). And where *Miss Julie* is concerned, the complexity underlying her identity is further enriched by the range of associations that she and Jean bear. Not only are they the swineherd and princess of fairy tale but Actaeon and Diana (the name of Julie's thoroughbred bitch which mates with the gatekeeper's mutt and prefigures her own fall, as the Nöjd episode foreshadows the principal action of *The Father*), Joseph and Potiphar's Wife and—even more ominously—Adam and Eve.[1] As Jean makes plain in the long, seductive speech to Julie with which the first phase of the play approaches its climax, the Count's estate represents the Garden of Paradise where young boys not only scrump apples but also dream of possessing beautiful young girls, and the play as a whole, in which Julie steps down from her elevated position into the mire of human sexual relations, is a rerun of the Fall of Man. The patriarchal Count, whose 'unhappy spirit hover(s) above and behind it all', is thus an Old Testament deity, kept artfully offstage but whose omnipresence makes itself felt through the riding boots that Jean has to polish, the bell at which he cringes, and the speaking tube via which, at the end of the play, the Count announces himself from on high to the fallen couple on stage.

The Dance of Death I

At first sight, Part 1 of *The Dance of Death*, which Strindberg wrote during October 1900, appears to be another naturalist play—a bleaker, more sardonic version of *The Father* perhaps. But this is seriously to misread the kind of drama that Strindberg began to write around the turn of the century when, in only four years, he deluged the Swedish theatre with eighteen new plays. This abundance was all the more striking since after 1892, when he completed a series of short plays on contemporary subjects and the fairy-tale play *The Keys of Heaven*, he had written nothing for the theatre until the first part of *To Damascus* in 1898.

Indeed, apart from a few essays there were no literary works of any significance during this period. Instead he devoted himself to a range of pursuits, including photography, painting, the natural sciences, and alchemy. The motives for this turn away from literature are complex. His disillusion with the kind of self-exploitative naturalist writing in which he implicated other people was probably one of the most important, and before returning to literature he needed to find a new moral and aesthetic basis on which to work. He was also

---

[1] In *A Madman's Defence* Strindberg's autobiographical hero identifies his mistress with the goddess Diana and is, like Jean, offended by the notion that she may regard him sexually as a reluctant Joseph.

depressed after the break-up of his marriage to Siri von Essen and separation from his children, to whom he was deeply attached. There was, too, a sense in which he was written out, and had exhausted the material exploited in composing his previous books. Quite simply, he needed to accumulate a further supply of experience on which to draw. Sweden, too, had proved a disappointment following his return from self-imposed exile in 1889. The theatres showed little interest in his plays, and the kind of scientific naturalism with which he was associated was in the process of being supplanted by the inward-looking neo-romanticism of a new generation of authors. In any case, imbued as he was with vestiges of his youthful pietism, he still found writing, which came so easily to him and gave him pleasure, problematic. As he told his brother, Axel, 'I still have probably 30 years to live. That's a whole lifetime, and Literature is something one should practise in one's youth . . . Science stands higher, and surely we must grow! not sink to the level of a literary man who has written himself dry' (ASB 7, 352).

Strindberg therefore turned his back on Sweden and went abroad again. He spent the following six years mainly in Berlin and Paris, but also in Austria at the home of Frida Uhl, the young Austrian journalist whom he married in 1893 and divorced in 1897—another subsequently productive experience where his writing was concerned. He consorted with other makers of the emerging modern movement in the arts like the painters Edvard Munch and Paul Gauguin and the composer Frederick Delius, but much of his time was spent, in great poverty, among a pot-pourri of alchemists, theosophists, Rosicrucians, and both white and black magicians like Gérard Encausse (Papus),[2] Allan Kardec, and Éliphas Lévi who occupied a prominent place in *fin-de-siècle* Paris, where symbolism had superseded naturalism as the most modern of artistic movements. Strindberg once claimed that Lévi's *Key to the Mysteries* could unlock all the signs and symbols in the *Occult Diary* he began to keep in 1896.

It was in Paris, between 1894 and 1896, that he underwent what, following his highly partial account of these years in the autobiographical fiction *Inferno* (1897), is generally called his 'Inferno

---

[2] Strindberg was so sanguine about Papus's powers that he claims to 'have suggested to [him] that I should "kill" myself with Cyanide and he recall me to life following my prescription; but he's reluctant to do so because a medical commission would only say: "All right, but as you see, he wasn't really dead"' (SL 2, 850).

Crisis'. Although this entailed moments of great mental suffering and instability, it may also be seen as another psychological experiment in which, sometimes with the assistance of alcohol and drugs, he organized a descent into himself to explore extreme psychological states, as well as an enormous act of will in which he fashioned himself anew. Strindberg exchanged the atheist standpoint with which he had been experimenting during the previous decade for a syncretic religion composed of elements from various Eastern religions and aspects of mystical experience as well as Christianity.[3] A complete account of these years would also require a detailed analysis of the way in which Strindberg used his painting, as described in the essay 'The New Arts! or The Role of Chance in Artistic Creation' (see SE 103–7), to transform naturalism into a new, associational *art fortuite* which was eventually to facilitate the emergence of his later modernist theatre.

It would also need to affirm the importance for these plays of the eighteenth-century scientist and mystic Emanuel Swedenborg (1688–1772), whose theory of 'correspondences' between the visible world here below and a higher world otherwise inaccessible to the living also informed the thought and sometimes the practice of Balzac, Baudelaire, and Yeats. In such works as *Heaven and Hell* Swedenborg presented Strindberg with a vision of the world that tallied with his own experience during the Inferno crisis, and helped form his later religious standpoint. So far as the plays are concerned, Swedenborg also provided him with a means of organizing his own experience of the earth as a kind of penal colony where the individual undergoes a period of purgation, or what Swedenborg calls 'vastation'; a satisfactory way of accounting for his fascination with the natural world, abandoning the naturalistic determinism in which the individual was irrevocably a part of nature, in favour of a universe ordered and governed by analogy or correspondences; and a basis for a new dramaturgy. The last is evident in the way that the vastation experience could be employed to dramatize a character's reversal of fortune; thus it becomes a central structuring device in many of the later plays, including, in *The Dance of Death*, the wordless scene in

---

[3] The best account remains Gunnar Brandell's *Strindberg in Inferno* (Cambridge, Mass., 1974), which shows that he also had recourse to the ideas and cosmologies of (among others) Hesiod, Dante, the Eddas, the Kabbala, and the *Metamorphoses* of Ovid, as well as to an idiosyncratic interpretation of contemporary scientific thought.

which Edgar tries to divest himself of his earthly goods. Moreover, Swedenborg's theory of correspondences allows him to see a parallel between his own artistic practice and that of the artist God whose hand Strindberg now discerned in every detail of the universe. For where until recently he had experienced only an anarchical chaos, he now perceived, as he emerged from the Inferno crisis, an underlying coherence in which he could discern a signifying order in nature on the one hand, and a moral order in the life of the individual on the other. As the protagonist of *To Damascus I* observes: 'Life—which before was a great nonsense—has taken on a purpose and I now see a design where once I only saw mere chance' (SV 39, 18).

On the one hand, therefore, *The Dance of Death* depicts a marital inferno with great realism, and numerous critics, who never tire of pointing to Strindberg's sister, Anna, and her husband, Hugo von Philp, as the models for Alice and Edgar, are in this respect correct in regarding it as a forerunner of Eugene O'Neill's *Long Day's Journey into Night* (1956) and Edward Albee's *Who's Afraid of Virginia Woolf?* (1962). Strindberg had spent the first two summers following his return to Stockholm in 1899 with the Philps at Furusund in the Stockholm archipelago. Like Alice, Anna had given up a career (in her case musical) to marry, and in January 1900 the irreligious Philp suffered a heart attack, and Strindberg sat up with him all night discussing death. That Strindberg was also deeply attracted to his sister gives an additional resonance to Kurt's role, and these links between life and art could easily be augmented (for example, the Philps celebrated their silver wedding a few days before Strindberg began work on the play). However, we also need to recognize that, as usual, Strindberg had numerous other models in mind, and that the finished play stands apart from them all. In particular, we should be aware of the way dialogue, setting and characters function on a symbolic as well as a realistic level. When, for example, Edgar asks Alice, 'Won't you play something for me?' in the play's opening line, the word 'play' has associations with his wife's past as an actress whose career marriage has cut short, and to the role-playing in which they both indulge. As to setting, the circular granite island fortress in which they are confined is only nominally a realistic location, and is designed to conjure up an image that is essentially the crux of the situation depicted in the play. As Strindberg observes in a manuscript note: 'If this existence is already purgatory or an inferno for crimes we have previously committed we are all demons, here to torment each other, and when we are driven against our will to do evil, we are only doing our duty, but suffer all the same from the fact that we have done wrong. This is the double curse of existence. No one has the opportunity of tormenting one another as thoroughly as a man and a woman who love one another (= hate one another)' (SgNM 6:14, 4). Thus, the curtain rises upon the red light of the setting sun glinting on the sabre of the sentry on watch outside the window. That he is there to guard those within as much as to protect them from a threat from without is a possibility which Edgar's reference to 'Baron Bluebeard with the maiden in his tower; and outside the sentry marches up and down with his sabre drawn, to guard the fair virgin' later confirms. It is an evening in autumn ('Outside and in,' as the Captain lugubriously remarks), and the surrounding sea is calm and still, although the gun batteries, seem to be defending those within from a hostile force without. Taken together, what is evoked in a multiplicity of ways is the fact of ageing, or extinguished vitality, and the imminent threat of death, not least in the appearance of the ailing Captain, who at the outset offers an image of impotent manhood. He has laid aside his parade uniform and is now dressed in a worn, undress uniform and fingering a spent cigar, all libidinal passion seemingly spent. Situated on the margin between land and sea, or life and death, the tower is thus a precarious last post where the Captain is poised for departure on that final journey which Strindberg so often portrayed in terms of a sea voyage.

Moreover, when Alice remarks of their situation, 'This is hell!', her words are not simply a commonplace; she is defining precisely where she and Edgar are confined, condemned to torment each other infernally until death, on an island from which they cannot escape. And to reinforce both this sense of enclosure and the feeling of descent into the self that they also present, the form of the play is, as many of Strindberg's post-Inferno dramas, circular rather than linear. Visually, at least, it ends as it began with Alice and Edgar alone and facing each other on stage, even though, given Strindberg's Swedenborgian scheme, Edgar has in fact undergone a crucial change. Having been briefly 'on the other side' following his heart attack, he is now dimly aware of a spiritual dimension and has consequently abandoned the materialism which made him regard death as leading only to 'a barrow load full [of muck] to wheel out and spread on the garden'.

The formal appropriateness of this ending is reason enough for the play to stand alone, unaccompanied by the much shorter and weaker *Dance of Death II* which Strindberg wrote later that winter. The drama as translated here was originally conceived as a single play, and it is likely that the sequel was written primarily to provide a more conciliatory ending after his German translator, Emil Schering, suggested that the first part was too grim to be performed as it stood. In fact, Schering was overlooking a vein of grotesque tragicomedy in the text that was to become commonplace in twentieth-century theatre. As Kurt remarks of Edgar, 'He'd be comic if he weren't tragic,' while in his concluding reflections on the action Edgar himself remarks that 'When it's a joke [life] can be most painful, when it's serious it can be quite tranquil and pleasant.'

A Dream Play

In the Preface to *Miss Julie* Strindberg drew attention to the way in which 'the dialogue . . . wanders, providing itself in the opening scene with material that is later reworked, taken up, repeated, expanded, and developed, like the theme in a musical composition'. If this ideal remains in many respects unrealized in the naturalistic plays of the 1880s, it is possible to see its implementation in post-Inferno dramas like *A Dream Play* and *The Ghost Sonata*. In this respect, there is some truth to Strindberg's reported assertion that he never ceased to be a naturalist ('People have said that *To Damascus* is simply dreams;' he remarked, 'certainly, but entirely naturalistic ones' (ASB XIV, 51)), and that he simply progressed naturally from the depiction of the social world and its domestic interiors to an exploration of the remote parts of that other interior, the mind. For the later, so-called dream plays are in fact as concerned with reality as *Miss Julie* is, but now it is the far more elusive reality of the unconscious mind that is Strindberg's principal concern. In *Miss Julie* the two main characters tell each other their private dreams in an exchange that can appear contrived if not performed with great skill; in *A Dream Play*, the inner life to which such dreams refer, or which is elsewhere to be determined between the lines, in the subtext of naturalist drama, is confronted full on by a dramatist who is well aware that such evanescent experience has long been a concern of the theatre.

In fact, the idea that life is a dream which may be most appropriately represented in the insubstantial world of the theatre is a traditional topos, and Strindberg has himself drawn attention to Calderón's *La vida es sueño* (*Life is a Dream*, 1635) and Shakespeare's *The Tempest*, where Prospero maintains that 'we are such stuff as dreams are made on', as two earlier plays in which the dream state becomes a metaphor for life (see note to p. 176). Apparently so revolutionary in structure and style, *A Dream Play* is consequently only extraordinary if the kind of realism that has dominated mainstream European theatre for many decades (and which continues to dominate television drama) is taken to be the norm. In many respects it merely restores to drama several of the features that distinguish it from other forms of writing, and especially from the novel, in which the kind of realism that came to dominate the genre during the nineteenth century remains the defining practice. In its fusion of speech, song, movement, gesture, lighting, visual effects, design, and music, *A Dream Play* not only places a renewed emphasis on the other, non-verbal languages of the theatre, and thus forms part of the turn-of-the-century theatrical revolution subsequently associated with directors like Edward Gordon Craig or Meyerhold, who were likewise concerned to 'retheatricalize the theatre'; it also recovers for the modern stage something of the theatrical poetry of Baroque drama or the romantic fairy-tale play.

A Dream Play was written in 1901, and has been readily associated with two very different people, the Norwegian actress Harriet Bosse and Sigmund Freud. The dual role of Agnes and Indra's Daughter was in fact created with Bosse in mind, and in due course she would perform it when it finally reached the stage on 17 April 1907. Graced with an exotic beauty which critics sometimes described as 'oriental', she had first come to Strindberg's attention as Puck in another dream play, *A Midsummer Night's Dream*. He promptly saw to it that she was given the part of The Lady in the 1900 première of *To Damascus I*, a role he then invited her to play in his life. She accepted and they were married in May 1901. However, for many reasons, and not least because of the discrepancy in their ages (Harriet was thirty years younger than Strindberg), the marriage soon foundered. According to the *Occult Diary*, by the end of the month they were sleeping apart, and in late June Harriet, who was infuriated by his refusal to accompany her on holiday abroad, left 'without saying goodbye, without

saying where she was going'. They were reconciled shortly afterwards, but although now pregnant she moved out again in August,
and for the next few weeks Strindberg, having begun a play which he
told Harriet was to be called 'The Growing Castle' ('grand, beautiful,
like a dream . . . It is of course about you—Agnes—who will free the
prisoner from the castle' (SL 2, 685)), put it aside to write another
history play, this time about the Swedish Queen Christina, in whose
capricious theatricality he recognized an affinity with his estranged
wife. (It was to become one of the latter's most celebrated roles.)
However, Harriet returned at the beginning of October and only
then, encouraged by recent events to regard life as 'ever more dreamlike and inexplicable' (SL 2, 689) and still captivated by her beauty,
which he described in his diary as 'ethereal', did he resume work on *A
Dream Play*, calling it 'my best loved Play, the child of my greatest
pain' (SL 2, 739). For, reconciled if only temporarily with Bosse, he
dreamt while writing it of reconciliation with the world through
woman.

Freud, meanwhile, had published his *The Interpretation of Dreams*
in 1899 (though portentously dated 1900), and it is naturally tempt-
ing to link two works on dreaming which were, in their respective
spheres, to exert so enormous an influence on the new century.
Though it must be remembered that Strindberg never read Freud,
in some respects he hardly needed to, so similar was the ground on
which they were both working. They had both read many of the same
books including the French psychologists Charcot (with whom
Freud had studied during the 1880s) and Bernheim, whose *De la
suggestion et de ses applications à la thérapeutique* he translated into
German, as well as the philosophers Schopenhauer and Eduard von
Hartmann, whose *Philosophie des Unbewußten* (*Philosophy of the
Unconscious*, 1869) Strindberg had helped to translate into Swedish.
They both not only recorded and speculated on their own dreams
(this was one of the purposes of the *Occult Diary*) but read accounts of
other people's, including Carl du Prel's discussion, in *Die Philosophie
der Mystik* (1885), of how in dreaming we experience a dramatic
sundering of the Ego and, as both actor and spectator, witness
different aspects of the self in conflict. Both of them had also devoted
the 1890s to self-analysis (Strindberg in *Inferno* and *To Damascus*,
Freud in *The Interpretation of Dreams*), while the technique of free
association that Freud developed during this period has an obvious

affinity with Strindberg's theory of 'l'art fortuite' in his essay on 'The New Arts!'. Moreover, Freud's retrospective method, in which the past is uncovered piecemeal to the present consternation of those who lived it, owes perhaps as much to the naturalist drama of Ibsen as it does to the *Oedipus* of Sophocles. The only reference to Strindberg in Freud's work comes in *The Psychopathology of Everyday Life*, where he quotes from the novel *Gothic Rooms* (1904), although not the passage in which, in one of many remarkable pre-echoes of Freudian motifs, the heroine makes love and then tells her partner, 'you seemed to be my father, and I feel ashamed and disgusted' (SS 40, 244).

Like Freud, Strindberg was indeed alert to the psychopathology of everyday life in which the ordinary was the starting-point for the extraordinary. He was fond of quoting an aphorism from the *Talmud*: 'If you would learn to know the invisible, observe the visible with open eyes'; there was, he argued, a latent esoteric realm concealed behind the manifest, or exoteric visible world, a distinction Freud would also use in his analysis of dreams. It is appropriate, then, that *A Dream Play* should be rooted in the specific and mundane detail of everyday life. Those interested in identifying Freudian symbols need look no further than to Agnes releasing the Officer from prison by depriving him of the sabre with which she finds him beating the table, or to the castle that rises out of a bed of manure, and which is topped by a flower-bud that bursts into flower in the final tableau. But far more telling is the way in which the fabric of the play is composed out of the residues of daily experience that occur in real dreams. *A Dream Play* brings together a kaleidoscope of motifs based upon old and recent memories. For example, the growing castle is the cavalry barracks that Strindberg could see from the window of his apartment in Karlavägen, where he wrote the play. It was topped by a golden, bud-like baldachin that to Strindberg seemed about to burst into flower. The modern Tower of Babel described by the Poet in the second Fingal's Cave scene was the new Telephone Tower in Malm-skillnadsgatan. Fairhaven (Fagervik—literally 'Fair Bay') was to be found at the resort of Furusund in the Stockholm archipelago while Foulstrand, or 'Skamsund' (literally 'Shame Sound') he adapted with a dreamer's typical linguistic ingenuity from Skarmsund, situated just across the bay from Fagervik. There he had seen the Baths Doctor, Elias Nordström, on his way to a ball wearing a Moorish mask, an image he recalled when creating the Quarantine Master Ordström, with his blackened face. The Blind Man, too, can be traced to a jeweller and art collector named Christian Hammer, who owned the island of Furusund and had lost his sight, while the Officer's mother resembles Strindberg's in having been a servant. In finding himself back at school, unable to multiply two by two, the Officer experiences one of Strindberg's recurring nightmares, and the scene in which degrees are conferred may derive from rumours reaching him at about this time that both the Universities of Lund and Uppsala were considering awarding him an honorary doctorate. Meanwhile, the scene outside the theatre recalls the numerous occasions on which he had waited for Siri von Essen or (more recently, and now with greying hair) for Harriet in a corridor of the Royal Theatre, where there was a door with a clover-leaf hole.

Consequently, the seemingly insubstantial, oneiric world of the play is sustained by a multitude of sharply observed details, hallucinatory in their precision and vivid focus. These are woven together according to the method outlined in the brief explanatory note which prefaces it, and which Strindberg glossed in a letter to Emil Schering: 'Understand *The* [sic] *Dream Play?* Indra's daughter has come down to earth in order to find out how mankind lives, and thus discovers how hard life is. And the hardest thing of all is hurting others, which one is forced to do if one wants to live. The form is motivated by the foreword; the jumble and confusion of a dream, in which there is, however, a certain logic! Everything absurd becomes probable. People flit past and a few traits are sketched in, the sketches merge, a single character dissolves into several, who merge into one again. Time and space do not exist; a minute is like many years; no seasons; the snow covers the countryside in summer, the lime tree turns yellow, and then green again, etc.' (SL 2, 692).

However, the crucial point is that the play is not a dream but an imitation of a dream. Whereas a dreamer lacks a conscious intent *A Dream Play* is shaped by the dramatist's concern to depict his vision of the world in the guise of the dream it appears to him to be. Strindberg therefore has recourse to a number of devices which convey the disjointed but apparently logical form of a dream in which time and place do not exist. Hence, for example, the sudden cinematic cuts and dissolves that mark the passage from one location to another—the way in which a wall abruptly disappears and a bed becomes a tent, an office a church, and an organ a cave; how the lime tree is transformed into a hat-stand and then a candelabrum, the Lawyer's desk into a lectern, and the door with the four-leafed clover into a filing-cabinet and then the vestry door. On the page the action is not broken into separate acts and scenes like a traditional dramatic text (there was originally no list of dramatis personae either); instead, it is designed to flow seamlessly from sequence to sequence by means of associations that are often visual and which are projected with the immediacy of dream. The visual dimension is crucial; it is not what he says but his appearance which conveys how the Officer ages and then grows young again, or the way that the bouquet withers and the lime tree gains or loses its leaves. Likewise, character is now seen to be truly 'characterless' as one identity continually shifts into another (it is not unreasonable, for example, to see the Officer, the Lawyer, and the Poet as three aspects of a single figure).

This material is subjected to the kind of condensation, displacement, secondary revision, association, and symbolism that occurs in the 'dream work' discussed by Freud in *The Interpretation of Dreams*, but which, as the Poet points out here, is also the domain of poetry. So, too, is the presence throughout the play of what has been called Strindberg's 'polyphonic mythology',[4] a blend of elements drawn from Hindu, Greek, and biblical mythology, Buddhism, Gnosticism, the chivalric quest traditions, the Arabian Nights, the stories and plays of Hans Christian Andersen, and the Indic image of the 'web' or 'veil' of Maya that Strindberg would know from his early reading of Schopenhauer, and which lies behind Agnes's attempt to answer the Poet's questions about the riddle of existence. Strindberg shared this general interest in Eastern religion and drama with the symbolist painters and writers he had known in Paris, but he utilized it according to the needs of his poetry (the God Indra, for example, never had a daughter). Agnes's account of creation, that he took from a discussion of Indian religion in Arvid Ahnfelt's *History of World Literature* (1875)— namely, that the world was one of appearances and had come into existence only through sin—was attuned both to his literary needs and to his post-Inferno ideas about the nature of human experience.

Nevertheless, although it imitates 'the inconsequent yet apparently logical form of a dream', the play retains the vestiges of

---

[4] Harry Carlson, *Strindberg and the Poetry of Myth* (Berkeley, 1982), 5.

a dramatic structure. For example, like the first part of *To Damascus*, it is in some respects circular. Leaving aside the Prologue, which was added later as a concession to an audience that might otherwise have difficulties locating itself in the shifting world of the play itself, the last scene returns us to the first setting outside the growing castle by way of Fingal's Cave and the theatre alley. It is also as if the opening images reproduce the stark visual images that accompany falling asleep, after which Indra's Daughter sinks deeper and deeper into the mire of existence as sleep becomes more profound, before she slowly ascends again into a waking state in the final scene where, since life has proved to be a dream and an illusion, she must die in order truly to live. Moreover, Agnes on her pilgrimage through life serves to link the different episodes together, and the final scene, in which many of the characters parade before her for the last time and cast their illusions upon the funeral pyre that she is about to ascend in order to purify herself in the flames, functions as a kind of flashback before waking, much as a man's life is supposed to pass before his eyes in the moment before he dies.

Of all Strindberg's plays, *A Dream Play* is the one that breaks most completely with the Aristotelian form of the well-made play and replaces a plot-oriented drama with one organized along musical lines, in terms of theme. The individual voices function as instruments in an ensemble that collectively articulates the play's themes, including the notions that human beings are to be pitied and love conquers all, the riddle of existence, the disturbing duality in which beauty (for example, a flower) has its roots in the dirt of the earth and pleasure is intimately linked with pain, a world of curious contradictions in which hopes entertained are always dashed, where even the Billposter's beloved fishing-net turns out to be the wrong shade of green. In the warp and weft with which such themes are woven together the spectator may finally discern a pattern which possesses the underlying coherence of dreams.

The Ghost Sonata

The Ghost Sonata was written in 1907, shortly after Strindberg moved into his final residence at 85 Drottninggatan, the so-called 'Blue Tower' which was situated close to the most important of his childhood homes. He wrote it in considerable physical pain for he was suffering both from the psoriasis with which he was periodically afflicted (his hands literally bled as he wrote it (SL 2, 735)) and from the first symptoms of the stomach cancer which brought about his death five years later. Moreover, although he still corresponded with Harriet Bosse, their physical relationship, which had continued intermittently even after their divorce in 1904, was now a thing of the past, and Harriet had instead to contend with the disconcerting notion that Strindberg expressed in his letters to her as well as in his *Occult Diary*, namely, that they remained partners on the 'astral' plane, where he claimed that she continued to visit him. In short, Strindberg was both lonely and confronting death (there is a death or funeral in each of the play's three scenes), and he now saw himself embarking upon a final stocktaking or balancing of accounts, in preparation for the journey that he customarily associated with death.

Like the other three plays that Strindberg wrote between January and June that year (*Thunder in the Air*, *The Burned House*, and *The Pelican*), he called *The Ghost Sonata* a 'chamber play'. The name partly derives from the size and style of the theatre for which he was now writing. He had been encouraged to resume dramatic writing again after another interval, this time of four years during which he wrote several major novels and volumes of short stories, by the prospect of at last having his own theatre. At the end of 1906 Strindberg had been approached by the young actor-manager August Falk, about the possibility of founding a theatre devoted primarily to his plays. Falck had been responsible for the first professional Swedish production of *Miss Julie* with which he had toured successfully earlier that year, and Strindberg, who thought he recognized a good omen in the name which Falck shared with the hero of his first novel, *The Red Room*, responded with enthusiasm. It would be the realization of a long-held dream.

The idea of a small-scale 'chamber' theatre specifically suited to such tightly structured, claustrophobic modern dramas as *The Dance of Death* or Ibsen's *Ghosts* was very much in keeping with developments elsewhere (Max Reinhardt, for example, had just opened his *Kammerspiele* in Berlin). Strindberg and Falck leased a large storehouse near the Central Station in Stockholm which, when renovated, housed a theatre seating 161 spectators. Called *Intima teatern* (the Intimate Theatre), it became, during the three years of its existence, a forum for theatrical experimentation and a proving-ground for many of Strindberg's plays, several of which (including *The Ghost Sonata*) received their premières there.

Something of what Strindberg had in mind in writing these plays may be gathered from a letter he sent to the Finland-Swedish author Adolf Paul in January 1907. He explained that a chamber play should be 'intimate in form, with a restricted subject, treated in depth, few characters, large points of view, free imagination, but based on observation, experience, carefully studied; simple, but not too simple; no great apparatus, no superfluous minor roles, no regular five-acters or "old machines", no long-drawn-out whole evenings' (SL 2, 734). And the following year, in one of the memoranda that he addressed to the predominantly young members of the Intimate Theatre, he observed: 'If anyone asks what an Intimate Theatre wishes to achieve, and what is meant by a "Chamber Play", I can answer as follows: in drama we seek the powerful, highly significant motif, but with limitations. In its treatment we try to avoid all show, all calculated effects, places for applause, star roles, solo numbers. No predetermined form is to restrict the author, for the motif determines the form. Consequently, freedom in treatment, restricted only by the unity of the ideas and the feeling for style' (SS 50, 12).

Thus, although several vestiges of traditional playmaking may still be discerned in *The Ghost Sonata* (for example, the reversal of fortune of the second scene in which the unmasker, Hummel, is himself unmasked, or the general movement from ignorance to insight that the Student undergoes), in stressing that 'the motif determines the form', Strindberg indicates an intention to pursue further the kind of thematic organization that he had employed in *A Dream Play*, and which he readily applies to other works, including *Hamlet*, which he compared to 'a symphony, polyphonically developed with independent motifs, which are beautifully woven together' (SS 50, 69). But here the analogy with music is stressed even more clearly in his conception of this new style of theatre as 'chamber music transposed to drama. The intimate action, the significant motif, treated in a sophisticated manner' (SS 50, 11). Each of the four chamber plays is therefore given an opus number, which suggests that, although each of them may stand alone, grouped together they form a kind of cycle, like a series of musical compositions (Strindberg once called them his 'Last Sonatas', SL 2, 735) or even the four parts of Wagner's Ring Cycle, one of which—*Die Walküre*—

forms part of the complex intertextuality of Strindberg's Opus 3, *The Ghost Sonata*.

The very speed with which they were composed links these plays from the outset, and certain themes, like the notion articulated throughout *The Ghost Sonata* that 'we are not what we seem', are common to all four of them. Meanwhile, other themes which are prominent in one or other of the plays may be given a secondary role in one or all of the others, and vice versa. These themes are stated, varied, and recapitulated in different rhythms and moods across the cycle as a whole. Thus, the final scene of *The Ghost Sonata* reviews material that has been presented in a different key earlier on in the play, while the Student's remark, 'the kitchen, that's where children's hearts are nipped in the bud, unless it's in the bedroom, of course', becomes the heart of the situation depicted in Strindberg's next play, *The Pelican*.

Given the privileged place that music occupied in Strindberg's thinking about drama during these years, it is not surprising that the attempt has been made to establish the form of the chamber plays in strict musical terms. But while the piano sonatas and chamber music of Beethoven that Strindberg so admired (see note to p. 249) may have helped him to find new ways of structuring and organizing a play, attempts to explain *The Ghost Sonata* in terms of sonata form, either as three separate sonata movements in different tempi or as aspects of a single movement with an exposition, development, recapitulation, and coda, remain—in spite of the play's title— impressionistic analogies. It may help the reader or the actor to see the first scene as a busy *allegro*, conceivably followed by a troubled *largo* punctuated by long silences (Scene 2), and a final *andante* which is rounded off with a Coda (the Student's long final speech) in which a number of the play's principal motifs are restated; but to insist on too exact a parallel runs the risk, not only of attributing to Strindberg a technical grasp of musical structure that he did not have, but also of closing down other possible ways of reading the play.

Again, it is possible to confer a certain coherence on a text that largely lacks a conventional narrative progression by regarding it as a kind of parodied fairy tale. Strindberg once remarked that in '*The Ghost Sonata* . . . I intended a fairy-tale or fantasy play set in the present and with modern houses' (ASB XVII, 151), and Hummel in fact encourages the reader or spectator to think in these terms when he observes that his 'whole life is like a book of fairy tales' in which, although all the stories are different, 'they hang together on a single thread, with a leitmotif that recurs over and over again'. In this reading, the heroic young Student (a Sunday Child who consequently sees clearly what others cannot, and whose role echoes that of Indra's Daughter in linking the different elements of the play) gains entry to a house that he mistakes for paradise with the aid of a mysterious and seemingly omnipotent fairy godfather (Hummel), in order to rescue a maiden from the room in which she is imprisoned under the venomous eyes of the vampire-like Cook. But here, of course, in a play where life on this 'madhouse, this prison, this charnel house the earth' is portrayed as a painful illusion—a kind of deathly somnambulism—to die is to awaken, and he liberates her by taking her life.

But on its own such a reading is also a reduction of the play's complex resonances to a single dimension. There are many other echoes—for example, of Wagner, *Faust*, *Hamlet*, the stories of E. T. A. Hoffmann, and the young student in Alain-René Lesage's novel *Le Diable boiteux* (1707) who is conducted behind the house façades of eighteenth-century Madrid by the lame demon Asmodeus—any one of which might be used to put a particular slant upon a play that inhabits the half-reality of Strindberg's best dream-play style, where the equivocal, disturbing power of a figure like Hummel is precisely linked to the mundane urban milieu in which the action is set. For on the one hand, the façade is that of a house in the fashionable suburb of Östermalm populated by some of the people that Strindberg used to encounter there on his morning walk, and about whose lives he used to speculate (one of them was a rich old man who dispensed charity to beggars, another a half-young man he had once seen through a window playing cards with three old people who appeared to him like mummies); on the other hand, out of the shards of such realistic detail, the 'observation' that he urged upon Adolf Paul but which he treats with almost contemptuous nonchalance himself, he fashions 'a world of Intimations' (SL 2, 741). Its characters are the grotesque and ghostly denizens of a designedly metaphorical, waking nightmare—the nightmare of everyday life where, as Strindberg notes, 'secrets like these are to be found in *every* home' (SL 2, 735). And while the menacing chiaroscuro of the play, emphasized in Max Reinhardt's staging of 1916, anticipates the expressionist cinema of Fritz Lang or Friedrich Murnau, it is worth remarking that a character like the Mummy, who has been reified from a figure of speech into the 'old parrot' she resembles, is no more extraordinary than (say) Miss Havisham in Dickens's *Great Expectations*, who still wears her wedding dress and veil and continues to live among the ruins of her wedding breakfast many years after her fiancé deserted her and time stopped at 'twenty minutes to nine'.

Otherwise, the play presents a characteristic late-Strindbergian blend of Christian and Eastern religion (here embodied in the Buddha that presides over the final scene), along with notions derived from theosophy (an early subtitle located the action to 'Kama Loka', the name given by theosophists to the first stage which the soul enters after death, where it is released from the 'ghosts' of earthly life), Swedenborg's theory of a correspondence in which the physical world is seen as symbolic of the spiritual world, and Schopenhauer's notion of the veil which in this world of illusion prevents us from seeing things as they really are—although in the bleakness of his vision Strindberg here goes further even than Schopenhauer. Unlike *The Dance of Death*, however, where the possible identification of the protagonists with Strindberg's sister Anna and her husband made it possible to reduce the predicament of the characters in the play to an act of personal revenge, here the implications remain universal. The world is one 'of folly and delusion (illusion), from which we must struggle to free ourselves' (SL 2, 735), and the characters have been consigned to an earthly purgatory, or hell, where the deliverance that death brings from the pains and trials of life is conveyed by the reproduction of Böcklin's once-fashionable painting *The Isle of the Dead* which descends at the close of the play. The imagery here is both conventional and yet highly personal. At one with the other chamber plays in presenting the release death brings as a sea voyage away from the contamination of earthly life to a state of post-mortem purity, *The Ghost Sonata* also associates it with a trip by steamer away from Stockholm out to the neighbouring archipelago, with its copious associations from Strindberg's early years of the summer and holidays, an escape from the city to a landscape which always remained for him as close to an earthly paradise as any he knew.

Moreover, in a play that is explicitly sceptical about the ability of language to convey the truth, and even more pessimistic about the capacity of people to use it to speak frankly, the action presents what the Student describes as 'this world of illusion, guilt, suffering, and death; this world of endless change, disappointment and pain' in a series of striking visual images: the death screen; the spider-like Hummel in his 'battle wagon' surrounded by a crowd of silent beggars, or breaking the silence by beating the table with his crutch; the monstrous Cook and her 'colouring bottle . . . with the scorpion-like lettering'; the Colonel who is not a colonel, and who is only held together beneath the uniform of which Hummel strips him by an iron corset; and the Mummy who arrests time's flow by literally stopping the clock, who lives in a cupboard in order not to see or be seen, and whose appearance brings her into poignant juxtaposition with the statue of the beautiful young woman she once was.

Such images focus the themes of the play and its concern with truth and lies, being and seeming, falsehood and unmasking, speech and silence, with food as a spiritual commodity as well as something to eat in a world where people prey upon each other, like the two vampires Hummel and the Cook. In the course of the play the Student penetrates further and further into the house, the house of life in which everyone is in some way related to everyone else, and where 'no one is who they seem to be' though all are bound to each other, as the Mummy says, by 'crimes and secrets and guilt'. 'Life is so horribly ugly,' Strindberg once noted, 'we human beings so abysmally evil, that if a writer were to depict *all* that he had seen and heard no one could bear to read it. . . . Breeding and education seem only to mask the beast in us, and virtue is a disguise. Life is so cynical that only a swine can be happy in it . . . [it] is a punishment! A hell. For some a purgatory, for none a paradise' (*Occult Diary*, 3 September 1904). In spite of the theatrical poetry in which the play is suffused, this is essentially what Strindberg depicts in the *Ghost Sonata*; for, like the Student's father, he could never remain silent. However, without the humour that characterizes *The Dance of Death*, it can appear one of the bleakest of his plays.

After the chamber plays of 1907 Strindberg was to write only one more major play, the dramatic epitaph *The Great Highway* (1909). But the dramas he had already produced in the wake of his Inferno crisis confirm him as the pivotal figure in the emergence of twentieth-century theatre. *A Dream Play* looks forward to Artaud, who directed it, and to the meta-theatrical tradition represented by Pirandello and

Genet; *To Damascus* establishes the expressionist genre of the pilgrim play or *Stationen* drama; *The Ghost Sonata* foreshadows the theatre of the absurd, from Witkiewicz to Beckett; and *The Dance of Death* offers an early but still unsurpassed vision of the kind of hell to which Sartre, Beckett, and Albee have variously condemned us. And more particularly, in all these late dramas, but perhaps especially in *A Dream Play* and *The Ghost Sonata*, Strindberg creates a true poetry of the theatre out of a combination of gestures, sounds, visual images, music, light, and spoken words. As he wrote in 1908 to the composer Tor Aulin: 'But *The Ghost Sonata* has another side! To extract atmosphere (poetry!) out of contemporary, everyday reality, without descending to the Orient or Medievalism of the Fairy-Tale play' (SL 2, 791). In so commenting, Strindberg justly recognizes his own achievement, and draws attention, quite properly, not to the minutiae of his life, but to his artistry.

NOTE ON THE TEXT

The texts on which these translations are based are those of the ongoing edition of Strindberg's Complete Works (*Samlade Verk*) under the general editorship of Lars Dahlbäck. The volumes containing these plays (vols. 27, 44, 46, and 58) have all been edited by Gunnar Ollén with the exception of *The Dance of Death*, for which Hans Lindström has been responsible. In this edition the text has been established wherever possible with direct reference to the original manuscript augmented by changes to the first edition only where these may safely be ascribed to Strindberg himself. This provides the most reliable text yet published, and in the case of *Miss Julie* it has meant the restoration of passages excluded from its first printing by the publisher, Joseph Seligmann. Of the works translated here the original manuscripts of *Miss Julie*, *The Dance of Death I*, *A Dream Play*, and *The Ghost Sonata* are all extant. In the case of *The Father*, the text has been established using the first edition published by Hans Österling (Helsingborg, 1887) with reference, too, to Strindberg's own French translation, *Père* (Helsingborg, 1888).

Using this new edition of Strindberg's works does present the translator with a problem, however. In the later plays, and most particularly in *The Ghost Sonata*, Strindberg employed an idiosyncratic system of *points suspensifs*, asterisks, single and triple dashes, semicolons and colons in the manner of musical notation to indicate shifts in tone and rhythm, pauses, or changes of focus in a character's thought pattern. In the case of the *points suspensifs* and the single or triple dashes these occur both within a speech and at the end of a line, and both with and without a full stop or other punctuation mark; meanwhile, the liberal use of commas or semicolons within a longer speech where a full stop might be expected also departs from established English practice.

Precisely what these diacritical marks signify is not always apparent, but with the musical inspiration of his last works in mind, Strindberg appears to have been working towards a notational system that would convey to actor and director the spoken values of the line in question. It would be relatively easy to smooth out the text by omitting these marks and where necessary to substitute more conventional punctuation, but—with the occasional necessary exception—I have, wherever possible, elected to retain them in the belief that they indicate how Strindberg saw (or heard) the movement of a speaker's mind. Very occasionally, where their retention within the body of a speech would obscure the meaning in translation, I have reluctantly dropped them, but otherwise such punctuation (or the lack of it) is Strindberg's. This applies even to his use of asterisks in the body of the text generally, as in the old French manner, to indicate the beginning or ending of a scene by the entry or exit of one or more of the characters; sometimes, however, asterisks are also employed as yet another indicator of a change of mood or direction, and therefore need to be retained on that account, too.

I have, however, elected not to reproduce every detail of the punctuation in one respect, namely Strindberg's liberal use of the exclamation mark, which is often attached to the mildest or most straightforward of utterances. This practice was taken up with enthusiasm by German expressionism but it can be misleading in English where, for example in *The Father* or *Miss Julie*, it suggests a melodramatic acting style at odds with the surface realism of these plays. Consequently, although I am aware that much of his dramatic pathos is achieved by exclamation, and that this needs to be reflected even in an English version, I have been more sparing with exclamation marks than Strindberg was. Even so, a considerable number remain.

Any other emphases in the spoken text, indicated by italics, are Strindberg's own and not the translator's.

Finally, my thanks to David McDuff for scrutinizing the text of the translation, James McFarlane for reading and commenting on an earlier version of the Introduction, and Clive Scott for reading and commenting on the notes. I am also grateful to Judith Luna and Jeff New for the care they have given this volume. Needless to say, they are in no way responsible for the shortcomings that remain.

SELECT BIBLIOGRAPHY

The great mass of scholarly writing about Strindberg is naturally in Swedish. With the exception of Torsten Måtte Schmidt's lavishly illustrated book on Strindberg's painting, this bibliography is restricted to works in English, with special emphasis on the texts in this volume.

Biography and Autobiography

Lagercrantz, Olof, *August Strindberg* (London, 1984).

Meyer, Michael, *Strindberg* (London, 1985).

Robinson, Michael, (ed. and trans.), *Strindberg's Letters*, 2 vols. (London and Chicago, 1992).

Strindberg, August, *Inferno* and *From and Occult Diary*, trans. Mary Sandbach (Harmondsworth, 1979).

Strindberg, August, *The Son of a Servant*, vol. 1, trans. Evert Sprinchorn (London, 1967).

Criticism

Benston, Alice, 'From Naturalism to the *Dream Play*', *Modern Drama*, 7/4 (1965), 382–98.

Bentley, Eric, *The Playwright as Thinker* (New York, 1946).

Bergman, Gösta M., 'Strindberg and the Intima Teatern', *Theatre Research*, 9/1 (1967), 14–47.

Blackwell, Marilyn Johns, (ed.), *Structures of Influence: A Comparative Approach to August Strindberg* (Chapel Hill, NC, 1981).

Brandell, Gunnar, *Strindberg in Inferno* (Cambridge, Mass., 1974).

Bulman, Joan, *Strindberg and Shakespeare* (London, 1933).

Carlson, Harry, *Strindberg and the Poetry of Myth* (Berkeley, 1982).

—— *Out of Inferno: Strindberg's Reawakening as an Artist* (Seattle, 1996).

Dahlström, C. E. W. L., *Strindberg's Dramatic Expressionism*, (2nd edn., New York, 1968).

Greenway, John L., 'Strindberg and Suggestion in *Miss Julie*', *South Atlantic Review*, 51/2 (1986), 21–34.

Hildeman, Karl-Ivar, 'Strindberg, *The Dance of Death* and Revenge', *Scandinavian Studies*, 25/4 (1963), 267–94.

Jacobs, Barry, 'Psychic Murder and Characterization in Strindberg's *The Father*', *Scandinavica*, 8/1 (1969), 19–34.

Jarvi, Raymond, '*Ett drömspel*: A Symphony for the Stage', *Scandinavian Studies*, 44/1 (1972), 28–42.

Jarvi, Raymond, 'Strindberg's *The Ghost Sonata* and Sonata Form', *Mosaic*, 5 (1972), 69–84.

Johannesson, Eric O., *The Novels of August Strindberg* (Berkeley, 1968).

Johnson, Walter, '*A Dream Play*: Plans and Fulfilment', *Scandinavica*, 10/2 (1971), 103–11.

—— *Strindberg and the Historical Drama* (Seattle, 1966).

Kvam, Kela, (ed.), *Strindberg's Post-Inferno Plays* (Copenhagen, 1994).

Lamm, Martin, *August Strindberg* (New York, 1971).

Madsen, Børge Gedsø, *Strindberg's Naturalistic Theatre* (Copenhagen, 1962).

Marker, F. J. and Marker, Lise-Lone, *The Scandinavian Theatre* (Cambridge, 1996).

Mays, Milton, 'Strindberg's *Ghost Sonata*: Parodied Fairy Tale on Original Sin', *Modern Drama*, 10/2 (1967), 189–94.

Parker, Gerald, 'The Spectator Seized by the Theatre: Strindberg's *The Ghost Sonata*', *Modern Drama*, 15/4 (1972), 373–86.

Plasberg, Elaine, 'Strindberg and the New Poetics', *Modern Drama*, 15/1 (1972), 1–14.

Powell, Jocelyn, 'Demons that Live in Sunlight: Problems in Staging Strindberg', *The Year's Work in English Studies*, 9 (1979), 116–34.

Reinert, Otto, (ed.), *Strindberg: A Collection of Critical Essays* (Eaglewood Cliffs, NJ, 1971).

Robinson, Michael, 'Prisoners at Play: Form and Meaning in Strindberg's *Dance of Death* and Beckett's *Endgame*', *Journal of European Studies*, 15/1 (1985), 31–48.

—— *Strindberg and Autobiography* (Norwich, 1986).

—— (ed.), *Strindberg and Genre* (Norwich, 1991).

Schmidt, Torsten Måtte, (ed.), *Strindbergs måleri* (Malmö, 1972).

Sondrup, Steven, 'Aspects of Musical Logic in Strindberg's *Spöksonaten*', *Scandinavian Studies*, 53 (1981), 154–64.

Sprinchorn, Evert, *Strindberg as Dramatist* (New Haven, 1982).

Steene, Birgitta, (ed.), *Strindberg and History*, (Stockholm, 1992).

Stockenström, Göran, 'The Journey from the Isle of Life to the Isle of Death', *Scandinavian Studies*, 50/2 (1978), 133–49.

Stockenström, Göran, (ed.), *Strindberg's Dramaturgy* (Minneapolis, 1988).

Strindberg, August, *Letters to the Intimate Theatre*, trans. Walter Johnson (Seattle, 1968).

—— *Selected Essays*, ed. and trans. Michael Robinson (Cambridge, 1996).

Strindberg Society, *Essays on Strindberg* (Stockholm, 1966).

—— *Strindberg and Modern Theatre* (Stockholm, 1981).

Templeton, Alice, '*Miss Julie* as "A Naturalistic Tragedy"', *Theatre Journal*, 42/4 (1990), 468–80.

Törnqvist, Egil, *Strindbergian Drama: Themes and Structure* (Stockholm, 1982).

—— and Jacobs, Barry, *Strindberg's Miss Julie. A Play and its Transpositions* (Norwich, 1988).

Valency, Maurice, *The Flower and the Castle* (New York, 1963).

Ward, John, *The Social and Religious Plays of Strindberg* (London, 1980).

Wilkinson, Lynn R., 'The Politics of the Interior: Strindberg's *Chamber Plays*', *Scandinavian Studies*, 65/4 (1993), 463–86.

Further Reading in Oxford World's Classics

Ibsen, Henrik, *Four Major Plays* (*A Doll's House*, *Ghosts*, *Hedda Gabler*, *The Master Builder*), trans. James McFarlane and Jens Arup, ed. James McFarlane.

—— *Peer Gynt*, trans. Christopher Fry and Johann Fillinger; ed. James McFarlane.

Synge, J. M., *The Playboy of the Western World and Other Plays*, ed. Ann Saddlemyer.

Three Pre-Surrealist Plays (Maeterlinck, *The Blind*, Apollinaire, *The Mammaries of Tiresias*, Jarry, *Ubu the King*), trans. and ed. Maya Slater.

A CHRONOLOGY OF
JOHAN AUGUST STRINDBERG

1849   Born 22 January at Riddarholmen in Stockholm, the fourth and eldest legitimate child of a shipping agent and a former servant girl and waitress, to whom eleven children are born in all, seven of them living to maturity.

1853   Father goes bankrupt but recoups his fortunes. By 1854 he is responsible for about one-third of the steamers plying out of Stockholm.

1856   Attends Klara School, a puritanical establishment for wealthy children, which Strindberg detests.

1860   Removed by his father to Jakob School, a school for poor children which Strindberg prefers.

1861   Moves to Stockholm Lyceum, a more liberal, private school where Strindberg makes good progress. Embraces Pietism during adolescence.

1862   Mother dies.

1863   Father marries Emilia Charlotte Petersson, his children's governess, whom Strindberg dislikes intensely.

1867–72   Matriculates and leaves for Uppsala to spend the first of several, ultimately fruitless spells at university. Supports himself between times by private tutoring, schoolteaching, and journalism. Studies medicine briefly and fails as an apprentice actor at the Royal Theatre in 1869.

1869   Writes first play, *A Nameday Gift*, now lost. Also completes first extant plays, *The Freethinker* and *Greece in Decline* (later reworked as *Hermione*).

1870   *In Rome*, a one-act comedy in verse, produced at the Royal Theatre. Reads Kierkegaard for the first time.

1871   Completes *The Outlaw*, premièred at the Royal Theatre in October. Receives a small grant from King Charles XV's private purse. Spends the first of several summers on the island of Kymmendö in the Stockholm archipelago. Takes up painting for the first time.

1872   Leaves Uppsala without a degree. Completes first major play, *Master Olof*, in prose. Unperformed until 30 December 1881, Strindberg rewrites it twice (1874; 1876), and is aggrieved that it remains unrecognized for so long.

1872–4 Supports himself mainly by journalism, including the editorship of an insurance journal, the *Svensk försäkringstidning*, translating, and art criticism; also trains as a telegraphist on the island of Sandhamn.

1874–82 Appointed assistant librarian in the Royal Library, where he studies sinology. Continues to eke out his salary with journalism and teaching.

1875 Meets Siri von Essen, a Finland-Swedish aristocrat with aspirations as an actress, currently married to Baron Carl Gustaf Wrangel, a guards officer.

1876 First visit to Paris. Introduces Swedish readers to French Impressionism. Completes revision of *Master Olof* in verse. Publishes a volume of short stories, *Town and Gown*, about Uppsala.

1877 Marries Siri von Essen, now divorced and engaged at the Royal Theatre.

1878 First child, a daughter, dies shortly after birth.

1879 Literary breakthrough with *The Red Room*, a satirical novel about contemporary Stockholm and a landmark in the emergence of modern Swedish literature. Continues his oriental studies. Receives silver medal of the St Petersburg Imperial Geographical Society for services to cartology and has a paper on relations between Sweden and China and Tartary read at the Académie des Inscriptions et Belles-Lettres in Paris.

1880 Daughter, Karin, born. *The Secret of the Guild* performed at the Royal Theatre. Begins serial publication of *Old Stockholm*, written with Claes Lundin.

1881 Daughter, Greta, born. Publishes *Studies in Cultural History*. Begins publication of *The Swedish People*, a major historical study in two volumes.

1882 Completes *The Swedish People*, writes fairy-tale play *Lucky Peter's Journey*, and *Sir Bengt's Wife*, a reply to Ibsen's *A Doll's House*, which is performed at the New Theatre with Siri von Essen in the title role. Publishes *The New Kingdom*, ten satirical sketches of contemporary society for which he is savagely criticized; begins writing *Swedish Destinies and Adventures*, a two-volume collection of historical short stories.

1883 Strindberg's father dies. He stays away from the funeral. Spends his last summer on Kymmendö. Publishes *Poems in Verse and Prose*. Leaves Sweden for France; will remain abroad for six years.

1884   Moves to Switzerland. Pays brief visit to Italy. Son, Hans, born. Reads anarchism and social theory. Publishes *Somnambulist Nights in Broad Daylight* (poetry) and volume 1 of *Getting Married*, twelve stories about married life, for which he is charged with blasphemy. Returns to Sweden to stand trial, is acquitted, but suffers great nervous strain; loses his publishers and henceforth suffers from severe penury, frequent vilification, and a sense of persecution.

1885   Writes *Getting Married II* (pub. 1886); is now a vehement anti-feminist. Publishes *Utopias in Reality* (four stories set in Switzerland). Moves back to France (Neuilly, Luc-sur-mer, and Grez sur Loing). Embraces atheism.

1886   Returns to Switzerland in May. Reads contemporary French and English psychology. Begins his self-analytical autobiographical novel, *The Son of a Servant*, of which volume 4 remains unpublished until 1909. Writes *Comrades*, his first naturalistic play. Spends September travelling through France gathering material for a sociological study, *Among French Peasants* (pub. 1889).

1887   Moves to Germany in January. Completes *The Son of a Servant*. Writes *The Father*, *Vivisections* (psychological stories and essays), and *The People of Hemsö*, a comic novel set on Kymmendö. His marriage is now under serious pressure; contemplates divorce. Moves to Denmark to attend the première of *The Father* (Copenhagen, 14 November). Consults a specialist about his mental health.

1888   Spent (apart from one brief retreat to Germany to avoid being arraigned for corrupting a minor) at various locations in Denmark. Writes *Life in the Skerries* (stories), *Flower Paintings and Animal Studies* (essays in natural history), *A Madman's Defence* (an autobiographical novel in French), *Miss Julie*, and *Creditors*. Founds the Scandinavian Experimental Theatre, loosely modelled on Antoine's Théâtre Libre in Paris. Corresponds with Nietzsche.

1889   Writes *The Stronger*, *Pariah*, and *Simoon*; dramatizes *The People of Hemsö*. The Scandinavian Experimental Theatre performs four of his plays, including *Miss Julie*, with Siri von Essen in the title role, before closing for good. Returns to Sweden.

1890   *By the Open Sea* (novel). The Berlin Freie Bühne performs *The Father*, the first production of a Strindberg play outside Scandinavia.

1891   Divorces Siri von Essen.

1892   Writes seven plays, *The Keys of Heaven*, *Debit and Credit*, *The First Warning*, *Facing Death*, *Motherly Love*, *Playing with Fire*, and *The Bond*, after which he virtually abandons literature for almost six years. Resumes painting (exhibiting in Stockholm, in July), experiments in photography (including colour photography), and devotes himself feverishly to science.

1892–3　Moves to Berlin in September and assumes a central role in the bohemian circle of writers, artists, and musicians, centred on the tavern Zum schwarzen Ferkel. Continues his experiments in painting, photography, and science; has a brief affair with Dagny Juel, the model for several of Edvard Munch's most famous paintings; meets the young Austrian journalist Frida Uhl (1872–1943), whom he marries in May 1893 on Heligoland. They spend a disastrous honeymoon in Gravesend and London. Paris première of *Miss Julie* at the Théâtre Libre, 16 January 1893. Spends several months as the guest of Frida's family at Dornach in Austria.

1894　Daughter, Kerstin, born. *Antibarbarus*, his most extended scientific tract, published. Resumes painting, and plans an exhibition in Paris; photographs the night sky with a pin-hole camera, conducts scientific experiments, and writes the first of many scientifically inflected essays. Moves to Paris in August. Gets to know Gauguin, Delius, Wedekind, Lugné-Poë, and Hamsun; parts irrevocably from Frida; continues to devote himself to a range of activities excluding (for the most part) literature or the theatre.

1894–6　The 'Inferno Crisis', during which Strindberg undergoes a period of severe mental anguish and sometimes suffers from pronounced paranoid delusions and acute psychotic states of mind. Living principally in Paris, but with journeys back to Sweden and Austria, his interest shifts from chemistry to alchemy (although like most makers of gold, he remains distressingly poor) and from naturalism to mysticism, occultism, theosophy, and religion. Begins to read Swedenborg seriously in 1896 and finds in him new ways of structuring his experiences; he also commences his *Occult Diary* and rediscovers his faith in a personal God.

1897　Writes *Inferno*, an account of his recent experiences, in French; follows it with two more autobiographical works, *Legends* and the unfinished *Jacob Wrestles*. Divorces Frida Uhl. Visits Paris for the final time in August.

1898　Returns to Sweden and settles in Lund. Writes *To Damascus I* and *II*, in which he finds a new dramatic style to match his new vision, and *Advent*, a morality play, as well as a further autobiographical novel, *The Cloister* (pub. 1966).

1899 Writes four major plays, *Crimes and Crimes*, *The Saga of the Folkungs*, *Gustav Vasa*, and *Erik XIV*. Settles in Stockholm.

1900 Writes six plays, *Gustav Adolf*, *Midsummer*, *Casper's Shrove Tuesday*, *Easter*, and *The Dance of Death I* and *II*. Meets Harriet Bosse (1878–1961), a young Norwegian actress who appears in the première of *To Damascus I*.

1901 Writes seven plays in a range of styles, *The Crown Bride*, *Swanwhite*, *Charles XII*, *To Damascus III*, *Engelbrekt*, *Queen Christina*, and *A Dream Play*. Marries Harriet Bosse, with whom he honeymoons in Denmark and Berlin.

1902 *Gustav III*, his last major play for five years. Daughter, Anne-Marie, born.

1903 Publishes *Alone*, an autobiographical novel, and a volume of *Fairy Tales*, and writes *The Nightingale of Wittenberg* (a history play about Luther) and the three 'World-Historical Dramas', *Moses*, *Socrates*, and *Christ*.

1904 Writes two novels, *Gothic Rooms* and *Black Banners*, a savage *roman à clef* (pub. 1907). Divorces Harriet, though they remain intimate for several more years.

1905 *Historical Miniatures* (short stories) and *Word-Play and Minor Art* (poems).

1906 Publishes two short novels, *The Roofing Feast* and *The Scapegoat*, and a collection of short stories, *Memories of the Chieftains*.

1907 Founds the Intimate Theatre (with August Falck); writes the Chamber Plays *Thunder in the Air*, *The Burned House*, *The Ghost Sonata*, and *The Pelican*. Publishes the first volume of *A Blue Book*, a compendious collection of brief essays on a variety of topics, scientific, religious, literary, alchemical, etc. Three more volumes appear before his death.

1908 Moves into his last home, 'The Blue Tower' at 85 Drottninggatan, now the Strindberg Museum. Harriet remarries. The *Occult Diary* concluded. Writes three plays, *Abu Casem's Slippers*, *The Last Knight*, and *The Protector of the Realm*.

1909 Publishes *Open Letters to the Intimate Theatre*, on drama and the theatre, his final history play, *Earl Birger of Bjälbo*, and *The Great Highway*, a dramatic epilogue and his last play. Is engaged briefly to Fanny Falkner, a 19-year-old art student who becomes his protégée at the Intimate Theatre.

1910 The Intimate Theatre closes. Commences the 'Strindberg Feud', a violent press polemic on political and religious issues with (among others) the explorer Sven Hedin and the nationalist poet Verner Von

Heidenstam. Strindberg's contributions later appear in book form as *Speeches to the Swedish Nation*.

1911 Signs a contract with Bonniers for the publication of his collected works, thus finally achieving financial security. Publishes *The Roots of World Languages*, one of several late works in comparative philology.

1912 His sixty-third birthday is the object of public celebration, including a torchlight procession of workers and students and numerous performances of his plays. The future socialist prime minister of Sweden, Hjalmar Branting, presents him with an 'Anti-Nobel Prize', some 50,000 crowns raised by a national subscription, including 11,000 contributions of less than 50 öre (1 shilling). Dies 14 May, of stomach cancer, three weeks after Siri von Essen.

THE FATHER
[Fadren]
A Tragedy

(1887)

CHARACTERS

The Captain
Laura, his wife
Bertha, their daughter
Doctor Östermark
The Pastor
The Nurse
Nöjd*
The Orderly

ACT 1

A living room in the CAPTAIN'*s house. At the back a door to the right leading to the entrance hall. In the middle of the room a large, round table with newspapers and journals. Stage right a leather sofa and table. In the right-hand corner a jib-door* covered in matching wallpaper leading to the* CAPTAIN'*s room above. Stage left a secretaire with a pendulum clock and a door leading to the rest of the house. Weapons on the walls; rifles and gamebags. By the door a clothes tree with military coats on it. On the large table a lamp is burning.*

SCENE 1

The CAPTAIN *and the* PASTOR *are sitting on the leather sofa. The* CAPTAIN *is in undress uniform, with riding boots and spurs. The* PASTOR *is in black, with a white neck collar but no lappets; he is smoking a pipe. The* CAPTAIN *rings.*

ORDERLY [*enters*]. You wanted something, sir?

CAPTAIN. Is Nöjd out there?

ORDERLY. Nöjd's in the kitchen, sir, awaiting orders.

CAPTAIN. The kitchen, again! Send him in right away!

ORDERLY. Very good, sir. [*Goes*

PASTOR. What's the matter now?

CAPTAIN. The rascal's been fooling about with the kitchen-maid again. He's a damned nuisance, that one!

PASTOR. Nöjd, you mean? He was in trouble last year, too, wasn't he?

CAPTAIN. Ah, you remember, do you? Now if you'd give him a friendly talking-to it might get through. I've sworn at him and given him a good drubbing too, but it has no effect.

PASTOR. So you want me to read him a sermon. What effect do you think God's word will have on a cavalryman?

CAPTAIN. Well, you may be my brother-in-law, but it's had none on me, as you know...

PASTOR. Indeed, I do!

CAPTAIN. But it might on him! Anyway, it's worth a try.

SCENE 2

The CAPTAIN. *The* PASTOR. NÖJD.

CAPTAIN. What have you been up to now, Nöjd?

NÖJD. Beg pardon, Captain, but I can't talk about it. Not in front of the Pastor here.

PASTOR. Don't let me embarrass you, my lad!

CAPTAIN. Out with it now, or you know what'll happen.

NÖJD. Well, you see, it was like this, we was dancing up at Gabriel's, and then, and then Ludvig said...

CAPTAIN. What's Ludvig got to do with it? Stick to the truth, man.

NÖJD. Well, and then Emma said we should go to the barn.

CAPTAIN. So, it was Emma who led you astray, I suppose?

NÖJD. We-ll, not exactly, but that weren't far off it, and I'll say this, if the girl don't want to, there's nothing doing.

CAPTAIN. Once and for all: are you the child's father or not?

NÖJD. How's a man to know that?

CAPTAIN. What do you mean? You don't know?

NÖJD. No, see, that's something a man can never know.

CAPTAIN. Weren't you the only one, then?

NÖJD. That time, yes, but how's a man to know he's always been the only one?

CAPTAIN. Are you trying to shift the blame onto Ludvig? Is that what you mean?

NÖJD. It's hard to know who to blame.

CAPTAIN. All right, but you've told Emma you want to marry her.

NÖJD. Oh, you always have to tell them that...

CAPTAIN [*to the* PASTOR]. This is outrageous!

PASTOR. It's the old story! But look here, Nöjd, surely you're man enough to know if you're the father?

NÖJD. Well, I had her all right, but you know well enough yourself, Pastor, that don't necessarily mean something has to happen!

PASTOR. Listen, my lad, it's you we're talking about now! And you'll surely not just abandon the girl alone with the child! You can't be forced to marry her, maybe, but you must take care of the child! That you must!

NÖJD. All right, but then so must Ludvig.

CAPTAIN. The case will have to go to court, then. I can't get to the bottom of it all, and I've really no wish to try. Right, dismiss!

PASTOR. Just a moment, Nöjd. Don't you think it's dishonourable to leave a girl in the lurch like that with a child? Don't you think so? Eh? Don't you consider such behaviour is... well...

NÖJD. Oh, if I knew I was the child's father, yes. But, you see, your reverence, that's something a man can never know. And sweating your whole life away for someone else's child, that's no joke! I'm sure you and the Captain both know what I mean!

CAPTAIN. Dismiss!

NÖJD. God save you, Captain! [*Exits*

CAPTAIN. But keep out of the kitchen, you rascal!

SCENE 3

The CAPTAIN. *The* PASTOR.

CAPTAIN. Well, why didn't you let him have it?

PASTOR. What do you mean? I thought I did!

CAPTAIN. Huh! You just sat there muttering to yourself!

PASTOR. To be honest, I really don't know what to say. It's hard on the girl, yes; but it's hard on the boy, too. Just suppose he isn't the father! The girl's only got to spend four months as a wet-nurse at the orphanage to get her child a permanent berth there.* The boy can hardly do that! The girl'll get a good place afterwards with a respectable family, but the boy's whole future might be ruined if he's discharged from the regiment.

CAPTAIN. Yes, I'm damned glad I'm not the magistrate who has to judge this case. I don't suppose the boy's that innocent, one just can't know, but one thing's for sure: the girl's guilty—if you can call it guilt.

PASTOR. Well, well, I'm judging no one. But what were we talking about now, before this blessed business interrupted us? Bertha's confirmation, wasn't it?

CAPTAIN. Not so much her confirmation; it's her whole upbringing that's at stake. This house is full of women, every one of whom wants to bring up my child. My mother-in-law wants to turn her into a spiritualist; Laura wants her to be an artist; the governess wants to make her a Methodist; old Margret wants her to be a Baptist; and the maids want to enroll her in the Salvation Army. It's no way to patch a soul together. Not when I'm the one who should be guiding her steps and I am constantly opposed in all my efforts. That's why I've got to get her out of this house.

PASTOR. You've too many women running your home.

CAPTAIN. You can say that again! It's like being in a cage full of tigers. If I didn't keep a red-hot iron in front of their noses they'd tear me to pieces the first chance they got! Yes, you can laugh, you rogue. It wasn't enough I married your sister, you had to palm your old stepmother off on me as well.

PASTOR. Oh good heavens, a man can hardly live under the same roof as his stepmother.

CAPTAIN. No, but a mother-in-law under someone else's is fine by you.

PASTOR. Yes, well, everyone has his lot in life.

CAPTAIN. Yes, but I've more than my fair share. I've my old nurse too, who treats me as though I were still wearing a bib. She's a dear old soul, God knows, but she doesn't belong here!

PASTOR. You should keep your women in line, Adolf; you let them run things far too much.

CAPTAIN. My dear fellow, will you kindly tell me how one keeps women in line?

PASTOR. Frankly speaking, Laura may be my own sister but she always was a bit trying.

CAPTAIN. No doubt Laura has her faults, but she's not so bad.

PASTOR. Oh, come on now, I know what she's like.

CAPTAIN. She's been brought up with a lot of romantic ideas and finds it hard to adjust, but after all she is my wife...

PASTOR. And because she's your wife, she's the best of women. No, Adolf, she's your greatest bane.

CAPTAIN. Yes, well, anyway, now the whole house has been turned upside-down. Laura won't let go of Bertha, and I can't let her stay in this madhouse.

PASTOR. So, Laura won't, eh? Well, in that case, I'm afraid things aren't going to be easy. When she was a child, she used to play dead until she got what she wanted. And when she'd got it, she'd hand it back, saying it wasn't the thing itself she wanted, just the fact of getting her own way.

CAPTAIN. Really, she was like that even then, eh? Hm! She gets so worked up at times, I'm really afraid she might be ill.

PASTOR. But what have you in mind for Bertha that she finds so unacceptable? Can't you meet each other halfway?

CAPTAIN. You mustn't think I want to turn her into a child wonder or remake her in my own image. I don't want to be my daughter's pimp, that's all—bring her up for marriage and nothing else. Then she'll have a hard time of it, if she remained single. On the other hand, I don't want to put her into some man's career, which requires years of study, because if she does decide to get married that would only prove a waste of time.

PASTOR. What do you want, then?

CAPTAIN. I want her to be a teacher. If she doesn't marry, then she can always fend for herself; she'll be no worse off than a poor schoolmaster with a family to support. If she marries, she can use what she's learned to bring up her own children. That's logical, isn't it?

PASTOR. Oh, perfectly! On the other hand, hasn't she shown such a talent for painting that it would go against the grain to repress it?

CAPTAIN. No! I showed some of her work to a well-known artist, and he says it's just the kind of thing everyone learns to do in school. But then last summer along comes some young whipper-snapper who knows better, and says she's a genius—and as far as Laura was concerned, that settled it.

PASTOR. Was he in love with the girl?

CAPTAIN. I take that for granted!

PASTOR. Then God help you, my dear fellow, for no one else can. This is all very sad, and Laura has her allies, of course... in there.

CAPTAIN. You can be sure of that! The whole household is up in arms, and just between you and me, they're not exactly fighting according to the rules.

PASTOR [*getting up*]. Do you think I don't know what it's like?

CAPTAIN. You, too?

PASTOR. Why not?

CAPTAIN. But the worst of it is, it seems to me Bertha's future is being decided in there out of pure spite. They keep on dropping hints about men finding out that women can do both this and that. It's man against woman, all day long, without end.—Are you going? No, do stay for supper. Nothing very grand, I suppose, but all the same; and you know I'm expecting the new doctor to come by. Have you seen him?

PASTOR. I caught a glimpse of him on my way over. He looked a decent enough sort, reliable.

CAPTAIN. Good, that's something. Do you think he might turn out my ally?

PASTOR. Who knows? It all depends how much he's had to do with women.

CAPTAIN. All right, but won't you stay?

PASTOR. No thanks, my dear fellow. I said I'd be home for supper, and my good lady gets anxious if I'm late.

CAPTAIN. Anxious? Angry, you mean! Well, as you will. Here, let me help you with your coat.

PASTOR. It's certainly very cold this evening. Many thanks. You should take care of yourself, Adolf, you seem a bit on edge!

CAPTAIN. Me, on edge?

PASTOR. Yes, are you sure you're feeling all right?

CAPTAIN. What's Laura been telling you? She's been treating me as if I'd one foot in the grave for twenty years.

PASTOR. Laura? No, no, it's just that you worry me. Take care of yourself. That's my advice. Goodbye, old chap. But didn't you want to talk to me about Bertha's confirmation?

CAPTAIN. Not really. I'm just going to let that take its normal course, according to convention. I've no intention of being a martyr to the truth. We're past all that. Goodbye, now. My regards to your wife!

PASTOR. Goodbye, Adolf. Give mine to Laura!

SCENE 4

The CAPTAIN, *then* LAURA.

CAPTAIN [*opens the secretaire and sits down at it, to do the accounts*]. Thirty-four—nine, forty-three—seven, eight, fifty-six.

LAURA [*enters from within the house*]. Would you mind...

CAPTAIN. Just a moment!—Sixty-six, seventy-one, eighty-four, eighty-nine, ninety-two, one hundred. What did you want?

LAURA. Am I interrupting?

CAPTAIN. Not at all! The housekeeping money, I suppose?

LAURA. Yes, the housekeeping.

CAPTAIN. Leave the accounts there, and I'll go through them.

LAURA. Accounts?

CAPTAIN. Yes.

LAURA. You want accounts now, do you?

CAPTAIN. Of course I do. We're in poor shape financially, and if things should come to a head, we'd need to produce them. Otherwise our creditors could sue me.

LAURA. It's not my fault if we're badly off.

CAPTAIN. That's just what the accounts will show.

LAURA. It's not my fault if that tenant of ours doesn't pay.

CAPTAIN. Who recommended him so highly? You! Why did you recommend a—let's just say—a good-for-nothing?

LAURA. Why did you take this good-for-nothing on then?

CAPTAIN. Because you wouldn't let me eat in peace, sleep in peace, or work in peace until you'd got him here. You wanted him because your brother wished to be rid of him, your mother wanted him because I didn't, the governess wanted him because he was a pietist, and old Margret because she'd known his grandmother from childhood. That's why we took him; and if I hadn't done so I'd be in the madhouse now, or lying in the family grave. All the same, here's the housekeeping and your pin money. You can let me have the accounts later.

LAURA [*curtseys*]. Thank you very much.—You keep a record of what you spend on yourself, do you?

CAPTAIN. That's none of your business.

LAURA. True—just like my child's upbringing. Have you gentlemen reached a decision yet after this evening's deliberations?

CAPTAIN. I'd already reached my decision. I merely wished to impart it to the only friend we seem have in common. Bertha is to live in town; she leaves in a fortnight.

LAURA. With whom is she to live, if I may ask?

CAPTAIN. With Säfberg, the lawyer.

LAURA. That freethinker!

CAPTAIN. As the law stands, children should be brought up in their father's faith.*

LAURA. And the mother has no say in the matter?

CAPTAIN. None at all. She's sold her birthright in a legal exchange, and relinquished all her rights; in return, her husband supports her and her children.

LAURA. So she has no rights over her own child?

CAPTAIN. None whatever!* Once you've sold something, you can't have it back and keep the money.

LAURA. But what if the father and mother were to reach a compromise...

CAPTAIN. And what might that be? I want her to live in town, you want her to stay at home. Take the arithmetic mean and she'd end up halfway, at the railway station. No, compromise is not a solution, you see!

LAURA. Then we'll have to try force!—What was Nöjd doing here?

CAPTAIN. That's a military secret.

LAURA. Which the whole kitchen knows.

CAPTAIN. Good, then you should know it too.

LAURA. I do.

CAPTAIN. And have already passed judgement?

LAURA. The law is quite specific.

CAPTAIN. It doesn't say who the child's father is.

LAURA. No, but one usually knows.

CAPTAIN. They say one can never really know that.

LAURA. How extraordinary! Not know who a child's father is?

CAPTAIN. So they say.

LAURA. Extraordinary! Then how can the father have all these rights over her child?

CAPTAIN. He has them only where he assumes responsibility, or has responsibility forced upon him. And in marriage, of course, paternity is not in doubt.

LAURA. Not in doubt?

CAPTAIN. I should hope not!

LAURA. Suppose the wife has been unfaithful?

CAPTAIN. That isn't the case here! Do you have any more questions?

LAURA. No!

CAPTAIN. Then I'll go up to my room. Will you let me know when the doctor arrives please.   [*Closes the secretaire and gets up*

LAURA. Yes sir!

CAPTAIN [*going out through the jib-door*]. The moment he arrives. I don't wish to appear discourteous. Understand?   [*Exits*

LAURA. I understand!

SCENE 5

LAURA *alone; looks at the banknotes in her hand.*

THE MOTHER-IN-LAW'S VOICE [*from within*]. Laura!

LAURA. Yes!

THE MOTHER-IN-LAW'S VOICE. Is my tea ready?

LAURA [*in the doorway to the living quarters*]. It's on its way!

LAURA *is moving towards the door at the rear when the* ORDERLY *opens it and announces 'Doctor Östermark'.*

DOCTOR. Madam!

LAURA [*going to meet him and extending her hand*]. Welcome, doctor. We're delighted to see you. The Captain is out, but he'll be back shortly.

DOCTOR. Forgive me for coming so late, but I've already had some patients to see.

LAURA. Won't you sit down? Please!—

DOCTOR. Thank you.

LAURA. Yes, there's a lot of sickness about just now. I do hope you'll like it here, though. Living out here in the country as we do, it's so important to find a doctor who takes an interest in his patients. And I've heard so many good things about you, Doctor, I do hope we shall get along well together.

DOCTOR. You're too kind, madam, although I hope for your sake that my visits here will not often be of a professional nature. Your family enjoys good health, I trust...

LAURA. No really serious illnesses, I'm glad to say, but all the same, things aren't quite as they should be...

DOCTOR. Indeed?

LAURA. Yes, unfortunately, things are not altogether as we might wish.

DOCTOR. Really? You alarm me!

LAURA. There are some things in family life that one is honour-bound to conceal from the world...

DOCTOR. But not from one's doctor.

LAURA. That's why it is my painful duty to tell you the whole truth right from the start.

DOCTOR. May we not postpone this conversation until I have had the honour of meeting the Captain?

LAURA. No! You must hear what I have to say before you see him.

DOCTOR. It concerns him, then?

LAURA. Yes, him—my poor, dear husband.

DOCTOR. This is most alarming. Believe me, you have my deepest sympathy!

LAURA [*taking out her handkerchief*]. My husband is mentally ill. Now you know everything. You may judge for yourself in due course.

DOCTOR. What are you saying! But I've read the Captain's papers on mineralogy with enormous admiration and always remarked in them a fine and lucid intellect.

LAURA. Really? I'd be delighted if we were all to be proved wrong.

DOCTOR. But it's possible his mind may be disturbed in some other way. Please, go on.

LAURA. That's just what we're afraid of. You see, he sometimes has the most peculiar ideas, to which as a scientist he might of course be entitled if they didn't threaten the well-being of his entire family. For example, he has a mania for buying all manner of things.

DOCTOR. That's worrying; what kind of things?

LAURA. Books! Whole crates of them, that he never reads.

DOCTOR. Well, there's nothing very odd in a scholar buying books.

LAURA. You don't believe me?

DOCTOR. I'm quite sure, madam, that you believe everything you're saying.

LAURA. But is it reasonable for a man to see through a microscope what's happening on another planet?

DOCTOR. Does he say he can do that?

LAURA. That's what he says.

DOCTOR. Through a microscope?

LAURA. Yes! A microscope!

DOCTOR. If that's so, then it is very worrying!

LAURA. If that's so! Here I am, doctor, confiding our family secrets to you, and you have no confidence in me...

DOCTOR. Now, now madam, I'm honoured by your confidence, but as a doctor I must conduct a thorough examination before I make a diagnosis. Has the Captain been given to sudden changes of mood or vacillation?

LAURA. Has he just? We've been married twenty years and he has never yet made a decision without reversing it!

DOCTOR. Is he stubborn?

LAURA. He always insists on having his own way, but once he gets it, he loses all interest and begs me to decide.

DOCTOR. This is worrying. I need to observe him closely. You see, madam, the will is the backbone of the mind; if it's impaired, the mind simply disintegrates.

LAURA. And God knows all I've done to meet his every wish during these long years of trial. Oh, if you only knew what I've had to put up with, living with him. If you only knew!

DOCTOR. Madam, your misfortune moves me deeply; I promise you I shall do whatever can be done. You have my most profound sympathy and may depend on me absolutely. But in the light of what I've heard, I must ask you one thing. Avoid touching upon any subjects that might excite the patient, for in an unstable mind they spread like wildfire, and easily turn into obsessions or fixed ideas. Do you understand?

LAURA. You mean I'm to avoid anything that might arouse his suspicion!

DOCTOR. Precisely! Just because he's so receptive to everything, a sick man will believe anything you tell him.

LAURA. I see! Yes, I see! Yes.—Yes! [*A bell rings within*] Excuse me, my mother wants a word with me. I won't be a moment... Ah, here's Adolf...

SCENE 6

The DOCTOR. *The* CAPTAIN *enters through the jib-door.*

CAPTAIN. Oh, you're here already, Doctor. Delighted to see you!

DOCTOR. Captain! It's a real pleasure to meet such a distinguished man of science.

CAPTAIN. Oh, please. My military duties don't allow me much time for serious research; nevertheless, I do think I'm on the track of an important discovery.

DOCTOR. Really!

CAPTAIN. Yes, you see, I've been submitting meteorites to spectral analysis* and found carbon, traces of organic life! What do you say to that?

DOCTOR. Can you see that in a microscope?

CAPTAIN. No, damn it, a spectroscope!*

DOCTOR. Spectroscope! Of course, I'm sorry! Well, then, you'll soon be able to tell us what's happening on Jupiter!

CAPTAIN. Not what's happening, but what has happened. If only that damned bookseller in Paris would send me those books—but I believe all the booksellers in the world have conspired against me. Would you credit it, two whole months and not a single reply to any of my orders or letters, not even my abusive telegrams! It'll drive me mad, I just don't understand what's going on!

DOCTOR. Oh, it's just common or garden carelessness, I suppose; you shouldn't take it too seriously.

CAPTAIN. Yes, but damn it all, I won't be able to get my paper finished in time, and I know they're working along the same lines in Berlin. But we're supposed to be talking about you now, not me! If you'd like to live here we've a small flat in the wing. Or do you want to live at the old doctor's place?

DOCTOR. Just as you wish.

CAPTAIN. No, it's as you wish. Just say!

DOCTOR. You must decide, Captain.

CAPTAIN. No, I'll decide nothing of the sort. It's up to you to say what you want. I've no preference, none at all!

DOCTOR. No, but I can't decide...

CAPTAIN. For Christ's sake, man, just say what you want. It's not up to me; I couldn't give a damn either way! Are you such a jellyfish you don't know what you want? Now, tell me, or I'll lose my temper!

DOCTOR. Since it's up to me, I'll live here!

CAPTAIN. Good! Thank you!—Oh!—Forgive me, Doctor, but nothing riles me more than hearing people say something's all the same to them.   [*Rings*

The NURSE *enters.*

CAPTAIN. Oh, it's you, Margret. Tell me, my dear, do you know if the wing is ready for the Doctor?

NURSE. Yes, it is, Captain!

CAPTAIN. Right! Then I won't keep you, Doctor, you must be tired. Goodbye for now. I look forward to seeing you again tomorrow.

DOCTOR. Goodnight, Captain!

CAPTAIN. I suppose my wife has told you something about the situation here, so you know more or less how the land lies.

DOCTOR. Your charming wife has given me a few pointers—things a newcomer ought to know. Goodnight, Captain.

SCENE 7

The CAPTAIN. *The* NURSE.

CAPTAIN. Well, my dear, is something the matter?

NURSE. Now, Master Adolf, just you listen to me.

CAPTAIN. All right, Margret. Go on, my dear, you're the only one I can listen to without being driven wild.

NURSE. Now, Master Adolf, listen: all this business about the child, couldn't you meet the mistress halfway? Remember she's a mother and...

CAPTAIN. And I'm a father, Margret!

NURSE. There, there, now, all right! But a father's got other things to think about beside his child, a mother only has her child.

CAPTAIN. That's precisely it. She's only got the one burden but I've got three, including hers. Don't you think I'd have been something more in life than an old soldier if I hadn't been saddled with her and her child?

NURSE. That's not what I meant.

CAPTAIN. No, I'm sure you didn't, you just wanted to put me in the wrong.

NURSE. Don't you think I want what's best for you, Master Adolf?

CAPTAIN. Yes, my dear, I'm sure you do, but you don't know what that is. You see, it's not enough for me to have given the child life; I want to give it my soul as well.

NURSE. Oh, all that's beyond me. But I still believe people should be able to get along together.

CAPTAIN. You're not my friend, Margret.

NURSE. Me? Goodness, Master Adolf, how can you say such a thing? Do you think I can ever forget you were my baby boy when you were little?

CAPTAIN. How could I ever forget it, my dear? You've been like a mother to me; up until now you've always supported me, even when everyone else was against me. But now, at the crucial moment, you betray me and go over to the enemy.

NURSE. Enemy!

CAPTAIN. Yes, the enemy! You know well enough how things are in this house, you've seen it all, from beginning to end.

NURSE. Indeed I have. But, dear God, why do two people have to torture each other to death; two people who are otherwise so good, and so kind to everyone else? The mistress is never like that to me or to other people. . .

CAPTAIN. Only to me, I know. But let me tell you, Margret, if you desert me now you commit a sin. There's a web being spun about me here, and that Doctor's no friend of mine!

NURSE. Oh, you think badly of everyone, Master Adolf, but that's
what comes of not having the true faith, you see. Yes, that's how
it is.

CAPTAIN. But you and your Baptists have found the one true faith, I
suppose. You're happy, anyway!

NURSE. Well, I'm certainly not as unhappy as you are, Master Adolf.
Just you humble your heart and you'll see how God will make you
happy, too, and love your neighbour.

CAPTAIN. It's strange, you know, you've only got to talk about God
and love, and your voice turns hard and your eyes fill with hate.
I'm sorry Margret, but that's certainly not the true faith.

NURSE. Oh yes, you're proud and stuck up enough with all your
book-learning, but that won't get you very far when it really
matters.

CAPTAIN. How haughtily speaks the humble of heart! At least I
know that learning's wasted on creatures like you!

NURSE. Shame on you! All the same, though, old Margret still loves
her big boy best, and when the storm breaks he'll come back to her
again, like the good little child he is.

CAPTAIN. Margret! I'm sorry—believe me, you're the only friend
I've got here. Help me! Something's about to happen here, I know
it is. I don't know what exactly, but it isn't right, whatever it is.
[*There is a scream from within*] What was that? Who screamed?

SCENE 8

As before. BERTHA *enters from within.*

BERTHA. Father, father, help me! Save me!

CAPTAIN. What is it, my child? Tell me!

BERTHA. Help! She wants to hurt me. I'm sure she does!

CAPTAIN. Who wants to hurt you? Come on, tell me!

BERTHA. Grandma! But it was my fault. I fooled her!

CAPTAIN. Go on!

BERTHA. Yes, but you mustn't say anything! Promise you won't!

CAPTAIN. All right. But tell me what it is!　　　[*The* NURSE *leaves*

BERTHA. Well, when evening comes she likes to turn the lamp down and sit me at the table holding a pen over a piece of paper. And then she says the spirits are going to write.

CAPTAIN. What's that! And you haven't told me about this before!

BERTHA. Forgive me, but I didn't dare to. Grandma says the spirits take their revenge if you do. And then the pen writes, but I don't know if it's me. And sometimes it goes all right, but at others not at all. And when I get tired, nothing comes, but it has to come all the same. And tonight I thought I was doing quite well, but then Grandma said it was straight out of Stagnelius,* and I'd been fooling her, and then she got so terribly angry.

CAPTAIN. Do you believe these spirits exist?

BERTHA. I don't know.

CAPTAIN. Well, I know they don't!

BERTHA. But Grandma says you don't understand, and that you've got much worse things that can see all the way to other planets.

CAPTAIN. She does, does she! What else does she say?

BERTHA. She says you can't do magic!

CAPTAIN. I've never said I could. You know what meteorites are, don't you? Stones that fall from other heavenly bodies. I can examine them and tell if they contain the same elements as our earth. That's all I can see.

BERTHA. But Grandma says there are things that she can see but you can't.

CAPTAIN. Then she's lying!

BERTHA. Grandma doesn't tell lies!

CAPTAIN. Why not?

BERTHA. Because in that case mummy tells lies too!

CAPTAIN. Hm!

BERTHA. If you say mummy tells lies, I'll never believe you again!

CAPTAIN. That's not what I said. Which is why you've got to believe me when I say that it's best for you and your entire future if you leave this house! Would you like that? Would you like to go and live in town and learn something useful?

BERTHA. Oh yes, I'd love to live in town—anywhere, away from here! As long as I can see you sometimes—often! It's always so gloomy in there, so horrible, like a winter night, but when you come home, father, it's like opening a window on a spring morning!*

CAPTAIN. My dear, my darling child!

BERTHA. But, father, you must be nice to mummy, do you hear? She cries such a lot!

CAPTAIN. Hm!—So you want to move to town?

BERTHA. Yes! Yes!

CAPTAIN. But what if your mother doesn't want you to?

BERTHA. But she must!

CAPTAIN. But supposing she doesn't?

BERTHA. Then I don't know what will happen. But she must, she must!

CAPTAIN. Will you ask her?

BERTHA. No, you must ask her, nicely, she doesn't take any notice of me!

CAPTAIN. Hm!—Well, if you want to, and I want you to, and she doesn't, what shall we do then?

BERTHA. Oh, then everything'll be so impossible again! Why can't you both...

SCENE 9

The CAPTAIN. BERTHA. LAURA.

LAURA. So, this is where you are, Bertha! Well, since it's her fate we're deciding, perhaps we might hear what she's got to say.

CAPTAIN. The child can scarcely have much to say about what the future holds for a young girl. You and I have seen a good many young girls grow up, though, so we shouldn't have too much trouble figuring it out.

LAURA. But since we don't agree, Bertha can decide.

CAPTAIN. No! I won't let anyone usurp my rights, neither woman nor child. Bertha, leave us. [BERTHA *leaves*

LAURA. You were afraid of what she might say. You thought it would be to my advantage.

CAPTAIN. I happen to know that she wants to leave home, but I know too that you have the power to change her mind any way you wish.

LAURA. Oh, am I so powerful?

CAPTAIN. Yes, you have a truly satanic power when it comes to getting your own way, but someone who doesn't care about the means always does. How did you get rid of old Dr Norling, for example, and then drum up this new fellow?

LAURA. Yes, how did I?

CAPTAIN. By insulting Norling until he left and getting your brother to canvass support for this one.

LAURA. Well, all very simple and quite above board. Is Bertha to leave?

CAPTAIN. Yes, in a fortnight.

LAURA. Is that final?

CAPTAIN. Yes!

LAURA. Have you spoken to Bertha about it?

CAPTAIN. Yes!

LAURA. Then I shall just have to try and prevent it!

CAPTAIN. You can't!

LAURA. Can't! Do you really think a mother is going to let her daughter go and live among evil-minded people who'll tell her that everything her mother has brought her up to believe is nonsense, so she'll despise her mother for the rest of her life?

CAPTAIN. And do you suppose a father is going to let a bunch of ignorant and superstitious women teach his daughter that he's a charlatan?

LAURA. It doesn't matter so much to a father.

CAPTAIN. How's that?

LAURA. Because a mother is closer to her child. After all, it's been established that no one can really know who a child's father is.

CAPTAIN. What has that to do with the present case?

LAURA. You don't know if you're Bertha's father!

CAPTAIN. Don't I!

LAURA. No, how can you know what other people don't!

CAPTAIN. Are you joking?

LAURA. No, I'm only applying your own principles. Besides, how do you know I haven't been unfaithful?

CAPTAIN. I can believe almost anything of you, but not that. Nor that you would talk about it if it were true.

LAURA. Suppose I was willing to endure everything, to be driven out, despised, anything just to keep my child and bring her up. Suppose I was telling the truth just now when I said that Bertha is my child, but not yours! Suppose...

CAPTAIN. Stop it!

LAURA. Just suppose: then your authority would be at an end!

CAPTAIN. You'd have to prove I wasn't the father!

LAURA. That wouldn't be so difficult! Do you want me to?

CAPTAIN. Stop it!

LAURA. I'd only need to give the name of the real father, specify the time and place; for instance—when was Bertha born?—Three years into our marriage...

CAPTAIN. I said stop it! Or else...

LAURA. Or else, what? All right, we'll stop! But think again before you decide to do anything! And above all, don't make yourself ridiculous!

CAPTAIN. I find all this extremely sad!

LAURA. Then you really are ridiculous!

CAPTAIN. But not you?

LAURA. No, we're not made like that.

CAPTAIN. That's why we can't fight with you.

LAURA. Why try to fight with a superior enemy?

CAPTAIN. Superior?

LAURA. Yes! It's strange, but I've never been able to look at a man without feeling I'm his superior.

CAPTAIN. Well, for once you're going to meet your match, and you'll never forget it.

LAURA. That will be interesting.

NURSE [*enters*]. Supper's ready. Won't you come and eat?

LAURA. Yes, thank you!

The CAPTAIN *hesitates; sits in an armchair next to the divan table.*

LAURA. Aren't you coming to supper?

CAPTAIN. No thank you, I don't want anything.

LAURA. What! You're not upset, are you?

CAPTAIN. No, I'm just not hungry.

LAURA. Come along now, or they'll start asking unnecessary questions.—Do be sensible, now!—Oh, all right then, sit there!

[*Exits*

NURSE. Master Adolf! What is all this?

CAPTAIN. I don't know. Can you tell me how you women can treat a grown man as if he were a child?

NURSE. Don't ask me. I suppose it's because you're all born of women, every one of you, big or small...

CAPTAIN. Whereas no woman is born of man. Yes, but I am Bertha's father. Tell me Margret, you do believe that? Don't you?

NURSE. Lord, what a baby you are. Of course you're your own child's father. Now come and eat, and don't sit there sulking! There, there, come along!

CAPTAIN [*gets up*]. Get out, woman! To hell with you, you witches! [*Goes to the hall door*] Svärd! Svärd!*

ORDERLY [*enters*]. Sir?

CAPTAIN. Harness the sleigh, at once!

NURSE. Captain! Now listen...

CAPTAIN. Get out, woman! At once!

NURSE. Lord preserve us, what's going to happen now?

CAPTAIN [*puts on his cap and equips himself to go out*]. Don't expect me home before midnight! [*Exits*

NURSE. Sweet Jesus, help us, how is this all going to end?

ACT 2

The same set as the previous act. The lamp is burning on the table; it is night.

SCENE 1

The DOCTOR. LAURA.

DOCTOR. Judging by my conversation with him, I'm still not entirely certain how things stand. In the first place, you were mistaken when you said he'd reached these startling conclusions about other heavenly bodies with a microscope. Now that I know it was a spectroscope, he's not only acquitted of any suspicion of mental instability; he also merits the highest praise as a scientist.

LAURA. Yes, but I never said that!

DOCTOR. Madam, I took notes of our conversation; I recall asking you specifically about the main point again because I thought I must have misheard you. One must be scrupulous about such accusations, when they could lead to a man being certified incapable of managing his affairs.

LAURA. Certified incapable?

DOCTOR. Yes, surely you know that someone who's declared insane loses his civil and family rights.

LAURA. No, I'd no idea.

DOCTOR. There's a further point which seems suspect to me. He mentioned that his letters to booksellers were going unanswered. May I ask if you—with the best of intentions—have been intercepting his mail?

LAURA. Yes, I have. But it was my duty to act in the family's best interest; I couldn't just stand idly by and let him ruin us all.

DOCTOR. Forgive me, but I don't think you could have foreseen the consequences of such an action. If he finds out you've been secretly meddling in his affairs his suspicions will be confirmed, and then they'll grow like an avalanche. What's more, by fettering his will you'll have further inflamed his impatience. You must know how painful it is to have one's dearest wishes frustrated, one's will thwarted.

LAURA. Don't I just!

DOCTOR. Well, then, judge how he must have felt.

LAURA [*getting up*]. Midnight, and he's still not home. Now we can expect the worst.

DOCTOR. But tell me, madam, what happened this evening after I left? I must know everything.

LAURA. Oh, he talked quite wildly and had the most bizarre ideas. Can you believe it—he got it into his head that he wasn't his own child's father.

DOCTOR. How very strange. Whatever gave him that idea?

LAURA. I really don't know—unless, well, he had been questioning one of the men about the parentage of some child or other, and when I took the girl's side he got excited and said that no one could tell who any child's father was. God knows, I did everything to calm him down, but now I think the whole thing's hopeless.   [*Weeps*

DOCTOR. But this can't be allowed to continue; something must be done, though without arousing his suspicions. Tell me, has the Captain had such wild fancies before?

LAURA. It was like this six years ago. Then he said himself that he feared for his sanity. He even wrote and told his doctor about it.

DOCTOR. Yes, yes, it's a deep-rooted problem, this. However, I'll not delve into it—the sanctity of family life, and so on—just confine myself to what may be observed. What's done can't be undone unfortunately; treatment should have been undertaken at the time.—Where do you think he is now?

LAURA. I've no idea. He's so unpredictable these days.

DOCTOR. Would you like me to await his return? To avoid arousing his suspicions, I could always say I was visiting your mother—that she'd been taken ill.

LAURA. That's an excellent idea! But don't leave us, Doctor. If you only knew how worried I am! Wouldn't it be better, though, to tell him right out what you think of his condition?

DOCTOR. One never says that to the mentally ill before they raise the subject themselves, and then only in exceptional cases. It depends entirely on what turn things take. But in that case we'd better not sit here. Perhaps I might slip into the next room, so it looks more natural.

LAURA. Yes, that would be better, then Margret can sit here. She always waits up for him when he's out; she's the only one who can do anything with him. [*Goes to the door, left*] Margret! Margret!

NURSE. What is it, madam? Is the master home?

LAURA. No, but you're to sit here and wait for him; and when he comes, you're to say that my mother's poorly and that's why the Doctor's here.

NURSE. Yes, yes. You just leave it to me.

LAURA [*opens the door to the inner rooms*]. Won't you please come in here, Doctor?

DOCTOR. Thank you.

SCENE 2

NURSE [*at the table; picks up her glasses and a hymnal*]. Yes, yes! Yes, yes!   [*Reads half to herself*

> A sorrowful and wretched thing
> Is life, whose end is swiftly nigh.
> Death's angel spreads his dark'ning wing
> And through the world resounds his cry:
> 'All is fleeting, All is vanity!'

Yes, yes! Yes, yes!

> All that on earth both breathes and lives
> To earth must fall before his might;

Sorrow alone proud death survives,
Above the fresh-laid grave to write:
'All is fleeting, All is vanity!'*

Yes, yes!

BERTHA [*has entered carrying a coffee-pot and a piece of embroidery;
speaks quietly*]. Can I sit with you, Margret? It's so horrible up
there!

NURSE. Heavens above, child; are you still up?

BERTHA. Oh, but I've got to finish father's Christmas present. And
here's something nice for you, too.

NURSE. But you dear, sweet child, this won't do; you've got to get up
in the morning; and it's past twelve o'clock.

BERTHA. What difference does that make? I daren't sit up there on
my own, I think it's haunted.

NURSE. You see! What did I say? Yes, you mark my words, there's
no good angel in this house. What did you hear?

BERTHA. I'm sure I heard someone singing in the attic.

NURSE. In the attic! At this time of night!

BERTHA. Yes. It was such a sad song, so sad, not like anything I've
ever heard before. And it sounded as if it came from the boxroom
where the cradle is, you know, to the left...

NURSE. Oh dear, oh dear! And what weather, too! I'm sure it'll
bring the chimneys down. 'Oh, what is this our earthly life?—
Lamentation, pain and strife.—Even at its very best.—It was only
trial and test.'*—Yes, dear child, God grant us a happy Christmas!

BERTHA. Margret, is it true that father's ill?

NURSE. Yes, I'm afraid he is.

BERTHA. That means no Christmas Eve* for us then. But if he's ill,
why isn't he in bed?

NURSE. Well, my child, when you're ill like he is, you can still be up.
Sshh! There's someone out in the hall. Go to bed now, and take
the coffee-pot with you, otherwise the master'll be angry.

BERTHA [*leaves with the tray*]. Good night, Margret!

NURSE. Good night, my child, God bless you!

SCENE 3

The NURSE. *The* CAPTAIN.

CAPTAIN [*taking off his greatcoat*]. Are you still up? Go to bed!

NURSE. I was only waiting till...

The CAPTAIN *lights a candle; opens the leaf of the secretaire; sits down and takes some letters and newspapers from his pocket.*

NURSE. Master Adolf.

CAPTAIN. What do you want?

NURSE. The old lady's sick. And the doctor's here!

CAPTAIN. Is it serious?

NURSE. No, I don't think so. Just a cold.

CAPTAIN [*gets up*]. Who was the father of your child, Margret?

NURSE. Oh, I've told you often enough, it was that good-for-nothing Johansson.

CAPTAIN. Are you sure it was him?

NURSE. Don't be so silly; of course I'm sure. He was the only one.

CAPTAIN. Yes, but was he sure he was the only one? No, you might be, but he couldn't. There's a difference, you see.

NURSE. I don't see any difference.

CAPTAIN. No, you can't see it; but it's there, all the same. [*Leafs through a photograph album on the table*] Do you think Bertha looks like me? [*Looks at a portrait in the album*

NURSE. Why, you're as like as two peas in a pod.

CAPTAIN. Did Johansson admit he was the father?

NURSE. Oh, but he had to.

CAPTAIN. How terrible!—Ah, here's the Doctor!

SCENE 4

The CAPTAIN. *The* NURSE. *The* DOCTOR.

CAPTAIN. Good evening, Doctor. How's my mother-in-law?

DOCTOR. Oh, it's nothing serious; a slight sprain to the left ankle, that's all.

CAPTAIN. I thought Margret said it was a cold. There seems to be some difference of opinion. Go to bed, Margret.

[*The* NURSE *leaves*

Pause.

CAPTAIN. Please sit down, Doctor.

DOCTOR [*sits*]. Thank you.

CAPTAIN. Is it true that if you cross a zebra with a mare, you get striped foals?*

DOCTOR [*surprised*]. That's perfectly correct.

CAPTAIN. Is it also true that if breeding then passes to a stallion, the foals may still be striped?

DOCTOR. Yes, that's also true.

CAPTAIN. So, under certain circumstances a stallion can sire a striped foal, and vice versa?

DOCTOR. So it seems, yes.

CAPTAIN. In other words, any resemblance the offspring may have to the father proves nothing.

DOCTOR. Oh...

CAPTAIN. In other words: paternity can't be proved.

DOCTOR. I... ah...

CAPTAIN. You're a widower, aren't you? Any children?

DOCTOR. Er—yes...

CAPTAIN. Didn't you ever feel ridiculous being a father? There's nothing as comical as the sight of a father holding his child's hand as they walk down the street, or hearing a father talk about his children. 'My wife's children', is what he ought to say. Didn't you ever feel there was something false about your position? Did you never have the least twinge of doubt—I won't say suspicions, because as a gentleman I assume your wife was above suspicion?

DOCTOR. I most certainly did not. But remember, Captain, a man must take his children on trust—isn't that what Goethe says?*

CAPTAIN. Trust, where a woman's concerned? That's risky.

DOCTOR. There are many different kinds of women, you know.

CAPTAIN. Recent research has shown there's only one!—When I was young I was strong and—dare I say it—handsome. I recall two fleeting incidents that gave me cause to ponder. Once I was travelling by steamer. Some friends and I were sitting in the forward saloon when the young waitress came and sat down opposite me, in tears. Her fiancé had been lost at sea, she said. We commiserated with her, and I ordered some champagne. After the second glass, I touched her foot; after the fourth her knee; and before morning I'd consoled her.

DOCTOR. One swallow doesn't make a summer!

CAPTAIN. Now my second example, and this was a real swallow. I was staying at Lysekil.* There was a young wife there, with her children—her husband was in town. She was a woman of strict principles and very devout; she preached morality to me and was quite honourable, I'm sure of that. I lent her a book, two books, in fact. Strangely enough, when she was leaving she returned them. Three months later I discovered a visiting card in one of them, with a fairly unambiguous declaration. It was innocent—as innocent as a declaration of love can be from a married woman to a stranger who's never made her any advances. Now comes the moral. Just don't trust them too much!

DOCTOR. Nor too little either!

CAPTAIN. Everything in moderation, eh? But you see, Doctor, that woman was so unaware of her own base motives that she told her husband how crazy she was about me. That's the danger, you see, their instinct for villainy is quite unconscious.* It's an extenuating circumstance, but it can't nullify their guilt, only mitigate it.

DOCTOR. Unhealthy thoughts, Captain; you should control them.

CAPTAIN. Don't use that word 'unhealthy'. Look, when the pressure gauge passes boiling point, any boiler will explode, but boiling point isn't the same for each and every boiler. Understand? However, you're here to keep an eye on me. If I weren't a man I'd have the right to complain, or explain, as it's so cunningly called. Then I might give you a complete diagnosis, my whole clinical history, but unfortunately I am a man, so it only remains for me to fold my arms across my breast like an ancient Roman and hold my breath until I die. Goodnight!

DOCTOR. Captain! If you're ill, it's no reflection on your honour to tell me everything. I must hear the other side!

CAPTAIN. I'd have thought one was enough.

DOCTOR. No, Captain. And you know, when I heard that Mrs Alving going on about her dead husband,* I thought to myself, 'It's a damned shame the man's dead!'

CAPTAIN. Do you think he'd have spoken out, if he'd been alive? If any man rose from the dead, do you think he'd be believed? Goodnight, Doctor. As you can see, I'm quite calm; you can sleep in peace.

DOCTOR. Goodnight then, Captain. I can have nothing further to do with all this.

CAPTAIN. Are we enemies?

DOCTOR. Far from it. It's just a pity we can't be friends. Goodnight.

[*Leaves*

CAPTAIN [*accompanies the* DOCTOR *to the hall door; then goes over to the stage-left door, and opens it a crack*]. Come in, and let's talk. I heard you listening out there.

SCENE 5

LAURA *enters, embarrassed. The* CAPTAIN *sits down at the secretaire.*

CAPTAIN. It's late, but we must have this out. Sit down! [*Pause.*] I've been to the post office this evening and picked up my letters. It's obvious from them that you've been withholding both my incoming and outgoing mail. The immediate consequence has been to delay and virtually destroy my work.

LAURA. It was an act of kindness on my part. You were neglecting your duties for this other work.

CAPTAIN. Hardly kindness, I think. You had a good idea that one day I stood to gain greater glory through my research than through my military career. And that's precisely what you didn't want, for that glory would only emphasize your own insignificance. What's more, I've confiscated some letters addressed to you.

LAURA. How noble of you!

CAPTAIN. You see, you do think well of me, after all. Anyway, these letters show just how long you've been setting all my former friends against me by spreading rumours about my state of mind. And your efforts have been successful, for there's scarcely anyone, from my commanding officer to the cook, who now believes I'm sane. Well, as far as my illness is concerned, these are the facts: my mind is, as you know, unaffected, so I can perform both my military duties and my responsibilities as a father. As long as my will remains relatively unimpaired, I still have my emotions more or less under control. But you've been gnawing away at it; soon it will slip its cogs and then the whole works will start spinning backwards. I won't appeal to your feelings, for you don't have any, that's your great strength. I do, however, appeal to your self-interest.

LAURA. Go on.

CAPTAIN. Your behaviour has succeeded in arousing my suspicion to the point where my judgement will soon be clouded, and my mind begin to wander. This is the onset of the madness that you've been waiting for; it may come at any moment. The question you now have to decide is: am I more use to you sane or insane? Think about it. If I have a breakdown I'll lose my position, and then where would you be? If I die, you'll get my life insurance. But if I should kill myself, you'll get nothing. It's therefore in your interest that I live out my life.

LAURA. Is this a trap?

CAPTAIN. Of course. It's up to you whether you walk round it or stick your head in it.

LAURA. You—commit suicide? You'll never do that!

CAPTAIN. Are you so sure? Do you believe a man can go on living when he's got nothing and no one left to live for?

LAURA. So you capitulate?

CAPTAIN. No, I propose an armistice.

LAURA. The conditions?

CAPTAIN. That I retain my sanity. Free me from my doubts and I'll lay down my arms.

LAURA. What doubts?

CAPTAIN. About Bertha's parentage.

LAURA. Are there any doubts about that?

CAPTAIN. For me there are, and it's you who raised them.

LAURA. I?

CAPTAIN. Yes, you've dropped them into my ear like henbane,* and circumstances have made them grow. Free me from uncertainty. Tell me straight out precisely what happened—I've already forgiven you.

LAURA. I can't very well confess to a crime I haven't committed.

CAPTAIN. What does it matter to you when you know I won't reveal it? Do you think a man would go about trumpeting his shame?

LAURA. If I say it isn't true, you still won't know for sure; but if I say it is, then you will. So you'd rather it was.

CAPTAIN. It's strange, but yes, I suppose it's because the former can't be proved while the latter can.

LAURA. Have you any grounds for your suspicions?

CAPTAIN. Yes and no.

LAURA. I think you'd like me to be guilty so you can throw me out and keep the child all to yourself. But I'm not falling into that trap.

CAPTAIN. Do you think I'd want to take over some other man's child if I knew you were guilty?

LAURA. No, I'm sure you wouldn't. That's why I realize you were lying just now when you said you'd already forgiven me.

CAPTAIN [*getting up*]. Laura, save me and my sanity. You don't understand what I'm saying. If the child's not mine, I don't have any rights over it, and nor do I want any. Isn't that what you're after? Well, isn't it? Or maybe you want something else? Power over the child, perhaps, but with me kept on as the breadwinner?

LAURA. Power, yes. What has this whole life-and-death struggle been about if not power?

CAPTAIN. Since I don't believe in a life to come, the child was my hereafter. She was my idea of immortality—perhaps the only one that has any basis in reality. Take that away and you cut off my life.

LAURA. Why didn't we part in time?

CAPTAIN. Because the child bound us together, until the bond became a chain. How did that happen? How? I've never thought about it, but now memories come flooding back, accusing, maybe even condemning. We'd been married two years and had no children—you best know why. I fell ill and was at death's door. In a lucid moment, I hear voices in the drawing room. It is you and the lawyer discussing the fortune I still possessed in those days. He explains that you stand to inherit nothing, since we have no children, and asks if you are pregnant. I didn't catch your reply. I got better, and we had a child. Who was the father?

LAURA. You!

CAPTAIN. No, I am not! There's a crime buried here that's starting to stink. A hellish crime! You women were soft-hearted enough to free your black slaves, but you keep your white ones. I've worked and slaved for you, your child, your mother, your servants; I've sacrificed my career and my prospects; I've been racked and scourged; I've gone without sleep; my hair has turned grey worrying about your future, all so you might lead an untroubled life and spend your old age enjoying it once again through your child. All this I've borne without complaint, because I believed I was father to this child. This is the lowest form of theft, the most cruel slavery. I've served seventeen years hard labour and was innocent. What can you give me in return?

LAURA. Now you *are* mad!

CAPTAIN [*sitting down*]. So you hope! And I've seen how you worked to hide your crime. I took pity on you because I didn't understand what was troubling you; I've often lulled your evil conscience to rest, believing I was driving away some morbid fancy; I've heard you cry out in your sleep without wanting to hear. Now I remember, the night before last—it was Bertha's birthday. It was between two and three in the morning and I was sitting up, reading. You screamed as if someone was trying to strangle you. 'Keep back, keep back!' I banged on the wall because—I didn't want to hear any more. I've long had my suspicions, but I didn't dare hear them confirmed. I've suffered all this for you. What will you do for me in return?

LAURA. What can I do? I'll swear in the name of God and everything I hold holy that you are Bertha's father.

CAPTAIN. What good is that when you've already said a mother can and should commit any crime for her child's sake? I beg you, in memory of all that's past, I beg you as a wounded man begs for the *coup de grâce*, tell me everything. Don't you see I'm as helpless as a child? Can't you hear me imploring your pity like a child its mother? Won't you forget I'm a man, a soldier, whose word both men and beasts obey? I ask only the pity you would show a sick man, I lay down the tokens of my power, and beg for mercy, for my life!

LAURA [*has approached him and lays her hand on his forehead*]. What? A man and crying!

CAPTAIN. Yes, I'm crying, even though I am a man. But has not a man eyes? Has not a man hands, organs, senses, affections, passions? Does he not live by the same food, is he not hurt with the same weapons, is he not warmed and cooled by the same winter and summer as a woman is? If you prick us, do we not bleed? If you tickle us, do we not laugh? If you poison us, do we not die? Why should a man not complain, a soldier weep?* Because it's unmanly! Why is it unmanly?

LAURA. Weep, my child, your mother's here with you again. Do you remember, it was as your second mother that I first entered your life? Your big strong body lacked backbone; you were a great child who'd either come into the world too early or perhaps arrived unwanted.

CAPTAIN. Yes, that's how it was, I suppose. My mother and father didn't want me and so I was born without a will. So I thought I was making myself whole when you and I became one, and therefore I let you rule. In the barracks, on the parade ground, I was the one who gave the orders; with you I was the one who obeyed. I became part of you, looked up to you as to a higher, more gifted being, listened to you as if I were your foolish child.

LAURA. Yes, that's how it was, and therefore I loved you as my child. But you know, I suppose you noticed it, every time your feelings changed and you stood before me as my lover, I felt ashamed. The ecstasy I always felt in your embrace was followed by pangs of conscience, as though my very blood felt the shame. The mother became the mistress—ugh!

CAPTAIN. I saw it, but didn't understand. And when I thought you despised me for my lack of masculinity, I sought to conquer you as a woman by being a man.

LAURA. Yes, but that was your mistake. The mother was your friend, you see, but the woman was your enemy; love between the sexes is a battle. Don't go thinking I gave myself; I didn't give, I took—what I wanted. Yet you held the advantage; I felt that and wanted you to feel it, too.

CAPTAIN. You always had the advantage; you could hypnotize me so that I neither saw nor heard but simply obeyed. You could give me a raw potato and make me believe it was a peach; you could force me to admire your silly whims as flashes of genius; you could have driven me to crime, yes, to the most contemptible actions. For you lacked sense, and instead of following my advice you did whatever came into your head. But later, when I awoke and thought things over, I felt my honour had been tarnished and sought to remove the stain by some great act, a noble deed, a discovery or an honourable suicide. I wanted to go to war, but was denied the opportunity. That's when I turned to science. And now, when I should only have to reach out and pluck the fruit, you cut off my arm. I'm dishonoured now, and cannot go on living, for a man cannot live without honour.

LAURA. But a woman can?

CAPTAIN. Yes, for she's got her children, he has none.—Yet you and I and everyone else have gone through life, unconsciously like children, stuffed full of fancies, ideals, and illusions. And then we awoke, yes, maybe, but with our feet on the pillow, and the one who woke us was himself a sleepwalker.* When women grow old and cease being women, they get beards on their chins; I wonder what men get when they grow old and cease to be men? Those who greeted the dawn were no longer cocks but capons, and those who answered were merely spayed hens,* so that when the sun was supposed to rise we found ourselves bathed in moonlight among ruins, just like in the good old days. There was no awakening: it had all been nothing but a short, morningside slumber with a few wild dreams.

LAURA. You should have been a poet, you know.

CAPTAIN. Maybe.

LAURA. Now I'm tired. If you've any more fantasies, they can keep till morning.

CAPTAIN. Just one word more—about realities. Do you hate me?

LAURA. Yes, sometimes. When you act the man.

CAPTAIN. It's like racial hatred, this. If we really are descended from the apes, it must have been from two different species. We've nothing in common, have we?

LAURA. What are you getting at?

CAPTAIN. Only that in this struggle one of us must go under.

LAURA. Which one?

CAPTAIN. The weaker, of course!

LAURA. And the stronger is in the right?

CAPTAIN. Always, since he has the power!

LAURA. Then I am in the right.

CAPTAIN. Do you already have the power then?

LAURA. Yes, and as of tomorrow, when I've had you placed under a guardian, I'll have it legally.

CAPTAIN. A guardian?

LAURA. Yes! And then I'll bring up my child myself, without having to listen to you and your hallucinations.

CAPTAIN. And what will you do for money when I'm no longer there?

LAURA. Your pension.

CAPTAIN [*making a threatening move towards her*]. How can you have me committed?

LAURA [*taking out a letter*]. With this letter, of which the court* now has a certified copy.

CAPTAIN. What letter?

LAURA [*retreating backwards towards the stage-left door*]. Yours! The one you wrote to your doctor, telling him you're insane!

The CAPTAIN *looks at her dumbly.*

LAURA. Now you've fulfilled your function as an unfortunately indispensable father and breadwinner. You're no longer needed; you can go. You can go now that you've seen my intelligence is equal to my will—not that you wanted to stay and acknowledge it!

The CAPTAIN *goes over to the table, picks up the burning lamp, and throws it at* LAURA, *who has retreated backwards through the door.*

ACT 3

The same set as in the previous act, but with another lamp. The jib-door is barricaded with a chair.

SCENE 1

LAURA. *The* NURSE.

LAURA. Did he give you the keys?

NURSE. Give me them? No, God help us, I took them from the coat that Nöjd had out for brushing.

LAURA. So it's Nöjd who's on duty today?

NURSE. That's right, Nöjd.

LAURA. Give me the keys!

NURSE. Very well, but it's no better than stealing. Oh, just listen to him walking about up there, madam. Back and forth, back and forth.

LAURA. Is the door safely locked?

NURSE. Oh yes, it's locked all right.

LAURA [*opens the secretaire and sits down at it*]. Get a grip on yourself, Margret. Our only hope is to remain calm. [*There is a knock on the door*] Who is it?

NURSE [*opening the hall door*]. It's Nöjd.

LAURA. Tell him to come in.

NÖJD [*enters*]. A despatch from the Colonel.

LAURA. Let me have it! [*Reads*] I see!—Nöjd, have you emptied all the guns and pouches?

NÖJD. That's done as ordered, ma'am.

LAURA. Then wait outside while I answer the Colonel's letter.

[NÖJD *exits*

LAURA *writes.*

NURSE. Listen, madam! Whatever's he doing up there?

LAURA. Quiet! I'm writing. [*The sound of someone sawing is audible*

NURSE [*half to herself*]. Oh, may God in his Mercy help us all! Where's this going to end?

LAURA. There. Give this to Nöjd. And my mother's to know nothing about all this! Do you hear?

The NURSE *goes to the door.* LAURA *opens the drawers of the secretaire and takes out some papers.*

SCENE 2

LAURA. *The* PASTOR *enters, takes a chair, and joins* LAURA *by the secretaire.*

PASTOR. Good evening, Laura. I suppose you know I've been away all day; I've only just got back. This is a bad business.

LAURA. Indeed it is—the worst night and day I've ever been through.

PASTOR. Well, I see no harm has come to you, at all events.

LAURA. No, thank God, but just think what could have happened.

PASTOR. Tell me one thing, though, what started it? I've heard such different stories.

LAURA. It started with some wild fantasy about him not being Bertha's father, and ended with his throwing a burning lamp in my face.

PASTOR. But this is terrible! This is insanity, pure and simple. What's to be done now?

LAURA. We must try to prevent any further outbreaks. The Doctor's sent to the hospital for a straitjacket. In the meantime I've informed the Colonel and am now trying to make sense of our financial situation, which he's mismanaged in the most reprehensible way.

PASTOR. What a wretched business! But then I've always expected something of the kind. Fire and water—why, there's bound to be an explosion. What's all that in the drawer there?

LAURA [*has pulled a drawer out of the desk*]. Look what he's kept hidden away.

PASTOR. Oh, my God! That's your doll; and there's your christening cap; and Bertha's rattle; and your letters; and your locket... [*drying his eyes*]. He must have loved you very much, Laura, all the same. I've never kept anything like that!

LAURA. I think he did love me once, but time—time changes so many things.

PASTOR. What's that paper there—the big one?—Why, it's the deed to a grave!—Well, better a grave than the asylum! Laura! Tell me: are you quite blameless in all this?

LAURA. Me? How am I to blame if a man goes mad?

PASTOR. Well, well! I shan't say anything. After all, blood is thicker than water!

LAURA. What do you mean by that?

PASTOR [*looks her in the eye*]. Listen!

LAURA. What?

PASTOR. Just listen to me! You can't deny all this fits in very nicely with your wanting to bring up your child yourself.

LAURA. I don't understand.

PASTOR. I really can't help admiring you!

LAURA. Me? Hm!

PASTOR. And I shall be that freethinker's guardian! You know, I've always regarded him as a tare among our wheat.*

LAURA [*with a brief, suppressed laugh; then quickly serious*]. And you dare say this to me, his wife?

PASTOR. My God, you're strong, Laura! Unbelievably strong! Like a fox in a trap: you'd rather bite off your own leg than allow yourself to be caught!—Like a master thief: no accomplice, not even your own conscience.—Look in the mirror! You don't dare!

LAURA. I never use a mirror!

PASTOR. No, you daren't!—Let me see your hand!—Not one spot of blood* to give you away, not a trace of that insidious poison! An innocent little murder that the law can't touch; an unconscious crime—unconscious? What a marvellous idea!— Listen to him working away up there, though!—Just you watch out! If that man gets out, he'll saw you in two!

LAURA. You talk too much, as if you had a bad conscience.— Accuse me, if you can!

PASTOR. I can't!

LAURA. You see! You can't, and so—I'm innocent!—Now you take care of your ward, and I'll look after mine!—Here's the Doctor!

SCENE 3

LAURA. *The* PASTOR. *The* DOCTOR.

LAURA [*rising*]. Good evening, Doctor. At least you want to help me. Isn't that so? Not that there's much to be done, I'm afraid. Do you hear how he's carrying on up there? Are you convinced now?

DOCTOR. I'm convinced an act of violence has been committed, but whether it is to be regarded as an outbreak of anger or insanity— that is the question.

PASTOR. Violence aside now, admit that he suffers from fixed ideas.

DOCTOR. I think your ideas are even more fixed, Pastor!

PASTOR. My firm convictions about the highest things...

DOCTOR. Let's forget them, shall we?—Madam, it rests with you whether your husband is fined and sent to prison or committed to an asylum. How would you describe his behaviour?

LAURA. I can't answer that now.

DOCTOR. You mean you have no firm opinion as to what is in the family's best interests? What do you say, Pastor?

PASTOR. Well, there'll be a scandal either way... it's hard to say.

LAURA. But if he's only fined for assault, he might act violently again.

DOCTOR. And if he goes to prison, he'll soon be released. So it seems best for all concerned that he's treated as insane.—Where's the nurse?

LAURA. Why do you ask?

DOCTOR. She must put the straitjacket on him, once I've had a word with him, and given her the order. But not before. I have the—er—garment outside! [*Goes out to the hall and returns with a large bundle*] Please ask the nurse to come in.

LAURA *rings*.

PASTOR. Dreadful! Simply dreadful!

The NURSE *enters*.

DOCTOR [*unpacks the straitjacket*]. Now pay attention, please! To prevent any further outbreaks of violence, you're to slip this jacket on to the Captain from behind, if and when I say so. As you can see, it's got unusually long arms, so as to restrict his movements. You tie them behind his back. These two straps here pass through these buckles which you then fasten to the frame of the chair or the sofa, whichever is more convenient. Will you do this?

NURSE. No, Doctor, I can't, I can't.

LAURA. Why don't you do it yourself, Doctor?

DOCTOR. Because the patient suspects me. You, madam, would be the most appropriate person, but I'm afraid he doesn't trust you either.

LAURA *grimaces*.

DOCTOR. Perhaps you, Pastor. . .

PASTOR. No, please, you'll have to excuse me!

<h2 style="text-align:center">SCENE 4</h2>

As before, plus NÖJD, *who enters at this point*.

LAURA. Have you already delivered my note?

NÖJD. As ordered, ma'am.

DOCTOR. Ah, it's you Nöjd! You know the situation here, don't you? You're aware the Captain is deranged. You must help us to take care of the patient.

NÖJD. If there's anything I can do for the Captain, he knows I'll do it.

DOCTOR. You're to put this jacket on him. . .

NURSE. No, he's not to touch him; Nöjd mustn't hurt him. I'd rather do it myself, gently, ever so gently! But Nöjd can wait outside and help me if need be. . . yes, that's what he can do.

There is a pounding on the jib-door.

DOCTOR. There he is! Put the jacket on the chair, under your shawl. Now, all of you, out of here. The Pastor and I will receive him— that door won't hold much longer.—Come on, out!

NURSE [*goes out to the left*]. Lord Jesus, help us!

[LAURA *closes the secretaire; then exits left.* NÖJD *exits upstage*

SCENE 5

The jib-door is propelled inwards so that the chair is thrown across the floor; the lock snaps. The CAPTAIN *enters with a pile of books under his arm.*

CAPTAIN [*puts the books on the table*]. It's all here in these books, every one of them. So I wasn't mad! Look here, the *Odyssey*, Book 1, line 215, page 6 in the Uppsala translation. Telemachus is speaking to Athena. 'My mother says I am surely his'—Odysseus', that is—'But I do not know. Nobody really knows his own father.' And Telemachus says this of Penelope, the most virtuous of women!* Delightful, eh? Here's the prophet Ezekiel: 'The fool says: "Lo here is my father", but who can know whose loins have begotten him?'* That's surely clear enough! What have I got here? Mersljakov's *History of Russian Literature*.* 'Alexander Pushkin,* Russia's greatest poet, died more of grief at the widespread rumours of his wife's infidelity than of the bullet he received in his breast in a duel. On his deathbed he swore she was innocent.' The ass! Oh, the ass! How could he swear to that? You see, I still read my books!—No, but Jonas, are you here? And the Doctor, naturally! Have you heard what I said to an English woman, who deplored the fact that Irishmen throw lighted lamps in their wives' faces?—'God, what women,' I said!—'Women?,' she lisped!— 'Yes, of course,' I replied. 'When things have come to such a pass that a man, a man who once loved and worshipped a woman, takes a lighted lamp and throws it in her face, then you really know!'

PASTOR. Know what?

CAPTAIN. Nothing! A man never knows anything, he only believes, isn't that so, Jonas? If you believe, you're saved. Yes, saved!

But I know that what a man believes can damn him, too. Indeed, I do!

DOCTOR. Captain!

CAPTAIN. Be quiet! I don't want to talk to you; I don't want to hear you report what they say in there, like some telephone. Yes, in there! You know!—Listen, Jonas, do you believe you're your children's father? I remember you had a tutor in your house, a good-looking boy, caused a lot of gossip.

PASTOR. Adolf! Take care!

CAPTAIN. Have a feel under that wig of yours and see if there aren't two bumps there. Upon my soul, I do believe he's turning pale! Yes, yes, they just talk, but my God, they've a lot to say. But we're all a bunch of ridiculous dogs all the same, we married men. Isn't that true, Doctor? How was your matrimonial bed? Wasn't there a lieutenant in your house, eh? Wait now, let me guess. He was called [*whispers in the* DOCTOR'S *ear*]. You see, he's turning pale, too! Now don't be sad. After all, she's dead and buried, and what's done can't be undone. I knew him, however, and he's now——— look at me, Doctor!—No, straight in the eyes—a major in the dragoons! By God, I do believe he's got horns as well!

DOCTOR [*pained*]. Captain, would you mind changing the subject!

CAPTAIN. You see! No sooner do I mention horns than he wants to change the subject!

PASTOR. You realize, Adolf, that you're insane.

CAPTAIN. Yes, I know that well enough. But if I could treat your crowned heads a while, I'd soon have you locked up too! Mad I may be, but how did I get that way? It doesn't concern you, it doesn't concern anyone! Let's talk about something else now. [*Takes the photograph album from the table*] Sweet Jesus, there's my child. Mine? Can we be sure of that? Do you know what we ought to do so as to be sure? First, get married, to gain social respectability; then divorce at once, and become lovers; and then adopt our children. Then at least a man'd know they were his by adoption! Isn't that right? But what good's all this to me now? What's the good of anything now that you've taken away my hope of immortality? What's the point of science and philosophy when I've nothing to live for? What use is my life to me, without honour? I grafted my right arm, half my brain, half my spinal chord onto another stem, because I believed they'd unite to form a single, more perfect tree, and then along comes someone with a knife and makes a cut just below the graft, and now I'm only half a tree—but the other half still goes on growing with my arm and half my brain, while I wither and die, for it was the best parts of myself I gave away. Now I want to die! Do what you will with me! I no longer exist!

The DOCTOR *whispers to the* PASTOR; *they go out to the left; shortly afterwards* BERTHA *comes in.*

SCENE 6

The CAPTAIN. BERTHA. *The* CAPTAIN *is sitting crumpled up over the table.*

BERTHA [*going up to him*]. Are you ill, father?

CAPTAIN [*looks up dully*]. Me?

BERTHA. Do you know what you've done? Do you know you threw a lamp at mother?

CAPTAIN. Did I?

BERTHA. Yes, you did! What if she'd been hurt?

CAPTAIN. What difference would that make?

BERTHA. You're not my father when you talk like that!

CAPTAIN. What's that you say? I'm not your father? How do you know? Who told you that? Who is your father, then? Who?

BERTHA. Well, not you, anyway!

CAPTAIN. Still not me! Who then? Who? You seem well informed. Who have you been talking to? That I should live to hear my own child tell me to my face I'm not her father! Don't you realize you're insulting your mother when you say that? Don't you understand that if it's true, it's to her shame?

BERTHA. Don't say anything bad about mother, do you hear?

CAPTAIN. No, you stick together, all of you against me. You've done so all along.

BERTHA. Father!

CAPTAIN. Don't use that word again!

BERTHA. Father, father!

CAPTAIN [*pulls her to him*]. Bertha, my dear, dear child, of course you're my child! Yes, yes, it can't be otherwise. It must be so! All the rest was just a morbid fancy carried on the wind like pestilence and fever. Look at me, so I may see my soul in your eyes.—But I can see her soul, too! You've got two souls, and you love me with one and hate me with the other. But you must love only me! You shall have but one soul, otherwise you'll never find peace, and nor shall I. You must have only one thought, which flows from mine, and only one will, which is also mine.

BERTHA. No, no! I want to be myself!

CAPTAIN. I won't let you! You see, I'm a cannibal, and I want to eat you up. Your mother wanted to eat me, but I didn't let her. I'm Saturn, who ate his children because it was foretold that otherwise they'd eat him.* To eat or be eaten! That is the question!* If I don't eat you, you'll eat me, you've already shown me your teeth. But don't be afraid, my darling child, I shan't hurt you!

Goes up to the collection of weapons and takes a revolver.

BERTHA [*tries to get away*]. Help, mother, help! He's going to kill me!

NURSE [*enters*]. Master Adolf, what's the matter?

CAPTAIN [*inspecting the revolver*]. Have you removed the bullets?

NURSE. Yes, I've tidied them away, but sit down here nice and quiet, and I'll bring them back again!

She takes the CAPTAIN *by the arm and seats him on the chair, where he remains sitting apathetically. Then she takes out the straitjacket and stations herself behind the chair.*

[BERTHA *steals out to the left*

NURSE. Do you remember, Master Adolf, when you were my dear little boy, and I tucked you up at night, and read you 'Gentle Jesus, meek and mild'? Do you remember, too, how I used to get up at night to give you a drink? Do you remember how I lit the candle and told you pretty stories when you had horrid dreams and couldn't sleep? Do you remember?

CAPTAIN. Go on talking, Margret, it soothes my head so. Go on talking.

NURSE. All right, but you listen carefully, then. Do you remember how you once took the big kitchen knife to go carving boats with, and how I came in and had to trick you into giving it me back? You were such a silly little boy and so we had to trick you, for you didn't believe we meant you well.—Give me that snake, I said, otherwise he'll bite you. And then you let go of the knife. [*Takes the revolver out of the* CAPTAIN*'s hand*] And the times you had to get dressed, and didn't want to. Then I had to jolly you along and say you'd get a gold coat and dress like a prince. And then I took your little undershirt, which was only made of green wool, and held it in front of you, and said: 'in with your arms now, both of them.' And then I said: 'sit still now and be a good boy while I button up the back.' [*She has got the straitjacket on him*] And then I said: 'get up now, and walk nicely across the floor so I can see how it fits'. . . [*She leads him over to the sofa*] And then I said: 'now it's time to go to bed.'

CAPTAIN. What did you say? Go to bed when he'd just got dressed?—Damnation! What have you done to me? [*Tries to free himself*] Oh, you damned cunning woman! Who'd have thought you were so clever? [*Lies down on the sofa*] Caught, clipped, and double-crossed*—and not even able to die.

NURSE. Forgive me, Master Adolf, forgive me, but I had to stop you killing the child!

CAPTAIN. Why not let me kill the child? After all, life is hell and death a heavenly paradise—children belong in heaven.

NURSE. How do you know what happens after death?

CAPTAIN. That's all one does know; about life one knows nothing. Oh, if we only knew that from the start!

NURSE. Master Adolf! Humble your stubborn heart and pray to God for mercy, it's still not too late. It wasn't too late for the thief on the cross when our Saviour said: 'Today shalt thou be with me in paradise.'*

CAPTAIN. Already croaking after carrion are you, you old crow?

The NURSE *takes her hymnal from her pocket.*

CAPTAIN. Nöjd! Is Nöjd there?

NÖJD *enters.*

CAPTAIN. Throw that woman out! She'll choke me to death with that hymn-book of hers. Throw her out the window or shove her up the chimney, anywhere you like!

NÖJD [*looks at the* NURSE]. God bless you, Captain, but I can't! I just can't! Half a dozen men, yes, but a woman. . .

CAPTAIN. Can't you manage a woman, eh?

NÖJD. 'Course I can. There's something special about them, though, as stops a man laying hands on them.

CAPTAIN. What's special about them? Haven't they lain hands on me?

NÖJD. Yes, but I can't, Captain. It's just as though you was to ask me to hit the Pastor. It's in a man's blood, like religion. I can't!

SCENE 7

As before plus LAURA, *who signals to* NÖJD *that he should leave.*

CAPTAIN. Omphale! Omphale! Now you're playing with the club while Hercules spins your wool.*

LAURA [*up to the sofa*]. Adolf! Look at me. Do you believe I'm your enemy?

CAPTAIN. Yes, I do. I believe you're all my enemies. My mother was my enemy—she didn't want to bring me into the world because of the pain I'd cause her. She denied me all nourishment in the womb and made a semi-cripple of me. My sister was my enemy when she taught me to defer to her. The first woman I ever held in my arms was my enemy, giving me ten years of disease for the love I gave her. My daughter became my enemy, when she had to choose between you and me. And you, my wife, you were my mortal enemy, for you didn't let go of me before there was no life left in me!

LAURA. I don't know that I ever thought much about, or intended, what you think I've done. I may have been moved by a vague desire to be rid of you for standing in my way. If you can see a plan in the way I've acted, then it's possible there was one, but I wasn't aware of it. I've never reflected upon what has happened; things just glided along on rails, which you yourself laid down, and before God and my conscience I believe I'm innocent, even if I'm not. You've been like a stone on my heart, pressing down upon me until my heart sought to shake off its burden. That's how it's been, and if I've hurt you without meaning to, I ask your forgiveness.

CAPTAIN. That sounds plausible enough. But how does it help me? And who's to blame? Perhaps our spiritual notion of marriage? In the old days a man married a wife; now he forms a business partnership with a career woman or moves in with a friend.— And then he seduces the partner or rapes the friend. Whatever happened to love, healthy sensual love? It died somewhere along the way. And what's the issue? Shares, dividends, placed with the bearer, with no joint liability. But who's the bearer when the crash comes? Who's the physical father of the spiritual child?

LAURA. So far as your suspicions about the child are concerned, they're completely unfounded.

CAPTAIN. That's just what's so horrible! If only they had some foundation, then at least there'd be something to hang on to. As it is, there are only shadows, hiding in the bushes and sticking out their heads to laugh—it's like fighting the air, a mock battle with blanks. Reality, however deadly, would have provoked resistance, mustered life and soul to action, but now... my thoughts dissolve into thin air, and my brain grinds on until it catches fire! Give me a pillow under my head! And put something over me, I'm cold! So terribly cold!

LAURA *takes her shawl and spreads it over him.** The NURSE *goes out to fetch a pillow.*

LAURA. Give me your hand, my friend.

CAPTAIN. My hand! Which you've tied behind my back... Omphale! Omphale! But I feel your soft shawl against my mouth; it's as warm and smooth as your arm, and it smells of vanilla like your hair did when you were young. Laura, when you were young and we walked in the birch woods among the primroses and thrushes—glorious, so glorious! How beautiful life was, and look at it now. You didn't want it to be like this. Neither did I, and yet it happened. Who rules our lives, then?

LAURA. God alone rules...

CAPTAIN. The God of battle, then. Or nowadays the goddess! Take away this cat that's lying on me! Take it away!

The NURSE *enters with the pillow, removes the shawl.*

CAPTAIN. Give me my tunic! Lay it over me!

The NURSE *takes his military tunic from the clothes hanger and lays it over him.*

CAPTAIN. Ah, my tough lion's skin that you would take from me. Omphale! Omphale! You cunning woman who loved peace and learnt to disarm us. Awake, Hercules, before they take your club away from you! You want to trick us out of our armour, too, and made believe it was only tinsel. It was iron, you know, before it was tinsel. It used to be the smith who forged the soldier's tunic; now it's the seamstress. Omphale! Omphale! Raw strength has given way before treacherous weakness. Damn you, woman! A curse upon all your sex! [*He raises himself to spit, but falls back upon the sofa*] What sort of pillow have you given me, Margret? It's so hard and so cold, so cold! Come and sit by me on this chair. There, like that! May I rest my head on your lap? So!—It's warm! Bend over me so I may feel your breast.—Oh, how sweet it is to sleep upon a woman's breast, whether a mother's or a mistress's—a mother's is sweetest, though!

LAURA. Would you like to see your child, Adolf? Say!

CAPTAIN. My child? A man has no children; only women have children. Therefore the future belongs to them, while we die childless.—'Gentle Jesus, meek and mild, Look upon this little child.'

NURSE. Listen, he's praying to God.

CAPTAIN. No, to you, to put me to sleep, for I'm tired, so tired! Good night, Margret, blessed art thou among women!

He raises himself, but falls back with a cry upon the NURSE'S *knee.*

SCENE 8

LAURA *crosses to the left and calls the* DOCTOR, *who enters with the* PASTOR.

LAURA. Help us, Doctor, if it's not too late! Look, he's stopped breathing!

DOCTOR [*examining the* CAPTAIN'S *pulse*]. It's a heart attack.

PASTOR. Is he dead?

DOCTOR. No, he may yet recover consciousness, but what kind of consciousness, we don't know.

PASTOR. 'Once to die, but after this the judgement'*...

DOCTOR. No judgement! And no accusations! You, who believe a God guides the destinies of men, may take the matter up with Him.

NURSE. Oh, Pastor, he prayed to God in his final hour!

PASTOR [*to* LAURA]. Is that true?

LAURA. Yes, it's true.

DOCTOR. If it is—and I can no more judge of that than of the cause of his illness—then my art is useless. Now you try yours, Pastor!

LAURA. Is that all you have to say beside this death-bed, Doctor?

DOCTOR. Yes, that's all! It's all I know. If anyone knows more, let him speak!

BERTHA [*enters from the left, runs to her mother*]. Mother, mother!

LAURA. My child! My own child!

PASTOR. Amen!

MISS JULIE

[Fröken Julie]

A Naturalistic Tragedy

(1888)

PREFACE

Like art in general, the theatre has long seemed to me a *Biblia pauperum*,* a Bible in pictures for those who cannot read what is written or printed, and the dramatist a lay preacher who peddles the ideas of the day in a popular form, so popular that the middle classes which form the bulk of the audience can, without too much mental effort, understand what is going on. That is why the theatre has always been an elementary school for the young, the semi-educated, and women, who still retain the primitive capacity for deceiving themselves or for letting themselves be deceived, that is, for succumbing to illusions and to the hypnotic suggestions of the author. Nowadays, therefore, when the rudimentary and undeveloped kind of thinking that takes the form of fantasy appears to be evolving into reflection, investigation, and analysis, it seems to me that the theatre, like religion, is about to be discarded as a dying form of art, which we lack the necessary preconditions to enjoy. This supposition is supported by the serious theatrical crisis now prevailing throughout Europe, and especially by the fact that in England and Germany, those cultural heartlands which have nurtured the greatest thinkers of our age, the drama is dead, along with most of the other fine arts.

Again, in other countries people have believed in the possibility of creating a new drama by filling the old forms with new contents; but this approach has failed, partly because there has not yet been time to popularize the new ideas, so the public has not been able to understand what was involved; partly because party differences have so inflamed emotions that pure, dispassionate enjoyment has become impossible in a situation where people's innermost thoughts have been challenged and an applauding or whistling majority has brought pressure to bear on them as openly as it can do in a theatre; and partly because we have not yet found the new form for the new content, and the new wine has burst the old bottles.

In the following play I have not tried to accomplish anything new, for that is impossible, but merely to modernize the form according to what I believe are the demands a contemporary audience would make of this art. To that end I have chosen, or let myself be moved by, a theme that may be said to lie outside current party strife, for the problem of rising or falling on the social ladder, of higher or lower, better or worse, man or woman is, has been, and always will be of lasting interest. When I took this theme from a real incident* that I heard about some years ago, it seemed to me a suitable subject for a tragedy, not least because of the deep impression it made on me; for it still strikes us as tragic to see someone favoured by fortune go under, and even more to see a whole family die out. But the time may come when we shall have become so highly developed, so enlightened, that we shall be able to look with indifference at the brutal, cynical, heartless drama that life presents, when we shall have laid aside those inferior, unreliable instruments of thought called feelings, which will become superfluous and harmful once our organs of judgement have matured. The fact that the heroine arouses our pity merely depends on our weakness in not being able to resist the fear that the same fate might overtake us. A highly sensitive spectator may still not feel that such pity is enough, while the man with faith in the future will probably insist on some positive proposals to remedy the evil, some kind of programme, in other words. But in the first place there is no such thing as absolute evil, for after all, if one family falls another now has the good fortune to rise, and this alternate rising and falling is one of life's greatest pleasures, since happiness is only relative. And of the man with a programme who wants to remedy the unpleasant fact that the bird of prey eats the dove and lice eat the bird of prey, I would ask: why should it be remedied? Life is not so idiotically mathematical that only the big eat the small; it is just as common for a bee to kill a lion or at least to drive it mad.

If my tragedy makes a tragic impression on many people, that is their fault. When we become as strong as the first French revolutionaries, we shall feel as much unqualified pleasure and relief at seeing the thinning out in our royal parks of rotten, superannuated trees, which have stood too long in the way of others with just as much right to their time in the sun, as it does to see an incurably ill man finally die. Recently, my tragedy *The Father* was criticized for being so tragic, as though tragedies were supposed to be merry.* One also hears pretentious talk about the joy of life,* and theatre managers commission farces as though this joy of life lay in behaving stupidly and depicting people as if they were all afflicted with St Vitus' dance or congenital idiocy.* I find the joy of life in its cruel and powerful struggles, and my enjoyment comes from getting to know something, from learning something. That is why I have chosen an unusual case, but an instructive one, an exception, in other words, but an important exception that proves the rule, even though it may offend those who love the commonplace. What will also bother simple minds is that my motivation of the action is not simple, and that there is not a single point of view. Every event in life—and this is a fairly new discovery!—is usually the result of a whole series of more or less deep-seated motives, but the spectator usually selects the one that he most easily understands or that best flatters his powers of judgement. Someone commits suicide. 'Business worries', says the business man. 'Unrequited love', say the ladies. 'Physical illness', says the sick man, 'Shattered hopes', says the failure. But it may well be that the motive lay in all of these things, or in none of them, and that the dead man concealed his real motive by emphasizing quite a different one that shed the best possible light on his memory.

I have motivated Miss Julie's tragic fate with an abundance of circumstances: her mother's 'bad' basic instincts; her father's improper bringing-up of the girl; her own nature and the influence her fiancé's suggestions had on her weak, degenerate brain; also, and more immediately: the festive atmosphere of Midsummer Night; her father's absence; her period; her preoccupation with animals; the intoxicating effect of the dance; the light summer night; the powerful aphrodisiac influence of the flowers; and finally chance that drives these two people together in a room apart, plus the boldness of the aroused man.

So my treatment has not been one-sidedly physiological nor obsessively psychological. I have not attributed everything to what she inherited from her mother nor put the whole blame on her period, nor just settled for 'immorality', nor merely preached morality—lacking a priest, I've left that to the cook!

I flatter myself that this multiplicity of motives is in tune with the times. And if others have anticipated me in this, then I flatter myself that I am not alone in my paradoxes, as all discoveries are called.

As regards characterization, I have made my figures fairly 'characterless' for the following reasons:

Over the years the word 'character' has taken on many meanings. Originally it no doubt meant the dominant trait in a person's soul-complex, and was confused with temperament. Later it became the middle-class expression for an automaton, so that an individual whose nature had once and for all set firm or adapted to a certain role in life, who had stopped growing, in short, was called a character, whereas someone who goes on developing, the skilful navigator on the river of life who does not sail with cleated sheets but tacks with every change in the wind in order to luff again, was called character-less. In a derogatory sense, of course, because he was so hard to catch, classify, and keep track of. This bourgeois concept of the immobility of the soul was transferred to the stage, which has always been dominated by the bourgeoisie. There a character became a man who was fixed and set, who invariably appeared drunk or comical or sad; and all that was needed to characterize him was to give him a physical defect, a club-foot, a wooden leg, a red nose, or some continually repeated phrase such as 'That's capital'* or 'Barkis is willin',* etc. This elementary way of viewing people is still to be found in the great Molière. Harpagon* is merely a miser, although he could have been both a miser and an excellent financier, a splendid father, and a good citizen; and even worse, his 'defect' is extremely advantageous to his daughter and his son-in-law, who are his heirs and therefore ought not to criticize him even if they do have to wait a while before jumping into bed together. So I do not believe in simple stage characters, and the summary judgements that authors pass on people—this one is stupid, that one brutal, this one jealous, that one mean—ought to be challenged by naturalists, who know how richly complicated the soul is, and who are aware that 'vice' has a reverse side, which is very much like virtue.

As modern characters, living in an age of transition more urgently hysterical at any rate than the one that preceded it, I have depicted the figures in my play as more split and vacillating, a mixture of the old and the new, and it seems to me not improbable that modern ideas may also have permeated down by way of newspapers and kitchen talk to the level of the servants. That is why the valet belches forth certain modern ideas from within his inherited slave's soul. And I would remind those who take exception to the characters in our modern plays talking Darwinism,* while holding up Shakespeare to our attention as a model, that the gravedigger in *Hamlet* talks the then-fashionable philosophy of Giordano Bruno* (Bacon),* which is even more improbable since the means of disseminating ideas were fewer then than now. Besides, the fact of the matter is, 'Darwinism' has existed in every age, ever since Moses's successive history of creation from the lower animals up to man; it is just that we have discovered and formulated it now!

My souls (characters) are conglomerates of past and present stages of culture, bits out of books and newspapers, scraps of humanity, torn shreds of once fine clothing now turned to rags, exactly as the human soul is patched together, and I have also provided a little evolutionary history by letting the weaker repeat words stolen from the stronger, and allowed these souls to get 'ideas', or suggestions as they are called, from one another, from the milieu (the death of the siskin), and from objects (the razor). I have also facilitated *Gedankenübertragung** via an inanimate medium (the Count's boots, the bell). Finally, I have made use of 'waking suggestion',* a variation of hypnotic suggestion, which is now so well known and popularized that it cannot arouse the ridicule or scepticism it would have done in Mesmer's time.*

Miss Julie is a modern character which does not mean that the man-hating half-woman has not existed in every age, just that she has now been discovered, has come out into the open and made herself heard. Victim of a superstition (one that has seized even stronger minds) that woman, this stunted form of human being who stands between man, the lord of creation, the creator of culture, [and the child],* is meant to be the equal of man or could ever be, she involves herself in an absurd struggle in which she falls. Absurd because a stunted form, governed by the laws of propagation, will always be born stunted and can never catch up with the one in the lead, according to the formula: A (the man) and B (the woman) start from the same point C; A (the man) with a speed of, let us say, 100 and B (the woman) with a speed of 60. Now, the question is, when will B catch up with A?—Answer: *Never!* Neither with the help of equal education, equal voting rights, disarmament, or temperance—no more than two parallel lines can ever meet and cross.

The half-woman is a type who thrusts herself forward and sells herself nowadays for power, decorations, honours, or diplomas as formerly she used to do for money. She is synonymous with degeneration. It is not a sound species for it does not last, but unfortunately it can propagate itself and its misery in the following generation; and degenerate men seem unconsciously to select their mates among them so that they increase in number and produce creatures of uncertain sex for whom life is a torment. Fortunately, however, they succumb, either because they are out of harmony with reality or because their repressed instincts erupt uncontrollably or because their hopes of attaining equality with men are crushed. The type is tragic, offering the spectacle of a desperate struggle against nature, a tragic legacy of Romanticism which is now being dissipated by Naturalism, the only aim of which is happiness. And happiness means strong and sound species. But Miss Julie is also a relic of the old warrior nobility that is now giving way to the new aristocracy of nerve and brain; a victim of the discord which a mother's 'crime' has implanted in a family; a victim of the errors of an age, of circumstances, and of her own deficient constitution, which together form the equivalent of the old-fashioned concept of Fate or Universal Law. The naturalist has erased guilt along with God, but he cannot erase the consequences of an action—punishment, prison, or the fear of it—for the simple reason that these consequences remain, whether or not he acquits the individual. For an injured party is less forbearing than those who have not been harmed may be, and even if her father found compelling reasons not to seek his revenge, his daughter would wreak vengeance on herself, as she does here, because of her innate or acquired sense of honour which the upper classes inherit—from where? From barbarism, from their original Aryan home,* from the chivalry of the Middle Ages, all of which is very beautiful, but a real disadvantage nowadays where the preservation of the species is concerned. It is the nobleman's *harakiri*, the inner law of conscience which makes a Japanese slit open his own stomach when someone insults him, and which survives in modified form in that privilege of the nobility, the duel. That is why Jean, the servant, lives, but Miss Julie, who cannot live without honour, does not. The slave has this advantage over the earl, he lacks this fatal preoccupation with honour, and there is in all of us Aryans a little of the nobleman or Don Quixote,* which means that we sympathize with the suicide who has committed a dishonourable act and thereby lost his honour, and we are noblemen enough to suffer when we see the mighty fallen and reduced to a useless corpse, yes, even if the fallen should rise again and make amends through an honourable act. The servant Jean is the type who founds a species, someone in whom the process of differentiation may be observed. He was a poor tied-worker's son* and has now brought himself up to be a future nobleman. He has been quick to learn, has finely developed senses (smell, taste, sight) and an eye for beauty. He has already come up in the world, and is strong enough not to be concerned about exploiting other people. He is already a stranger in his environment, which he despises as stages in a past he has put behind him, and which he fears and flees, because people there know his secrets, spy out his intentions, regard his rise with envy, and look forward to his fall with pleasure. Hence his divided, indecisive character, wavering between sympathy for those in high positions and hatred for those who occupy them. He calls himself an aristocrat and has learnt the secrets of good society, is polished on the surface but coarse underneath, and already wears a frock coat with style, although there is no guarantee that the body beneath it is clean.

He respects Miss Julie but is afraid of Kristin because she knows his dangerous secrets, and he is sufficiently callous not to allow the events of the night to interfere with his future plans. With the brutality of a slave and the indifference of a master he can look at blood without fainting, and shake off misfortune without further ado. That is why he escapes from the struggle unscathed and will probably end up the proprietor of a hotel; and even if *he* does not become a Romanian count, his son will probably go to university and possibly become a government official.

Moreover, the information he gives about life as the lower classes see it from below is quite important—when he speaks the truth, that is, which he does not often do, for he tends to say what is to his own advantage rather than what is true. When Miss Julie supposes that everyone in the lower classes finds the pressure from above oppressive, Jean naturally agrees since his intention is to gain sympathy, but he immediately corrects himself when he sees the advantage of distinguishing himself from the common herd.

Apart from the fact that Jean is rising in the world, he is also superior to Miss Julie in that he is a man. Sexually he is the aristocrat because of his masculine strength, his more finely developed senses, and his ability to take the initiative. His inferiority arises mainly from the social milieu in which he temporarily finds himself and which he will probably discard along with his livery.

His slave mentality expresses itself in his respect for the Count (the boots) and his religious superstition; but he respects the Count mainly as the occupant of the high position that he covets; and this respect remains even when he has conquered the daughter of the house and seen how empty that pretty shell is.

I do not believe there can be any love in a 'higher' sense between two such different natures, so I let Miss Julie imagine she loves him as a means of protecting or excusing herself; and I let Jean suppose he could fall in love with her if his social circumstances were different. I suspect that love is rather like the hyacinth, which has to put its roots down into the darkness *before* it can produce a strong flower. Here it shoots up, blooms, and goes to seed all in a moment, and that is why it dies so quickly.

Kristin, finally, is a female slave. Standing over the stove all day has made her subservient and dull; like an animal her hypocrisy is unconscious and she overflows with morality and religion, which serve as cloaks and scapegoats for her sins whereas a stronger character would have no need of them because he could bear his guilt himself or explain it away. She goes to church to unload her household thefts onto Jesus casually and deftly, and to recharge herself with a new dose of innocence.

Moreover, she is a minor character, and therefore my intention was only to sketch her in as I did the Pastor and the Doctor in *The Father*, where I just wanted to depict ordinary people as country parsons and provincial doctors usually are. And if some people have found my minor characters abstract,* that is because ordinary people are to some extent abstract when working; which is to say, they lack individuality and show only one side of themselves while performing their tasks, and as long as the spectator feels no need to see them from several sides, my abstract depiction will probably suffice.

Finally, where the dialogue is concerned I have somewhat broken with tradition by not making my characters catechists who sit around asking stupid questions in order to elicit a witty reply. I have avoided the symmetrical, mathematical artificiality of French dialogue and allowed my characters' brains to work irregularly as they do in real life, where no subject is ever entirely exhausted before one mind discovers by chance in another mind a cog in which to engage. For that reason the dialogue also wanders, providing itself in the opening scenes with material that is later reworked, taken up, repeated, expanded, and developed, like the theme in a musical composition.

The action is sufficiently fecund, and since it really concerns only two people I have restricted myself to them, introducing only one minor character, the cook, and letting the father's unhappy spirit hover above and behind it all. I have done this because it seems to me that what most interests people today is the psychological process; our inquiring minds are no longer satisfied with simply seeing something happen, we want to know how it happened. We want to see the strings, look at the machinery, examine the double-bottomed box, try the magic ring to find the seam, and examine the cards to discover how they are marked.

In this regard I have had in mind the monographic novels of the Goncourt brothers,* which have attracted me more than anything else in contemporary literature.

As for the technical aspects of the composition, I have, by way of experiment, eliminated all act divisions. I have done this because it seems to me that our declining susceptibility to illusion would possibly be disturbed by intervals, during which the spectator has time to reflect and thereby escape from the suggestive influence of the dramatist-hypnotist. My play probably runs for about an hour and a half, and since people can listen to a lecture, a sermon, or a conference session for that length of time or even longer, I imagine that a ninety-minute play should not exhaust them. I attempted this concentrated form as long ago as 1872, in one of my first attempts at drama, *The Outlaw*,* but with scant success. I had written the piece in five acts, but when it was finished I noticed what a disjointed and disturbing effect it had. I burned it and from the ashes arose a single, long, carefully worked-out act of fifty printed pages, which played for a full hour. Consequently the form is not new, though it seems to be my speciality, and current changes in taste may well have made it timely. In due course I would hope to have an audience so educated that it could sit through a single act lasting an entire evening, but this will require some preliminary experimentation. Meanwhile, in order to provide resting places for the audience and the actors without breaking the illusion for the audience I have used three art forms that belong to the drama, namely the monologue, mime,* and ballet, all of which were part of classical tragedy, monody* having become monologue and the chorus, ballet.

Nowadays our realists have banished the monologue as implausible, but given appropriate motivation it becomes plausible, and I can therefore use it to advantage. It is perfectly plausible for a speaker to walk up and down alone in his room reading his speech aloud, that an actor should run through his role aloud, a servant girl talk to her cat, a mother prattle to her child, an old maid chatter to her parrot, or a sleeper talk in his sleep. And in order to give the actor a chance, for once, to work on his own and to escape for a moment from the hectoring of an author, I have not written out the monologues in detail but simply suggested them. For, in so far as it does not influence the action, it is quite immaterial what is said while asleep or to the cat, and a talented actor who is absorbed in the situation and mood of the play can probably improvise better than the author, who cannot calculate in advance just how much needs to be said, or for how long, before the theatrical illusion is broken.

As we know, some Italian theatres have returned to improvisation,* producing actors who are creative in their own right, although in accordance with the author's intentions. This could really be a step forward or a fertile, new form of art that may well deserve the name *creative*.

Where a monologue would be implausible, I have resorted to mime, and here I leave the actor even greater freedom to create— and so win independent acclaim. But in order not to try the audience beyond its limits, I have let the music—well-motivated by the Midsummer dance, of course—exert its beguiling power during the silent action, and I would ask the musical director to select this music with great care so that the wrong associations are not aroused by recollections of the latest operettas or dance tunes or by the use of ultra-ethnographic folk music.

I could not have substituted a so-called crowd scene for the ballet I have introduced because crowd scenes are always badly acted, with a pack of simpering idiots seeking to use the occasion to show off and so destroy the illusion. Since ordinary people do not improvise their malicious remarks but use ready-made material that can be given a double meaning, I have not composed a malicious song but taken a little-known singing game* which I noted down myself in the neighbourhood of Stockholm. The words do not hit home precisely, but that is the intention, for the cunning (weakness) of the slave does not permit him to attack directly. So: no speaking buffoons in a serious play, no coarse smirking over a situation that puts the lid on a family's coffin.

As for the scenery, I have borrowed the asymmetry and cropped framing of impressionist painting,* and believe I have thereby succeeded in strengthening the illusion; for not being able to see the whole room or all the furniture leaves us free to conjecture, that is, our imagination is set in motion and we complete the picture ourselves. This also means that I have avoided those tiresome exits through doors, particularly stage doors that are made of canvas and sway at the slightest touch; they do not even permit an angry father to express his anger after a bad dinner by going out and slamming the door behind him 'so the whole house shakes'. (In the theatre it sways!) I have likewise restricted myself to a single set, both to allow the characters time to merge with their milieu and to break with the custom of expensive scenery. But when there is only a single set, one is entitled to demand that it be realistic. Yet nothing is more difficult than to get a room on stage to resemble a real room, no matter how easy the scene-painter finds erupting volcanoes and waterfalls. Even if the walls do have to be of canvas, it is surely time to stop painting shelves and kitchen utensils on them. There are so many other stage conventions in which we are asked to believe that we might be spared the effort of believing in painted saucepans.*

I have placed the rear wall and the table at an angle so that the actors have to play face on or in half profile when they are seated opposite each other at the table. In a production of *Aida** I have seen an angled backdrop which led the eye out into an unknown perspective, nor did it give the impression of having been put there simply to protest the boredom of straight lines.

Another perhaps desirable innovation would be the removal of the footlights. I understand that the purpose of lighting from below is to make the actors' faces fatter, but I would like to ask: why all actors have to have fat faces? Does not this underlighting obliterate a great many features in the lower parts of the face, especially around the jaws, distort the shape of the nose, and cast shadows over the eyes? Even if this is not the case, one thing is certain: it hurts the actors' eyes, so that their full expressiveness is lost, for footlights strike the retina in places that are normally protected (except in sailors, who cannot avoid seeing the sun reflected in water), and therefore we seldom see any other play of the eyes except crude glances either to the side or up to the balcony, when the white of the eye is visible. This probably also accounts for the tiresome way that actresses in particular have of fluttering their eyelashes. And when anyone on stage wants to speak with the eyes, the actor has sadly no alternative but to look straight at the audience, with which he or she then enters into direct contact outside the frame of the set—a bad habit rightly or wrongly called 'counting the house'.

Would not sufficiently strong side lighting (using parabolic reflectors or something similar) give the actor this new resource, of strengthening his facial expression by means of the face's greatest asset: the play of the eyes?

I have hardly any illusions about getting the actor to play for the audience and not with it, although this would be desirable. Nor do I dream of seeing the full back of an actor* throughout an important scene, but I do fervently wish that vital scenes should not be performed next to the prompter's box, as duets designed to elicit applause, but rather located to that part of the stage the action dictates. So, no revolutions, simply some small modifications, for to turn the stage into a room with the fourth wall removed and some of the furniture consequently facing away from the audience, would probably have a distracting effect, at least for the present.

When it comes to a word about make-up I dare not hope to be heard by the ladies, who would rather be beautiful than truthful. But the actor really might consider whether it is to his advantage to paint his face with an abstract character that will sit there like a mask. Picture an actor who gives himself a pronounced choleric expression by drawing a line with soot between his eyes, and suppose that, in spite of being in so permanently enraged a state, he needs to smile on a certain line. What a horrible grimace that would be! And how can the old man get the false forehead of his wig to wrinkle with anger when it is as smooth as a billiard ball?

In a modern psychological drama, where the subtlest movements of the soul should be mirrored more in the face than in gestures and sounds, it would probably be best to experiment with strong side lighting on a small stage and with actors wearing no make-up, or at least a bare minimum.

If we could then dispense with the visible orchestra* with its distracting lights and faces turned towards the audience; if we could have the stalls raised so that the spectator's eyes were on a line higher than the actor's knees; if we could get rid of the private proscenium boxes with their giggling drinkers and diners; if we could have complete darkness in the auditorium;* and finally, and most importantly, if we had a *small* stage and a *small* auditorium, then perhaps a new drama might arise, and the theatre would at least be a place where educated people might once again enjoy themselves. While waiting for such a theatre, we shall just have to go on writing for our desk drawers, preparing the repertoire whose time will come.

I have made an attempt! If it fails, there will surely be time to try again!

CHARACTERS

Miss Julie,* 25
Jean, a servant, 30
Kristin, a cook, 35

The action takes place in the Count's kitchen, on Midsummer Night.

A large kitchen, the ceiling and side walls of which are masked by draperies and top borders. The rear wall is slanted inwards and upstage from the left; on it, to the left, are two shelves with utensils of copper, bronze, iron, and pewter. The shelves are lined with goffered paper. Some way to the right three-quarters of the large, arched exit with two glass doors, through which is seen a fountain decorated with a cupid, lilac bushes in bloom, and some tall Lombardy poplars.

Stage left the corner of a big tiled stove with a section of its hood.

Stage right there protrudes one end of the servants' dining-table, of white pine, with some chairs.

The stove is decorated with bunches of birch leaves;* the floor is strewn with juniper.

On the end of the table a large Japanese spice-jar containing lilacs in flower.

An ice-box, a scullery table, a sink.

Above the door there is a big, old-fashioned bell, and emerging to the left of this a speaking-tube.

KRISTIN *is standing at the stove, frying something in a frying pan; she is wearing a light-coloured cotton dress, covered before with an apron;* JEAN *enters, dressed in livery and carrying a pair of large riding boots, with spurs, which he puts down on the floor where they remain clearly visible.*

JEAN. Miss Julie's quite crazy again tonight; absolutely crazy!*

KRISTIN. Oh, so you're back then, are you?*

JEAN. I went with the Count to the station and on my way back past the barn I just stopped by for a dance. And who do I see but her ladyship with the gamekeeper, leading the dance? But as soon as she claps eyes on me, she comes rushing straight on over and invites me to join her in the ladies' waltz. And how she waltzed!—I've never known the like. She's crazy!

KRISTIN. She always has been, but nothing like these last two weeks, since her engagement ended.

JEAN. Yes, what about all that? He was a fine enough fellow after all, even though he wasn't rich. But they've got so many airs and graces, her sort. [*He sits down at the end of the table*] All the same, it's odd that a young lady like her should want to stay at home with the servants, eh? Rather than visit her relations with her father. At midsummer, too!

KRISTIN. She's maybe a bit embarrassed after that to-do with her young man.

JEAN. Could be. But he knew how to stand up for himself, at any rate. Do you know what happened, Kristin? I saw it, even though I took care not to let on.

KRISTIN. No, you never?

JEAN. Didn't I just.—They were down at the stables one evening, and Miss Julie was training him—that's what she called it. Do you know how? She made him leap over her riding crop, the way you teach a dog to jump. Twice he jumped, and got a cut each time; but the third time, he snatched the whip out of her hand, broke it into a thousand pieces;* and off he went.

KRISTIN. Is that what happened? No! You don't say!*

JEAN. That was it, all right!—But what have you got for me now, Kristin, something tasty?

KRISTIN [*serves from the pan and sets a place for* JEAN]. Oh, just a bit of kidney, off the veal roast!

JEAN [*smells the food*]. Lovely! That's my great *délice*!* [*Feels the plate*] You might have warmed the plate, though!

KRISTIN. You're worse than his Lordship, once you start.

Rumples his hair affectionately.

JEAN [*crossly*]. Stop mussing my hair! You know how sensitive I am!

KRISTIN. Now, now, you know it's only love.

JEAN *eats.* KRISTIN *opens a bottle of beer.*

JEAN. Beer? On Midsummer Eve? No thank you! I can do better than that. [*He opens a drawer in the table and takes out a bottle of red wine, sealed with yellow wax*] Yellow seal, see*—the best!—Now get me a glass. A wine glass, of course, when I'm drinking *pur*!*

KRISTIN [*returns to the stove, and puts on a small saucepan*]. Heaven help whoever gets you for a husband. What a fusspot!

JEAN. Rubbish! You'd be glad enough to get a fine fellow like me; and it's done you no harm people calling me your fiancé. [*Tastes the wine*] Good! Very good! A little more *chambré*,* perhaps. [*Warms* *the glass with his hands*] We bought this in Dijon. Four francs a litre it was, before bottling; and then there was the duty. What's that you're cooking? It smells foul.

KRISTIN. Oh, just some filthy muck Miss Julie wants for Diana.*

JEAN. You should watch your language, Kristin. Why are you cooking for that little cur on a holiday, though? Is it ill, or what?

KRISTIN. Oh it's ill, all right! She slunk off with the gate-keeper's mutt—now she's up the spout—and Miss Julie won't have it!

JEAN. She's so stuck-up about some things, and not proud enough about others, just like her Ladyship when she was alive. She was more at home in the kitchen and around the barn, but always demanded a carriage and pair. She went around with dirty cuffs, but had to have the Count's crest on every button.—And talking of Miss Julie, she takes no care of herself or her person. To my mind she's no lady. Just now, dancing in the barn, she grabbed the gamekeeper away from Anna and made him dance with her. We'd not behave like that; but that's how it is when the gentry try to act common—they become common. What a splendid creature, though! Quite magnificent! Oh! What shoulders and— etcetera!

KRISTIN. All right, don't go on. I've heard what Klara says, and she dresses her.

JEAN. Oh, Klara! You women are always jealous of one another. I've been out riding with her... And then, the way she dances!

KRISTIN. Listen, Jean; don't you want to dance with me when I'm done...

JEAN. I said so, didn't I?

KRISTIN. Promise?

JEAN. Promise? When I say I'll do a thing, I do it. But thanks for dinner now. It was very nice.   [*Recorks the bottle*

MISS JULIE [*in the doorway, talking to someone outside*]. I'll be back right away. You carry on now.

JEAN *hides the bottle away in the drawer of the table; gets up respect-fully.*

MISS JULIE [*enters; approaches* KRISTIN *at the stove*]. Well, is it ready?

KRISTIN *indicates that* JEAN *is present*.

JEAN [*gallantly*]. You ladies have your secrets, perhaps?

MISS JULIE [*flips him in the face with her handkerchief*]. Nosey!

JEAN. Oh, what a lovely smell of violets!

MISS JULIE [*coquettishly*]. Cheeky! So you know about perfumes, too! You certainly know how to dance... no looking now. Go away!

JEAN [*impertinently, yet respectfully*]. Some magic potion* you ladies are cooking up this Midsummer Eve, is that it? Foretell the future? Like those cards which show you who you'll marry?*

MISS JULIE [*sharply*]. You'd need good eyes to see *that*. [*To* KRISTIN] Pour it into a half-bottle, and cork it well.—Come and dance a schottische* with me, Jean...

JEAN [*hesitating*]. I don't wish to appear impolite, but I'd promised this dance to Kristin...

MISS JULIE. Well, she can have another, can't you Kristin? You'll lend me Jean, won't you?

KRISTIN. That's hardly up to me. If your Ladyship condescends, it's not for him to refuse. Go on, you, and be grateful for the honour.

JEAN. To be frank, and without wishing to offend, I wonder if it would be wise for your Ladyship to dance twice running with the same partner, especially as these people aren't slow to jump to conclusions...

MISS JULIE [*flaring up*]. What? What conclusions? What do you mean?

JEAN [*politely*]. If your Ladyship doesn't wish to understand, I must speak more plainly. It doesn't look right to prefer one of your retainers before others awaiting the same rare honour...

MISS JULIE. Prefer! What an idea! I'm astonished! I, the lady of the house, honour this dance of yours with my presence, and now, when I really feel like dancing, I want someone who knows how to lead, and who won't make me look ridiculous.

JEAN. As your Ladyship commands. I am at your service.

MISS JULIE [*softly*]. Don't take it as a command. This evening we are all just enjoying ourselves together, and any rank is laid aside. So, give me your arm.—Don't worry, Kristin! I shan't run off with your fiancé!

[JEAN *offers* MISS JULIE *his arm, and conducts her out*

PANTOMIME*

This should be played as if the actress were really alone; when necessary she should turn her back on the audience; she does not look towards the auditorium nor hurry, as if afraid the audience might become impatient.

KRISTIN *alone. The faint sound of a violin at a distance, playing a schottische.*

KRISTIN *humming to the music; clears up after* JEAN, *washes the plate at the sink, dries it, and puts it away in a cupboard.*

Then she removes her apron, takes out a small mirror from a drawer in the table, places it against the pot of lilac on the table, lights a candle, and heats a hairpin, with which she crisps the hair on her forehead.

Then she goes to the door and listens. Returns to the table. Finds MISS JULIE's *forgotten handkerchief, which she picks up and sniffs; then she spreads it out, as though wrapped in thought, stretches it, smooths it out, and folds it into quarters, etc.*

JEAN [*enters, alone*]. But she really *is* crazy! What a way to dance! And everyone guffawing at her from behind the doors. What do you make of it, Kristin?

KRISTIN. Well, she's got her monthly now; then she always acts this strange. Now, are you going to dance with me?

JEAN. You're not mad at me for going off like that, are you?

KRISTIN. No!—Not for a little thing like that; besides, I know my place...

JEAN [*putting his arm about her waist*]. You're a sensible girl, Kristin, you'd make a good wife...

MISS JULIE [*enters; is disagreeably surprised; with forced jocularity*]. Charming partner you are, running away from your lady like that.

JEAN. On the contrary, Miss Julie, as you see, I've hurried to find the one I just left.

MISS JULIE [*changing her tone*]. You know, you're an incomparable dancer.—But why are you wearing livery? It's a holiday! Take it off at once!

JEAN. Then I must ask you to withdraw for a moment, Miss Julie, my black coat is right here. . .   [*Gestures as he moves to the right*

MISS JULIE. Do I embarrass you? It's just a coat. Go into your room, then, and be quick about it. Or you can stay and I'll turn my back.

JEAN. With your permission, then.

[*Goes to the right; his arm is visible as he changes his coat*

MISS JULIE [*to* KRISTIN]. Well, Kristin; he's very familiar, are you and Jean engaged?

KRISTIN. Engaged? If you like. We call it that.

MISS JULIE. Call?

KRISTIN. Well, your Ladyship, you've been engaged yourself, and. . .

MISS JULIE. We were properly engaged. . .

KRISTIN. But it still didn't come to anything. . .

[*JEAN enters in black tail coat and a black derby hat.*]

MISS JULIE. *Très gentil, monsieur Jean! Très gentil!*

JEAN. *Vous voulez plaisanter, madame!*

MISS JULIE. *Et vous voulez parler français!** Where did you learn that?

JEAN. In Switzerland while I was a *sommelier!** at one of the biggest hotels in Lucerne.*

MISS JULIE. You look quite the gentleman in that frock-coat. *Charmant!**   [*She sits at the table*

JEAN. Oh, you're flattering me.

MISS JULIE [*offended*]. Flattering you?

JEAN. My natural modesty forbids me to believe that you would pay someone like me a true compliment, and therefore I permitted myself to suppose that you were exaggerating, or as it is called, 'flattering'.

MISS JULIE. Where did you learn to speak like that? You've spent a lot of time at the theatre, is that it?

JEAN. Among other things. I've been around, you know!

MISS JULIE. But you come from round here, don't you?

JEAN. My father was a labourer* on the next estate, the attorney's place. I used to see you as a child, though you never noticed me.

MISS JULIE. No, really?

JEAN. Yes, I remember one time especially... but I can't tell you that.

MISS JULIE. Oh yes! Do! Why not? Just this once!

JEAN. No, I really couldn't, not now. Another time, perhaps.

MISS JULIE. Another time means never. Is now so dangerous?

JEAN. Dangerous, no, but I'd rather not.—Just look at that!

He indicates KRISTIN, *who has fallen asleep in a chair by the stove.*

MISS JULIE. She'll make a delightful wife, that one! Perhaps she snores, too?

JEAN. No, she doesn't, but she talks in her sleep.

MISS JULIE [*indelicately*]. How do you know?

JEAN [*coolly*]. I've heard her!

Pause, while they look at each other.

MISS JULIE. Why don't you sit down?

JEAN. Not in your presence. I wouldn't take the liberty.

MISS JULIE. But if I were to order you to?

JEAN. Then I'd obey.

MISS JULIE. Then sit.—But wait! Can you get me something to drink first?

JEAN. I don't know what we've got in the ice-box here. Just beer, I think.

MISS JULIE. What do you mean, 'just'? I've simple tastes; I prefer it to wine.

JEAN [*takes a bottle of beer from the ice-box; finds a glass and plate from the cupboard, and serves her*]. My compliments!

MISS JULIE. Thank you. Won't you have something to drink yourself?

JEAN. I'm not really a beer drinker; but if it's an order.

MISS JULIE. Order?—As a gentleman you should keep your lady company, I think.

JEAN. You're right, of course.   [*Opens another bottle, takes a glass*

MISS JULIE. Now drink my health! [JEAN *hesitates*] I do believe you're shy!

JEAN [*kneeling, in a humorous parody; raises his glass*]. My mistress's health!

MISS JULIE. Bravo!—Now finish things off properly and kiss my shoe as well!

JEAN *hesitates, but then boldly grasps her foot, which he kisses lightly.*

MISS JULIE. Excellent! You should have been an actor.

JEAN [*getting up*]. This can't go on, Miss Julie; someone might come in and see us.

MISS JULIE. So what?

JEAN. People would talk, that's what! And if you knew how their tongues were wagging up there just now, then...

MISS JULIE. What were they saying? Tell me!—Sit down!

JEAN [*sits*]. I don't want to hurt you, but they were using expressions which suggested that... well, you can guess yourself. You're no child, and when a woman's seen drinking alone at night with a man—a servant or not—then...

MISS JULIE. Then what? Besides, we're not alone. Kristin's here.

JEAN. Asleep.

MISS JULIE. Then I'll wake her. [*Gets up*] Kristin! Are you asleep?

KRISTIN *babbles in her sleep.*

MISS JULIE. Kristin!—She's well away!

KRISTIN [*in her sleep*]. His Lordship's boots are brushed—put on the coffee—right away, right away, right...

[*Mumbles incoherently*

MISS JULIE [*takes her by the nose*]. Will you wake up?

JEAN [*sharply*]. Let her alone, she's sleeping!

MISS JULIE [*sharply*]. What?

JEAN. Someone who's been standing over a stove all day has the right to be tired when night comes. Sleep should be respected...

MISS JULIE [*changes her tone*]. That's nobly put, it does you credit—thank you! [*Holds out her hand to* JEAN] Come outside now and pick me some lilac.

JEAN. With you?

MISS JULIE. With me.

JEAN. That's impossible! We can't!

MISS JULIE. I don't understand what you mean. You surely don't imagine that...

JEAN. Me, no, but the others.

MISS JULIE. What? That I should be *verliebt** with my servant?

JEAN. I'm not given to conceit, but it's been known to happen—and nothing's sacred to these people.

MISS JULIE. I do believe you're an aristocrat!

JEAN. Yes, I am!

MISS JULIE. I step down...

JEAN. Don't step down, Miss Julie, take my advice. No one will believe you did so freely; people will always say you fell.

MISS JULIE. I've a higher opinion of people than you. Come and see.—Come on! [*She gives him a long, steady look*

JEAN. You know, you're strange.

MISS JULIE. Perhaps. But then so are you.—Besides, everything's strange. Life, people, everything's a scum that drifts, drifts on across the water, until it sinks, sinks. There's a dream I have from time to time; I'm reminded of it now.—I'm sitting on top of a pillar that I've climbed, and can see no way of getting down; when I look down, I get dizzy, but down I must, though I haven't the courage to jump; I can't stay where I am and I long to fall; but I don't; and yet I'll get no peace until I come down, no rest until I come down, down to the ground, and were I to reach the ground I'd want to bury myself in the earth... Have you ever felt anything like that?

JEAN. No! I usually dream I'm lying under a tall tree in a dark wood. I want to climb up, up to the top, and look around over the bright landscape where the sun is shining, plunder the bird's nest up there where the gold eggs lie. I climb and climb, but the trunk is so thick, and so slippery, and it's so far to the first branch. But I know that if I could only reach that first branch I'd get to the top like on a ladder. I haven't reached it yet, but I will do one day, even if it's just a dream.

MISS JULIE. Here I am swapping dreams with you. Come on! Just into the park!   [*She offers him her arm, and they go*

JEAN. If we sleep on nine Midsummer flowers tonight, Miss Julie, our dreams will come true.*

JULIE *and* JEAN *turn in the doorway*. JEAN *puts a hand to one of his eyes.*

MISS JULIE. Something in your eye? Let me see.

JEAN. It's nothing—only a speck of dust—it'll be all right.

MISS JULIE. My sleeve must have caught you; sit down and I'll help you. [*She takes him by the arm and sits him down; takes his head and pushes it backwards; with the tip of her handkerchief she tries to remove the speck of dust*] Sit still now; absolutely still!—[*Slaps his hand*] There! Will you obey me!—I do believe you're trembling, a big strong fellow like you! [*Feels his upper arm*] With arms like that!

JEAN [*warning her*]. Miss Julie!

KRISTIN *has woken up, walks heavy with sleep to the right, to go to bed.*

MISS JULIE. Yes, Monsieur Jean?

JEAN. *Attention! Je ne suis qu'un homme!**

MISS JULIE. Will you sit still!—There! Now it's gone. Kiss my hand, and say thank you!

JEAN [*gets up*]. Miss Julie, listen to me.—Kristin's gone to bed now.—Will you listen to me!

MISS JULIE. Kiss my hand first.

JEAN. Listen to me!

MISS JULIE. Kiss my hand first!

JEAN. All right. But blame yourself.

MISS JULIE. For what?

JEAN. For what? Are you a child? At twenty-five? Don't you know it's dangerous to play with fire?

MISS JULIE. Not for me; I'm insured.

JEAN [*boldly*]. No, you're not. And even if you are, there's more inflammable material around.

MISS JULIE. Meaning you?

JEAN. Yes! Not because I'm me, but because I'm a young man—

MISS JULIE. With a prepossessing appearance—what incredible conceit! A Don Juan, perhaps? Or a Joseph! Yes, upon my soul, I do believe you're a Joseph!*

JEAN. Do you?

MISS JULIE. I almost fear it!

JEAN *boldly forward and tries to take her round the waist to kiss her.*

MISS JULIE [*slaps him*]. Cheek!

JEAN. Are you joking or serious?

MISS JULIE. Serious!

JEAN. Then you were serious just now, too. You play far too seriously—that's dangerous. Now I'm tired of this game, and with your permission I'll get back to my work. The Count'll be needing his boots, and it's long past midnight.

MISS JULIE. Put those boots down!

JEAN. No. They're one of my duties, which don't include being your plaything. And I never shall be. I hold myself too good for that.

MISS JULIE. Aren't we the proud one!

JEAN. In some respects, yes; in others, no.

MISS JULIE. Have you ever been in love?

JEAN. That's not a word we use, though I've fancied lots of girls, and was once quite sick when I couldn't get the one I wanted. Sick, you know, like those princes in the Arabian Nights, who couldn't eat or drink for love.

MISS JULIE. Who was she? [JEAN *remains silent*] Who was she?

JEAN. You can't make me tell you.

MISS JULIE. Suppose I ask you as an equal, as a—friend? Who was she?

JEAN. You!

MISS JULIE [*sits*]. How priceless!

JEAN. Yes, if you like. It was ridiculous.—You see, this is the story I didn't want to tell you just now, but now I'm going to. Do you know what the world looks like from down below?—No, you don't. Like hawks and falcons, whose backs we seldom see because they mostly soar on high. I lived in a hovel with seven brothers and sisters, and a pig out in the grey fields, where there wasn't a single tree. But from the window I could see the wall of his Lordship's park, overhung with apple trees. It was the garden of paradise, surrounded by angry angels who watched over it with flaming swords. All the same, along with the other boys I found a way to the tree of life*—now you despise me—

MISS JULIE. Oh! All boys steal apples.

JEAN. You say that now, but you still despise me. Never mind. One day I went into this paradise, along with my mother, to weed the onion beds. Alongside this patch of garden there was a Turkish pavilion,* shaded by jasmines, and overgrown with honeysuckle. I'd never seen such a beautiful building, and had no idea what it was for. People used to go in and come out, and one day the door was left ajar. I stole in. The walls were all covered with portraits of kings and emperors, and over the windows there were red curtains with tassles on them—now you know what I'm talking about. I [*he breaks off a spray of lilac and holds it under* MISS JULIE'*s nose*], I'd never been inside the Hall, never seen anything except the church—but this was more beautiful; and wherever my thoughts strayed, they always came back—there. Gradually I was overcome by a longing just once to experience the full delight of—*enfin*,* I crept inside, saw, and marvelled. But then I heard someone coming! There was only one way out for the gentry, but for me there was another, and I had no choice but to take it.

MISS JULIE, *who has taken the lilac blossom, lets it fall on the table.*

JEAN. Then I began to run, bursting through the raspberry bushes, and across a strawberry patch, until I arrived at the rose-garden. There I saw a pink dress and a pair of white stockings—it was you. I lay down under a pile of weeds, under—can you imagine it?— under thistles which pricked me, and wet earth that stank, and I thought: if it's true that a thief can enter heaven and dwell with the angels, then it's strange that a labourer's child here on God's earth cannot enter the Hall park and play with the Count's daughter.

MISS JULIE [*sentimentally*]. Do you suppose all poor children feel the way you did on that occasion?

JEAN [*at first hesitant, then with conviction*]. If *all* poor—yes—of course. Of course!

MISS JULIE. It must be a tremendous misfortune to be poor.

JEAN [*with deep pain, and powerful emotion*]. Oh, Miss Julie! Oh!—A dog may lie on the Countess's sofa, a horse may have its nose stroked by a young lady's hand, but a common drudge!—[*He changes tack*] Oh, all right, now and then a man has what it takes to hoist himself up in the world, but how often is that?—Do you know what I did then, though?—I ran down into the millstream with all my clothes on, got dragged out, and was given a thrashing. But the following Sunday, when father and all the others went to call on my grandmother, I saw to it that I was left at home. Then I washed myself in soap and warm water, put on my best clothes, and went to church—to see you. And when I'd seen you I returned home, determined to die. But I wanted to die beautifully and pleasantly, without pain. I remembered it was dangerous to sleep under an elder bush. We had a big one, just then in flower. I stripped it of everything it held, and made up a bed for myself in the oat-bin. Have you ever noticed how smooth oats are; soft to the touch like human skin?— — —Anyway, I shut the lid, closed my eyes, and fell asleep. When they woke me up I really was very ill. But as you see, I didn't die. I don't know what I was after, really. There was no hope of winning you, of course, but you stood for how hopeless it was ever to escape from the class in which I was born.

MISS JULIE. You're a charming storyteller, you know. Did you go to school?

JEAN. A bit. But I've read lots of novels and been to the theatre. Besides, I've heard posh people talk. That's what's taught me most.

MISS JULIE. Do you listen to what we say?

JEAN. Of course! And I've heard plenty too, sitting on the coachman's box or rowing the boat. Once I heard you and a girlfriend...

MISS JULIE. Indeed?—What did you hear?

JEAN. Really, it wouldn't bear repeating. All the same, I was a bit surprised. I couldn't understand where you'd learned all those words. Maybe at bottom there isn't such a big difference as they say there is between people and—well, people.

MISS JULIE. Shame on you! We don't behave like you when we're engaged.

JEAN [*stares at her*]. Is that so?—It's no good playing the innocent with me, you know...

MISS JULIE. That man was a swine. And I loved him!

JEAN. That's what you always say—afterwards.

MISS JULIE. Always?

JEAN. Always, yes, I'd say so. I've heard the expression several times before, on similar occasions.

MISS JULIE. What occasions?

JEAN. Like the one in question. The last time— — —

MISS JULIE [*gets up*]. Be quiet! I don't wish to hear any more.

JEAN. *She* didn't wish to, either—it's strange. Well, in that case, have I your permission to go to bed?

MISS JULIE [*softly*]. To bed! On Midsummer Night?

JEAN. Yes! Dancing with that lot up there doesn't exactly amuse me.

MISS JULIE. Get the key to the boat and row me out on the lake; I want to see the sunrise.

JEAN. Is that wise?

MISS JULIE. You sound as though you're worried about your reputation.

JEAN. Why shouldn't I be? I don't want to become a laughing-stock nor be dismissed without a reference, not now that I'm beginning to get on in the world. And I've a certain duty to Kristin, I believe.

MISS JULIE. Oh, so it's Kristin now— — —

JEAN. Yes, but you too.—Take my advice, and go back up to bed.

MISS JULIE. Me? Take your advice?

JEAN. Just this once; for your own sake! I beg you! It's late, you're tired and therefore drunk and hot-headed. Go to bed! Besides—if my ears don't deceive me—they're coming here to look for me. And if they find us here together, you're lost!

> *Voices singing in unison are heard approaching.*

> There came two women from out the wood
> Tridiridi-ralla tridiridi-ra.
> One with her feet both bare and cold
> Tridiridi-ralla-la.

> And money it seems was all their game
> Tridiridi-ralla tridiridi-ra.
> Though neither had a sou to her name.
> Tridiridi-ralla-la.

> The bridal wreath I'll give to you,
> Tridiridi-ralla tridiridi-ra.
> But to another I'll be true.
> Tridiridi-ralla-la.*

MISS JULIE. I know these people, and I love them, just as they love me. Let them come, you'll see!

JEAN. No, Miss Julie, they don't love you. They eat your food, but afterwards they spit. Believe me! Listen to them, just listen to what they're singing!—No, don't!

MISS JULIE [*listens*]. What are they singing?

JEAN. It's an obscene song! About you and me!

MISS JULIE. How horrible! Oh, how two-faced!—

JEAN. That's the rabble for you, they're all cowards! You can't fight them. Better run away.

MISS JULIE. Run away? But where? We can't get out! Or go in to Kristin!

JEAN. Into my room, then? Necessity knows no law; and you can trust me, I'm your true, loyal, and respectful friend.

MISS JULIE. But suppose—suppose they were to look for you there?

JEAN. I'll bolt the door, and if anyone tries to break in, I'll shoot!— Come! [*Kneeling*] Come on!

MISS JULIE [*significantly*]. You promise— — —

JEAN. I swear!

[MISS JULIE *exits rapidly stage right.* JEAN *quickly after her*

BALLET

The peasants enter, dressed in their best clothes, with flowers in their hats; a fiddler at their head; a cask of small beer and a small keg of acquavit, garlanded with leaves, are placed on the table; glasses are produced. They drink. Then a circle is formed and they sing and dance the dancing game, 'There came two women from out the wood'. *When this is finished, they exit again, still singing.*

MISS JULIE *enters alone; sees the havoc in the kitchen; clasps her hands together; then takes out a powder puff and powders her face.*

JEAN [*enters, excited*]. There, you see! And heard! Do you think it's possible to stay here now?

MISS JULIE. No. I don't. But what can we do?

JEAN. Leave, travel. Far away from here.

MISS JULIE. Travel? Yes, but where?

JEAN. To Switzerland, to the Italian lakes;—have you never been there?

MISS JULIE. No. Is it beautiful there?

JEAN. Eternal summer, oranges, laurel trees, ah!

MISS JULIE. But what would we do there?

JEAN. I'll start a hotel—tip-top service and a first-class clientele.

MISS JULIE. Hotel?

JEAN. That's the life, believe you me; a never-ending stream of new faces, new languages; no time for worry or nerves; no wondering what to do, when there's always work to be done; bells ringing night and day, trains whistling, the bus coming and going; and all the while the money just rolling in! That's the life!

MISS JULIE. That's as may be. But what about me?

JEAN. The mistress of the house; the jewel of the establishment. With your looks, and your style—why—we've got it made! Tremendous! You'll sit in the office like a queen, setting your slaves in motion at the push of a bell; and the guests will file past your throne and humbly leave their tribute on your table—you've no idea how people tremble when they're handed a bill.—I'll salt them all right, and you'll sugar them with your sweetest smile.— Oh! let's get away from here [*Takes a timetable from his pocket*] at once, by the next train!—We'll be in Malmö at six-thirty; Hamburg at eight-forty tomorrow morning; Frankfurt to Basel takes a day, and Como* via the Gotthard Pass,* let me see, three days. Three days!

MISS JULIE. That's all very well. But Jean—you must give me courage.—Tell me you love me! Come and take me in your arms!

JEAN [*hesitating*]. I'd like to—but I daren't! Not in this house, not again! I love you—of course I do—you don't doubt that, do you, Miss Julie?

MISS JULIE [*shyly, with genuine femininity*]. Miss! Call me Julie.* There are no barriers between us now. Call me Julie!

JEAN [*tormented*]. I can't!—There are still barriers between us, as long as we remain in this house—there's the past, there's his Lordship—I've never met anyone I respected as much as him— I only have to see his gloves lying on a chair, and I feel so small—I only have to hear that bell up there, and I start like a frightened horse—and now, when I see his boots standing there so high and mighty, it sends a shiver down my spine! [*Kicks the boots*] Superstition, prejudices, dinned into us from childhood—but they can easily be forgotten, too. Some other country, as long as it's a republic, and people will bow down before my porter's livery— bow down, you'll see. But *I* shan't! I wasn't born to bow and scrape, there's something to me, I've got character, just let me get hold of that first branch, and you'll soon see me climb! I may be a servant today, but next year I'll have my own place, and in ten years I'll be a landed gentleman. Then I'll go to Romania and get myself a decoration; why I might—only *might*, mind you—end up a count!

MISS JULIE. Gently does it!

JEAN. In Romania you can buy a title, so you'd be a countess all the same. My countess!

MISS JULIE. What do I care about all that? That's what I'm leaving behind.—Say you love me, otherwise—yes, what am I otherwise?

JEAN. I'll say it a thousand times—but later—not here! And above all, no scenes or we're lost. We must approach things coolly, like sensible people. [*Takes a cigar, cuts and lights it*] Now you sit there and I'll sit here, and we'll talk, as if nothing had happened.

MISS JULIE [*desperately*]. Oh, my God! Have you no feelings?*

JEAN. Me? No one's got more feelings than I have; but I can control mine.

MISS JULIE. A moment ago you could kiss my shoe—and now!

JEAN [*harshly*]. That was a moment ago. We've other things to think about now.

MISS JULIE. Don't speak so harshly to me!

JEAN. I'm not, just sensibly. One folly's enough, don't commit any more. The Count may return at any moment and by then we've got to have this sorted. What do you think of my plans for the future? Do you approve?

MISS JULIE. They seem quite sensible to me. Just one question, though: a big project like that requires a lot of capital. Have you got it?

JEAN [*chewing his cigar*]. Me? Sure! I've my professional expertise, my vast experience, my knowledge of languages. That's capital enough, I'd say.

MISS JULIE. But that won't even buy you a railway ticket.

JEAN. True enough! That's why I'm looking for a backer, someone who'll advance me the money.

MISS JULIE. Where will you find one in such a hurry?

JEAN. That's up to you, if you want to be my partner.

MISS JULIE. I can't, and I've nothing myself.

Pause.

JEAN. Then you can forget the whole thing— — —

MISS JULIE. And— — —

JEAN. Things will stay as they are.

MISS JULIE. Do you think I'll stay under this roof as your easy lay? Do you think I'll let people point their fingers at me; that I can look my father in the face after this? No! Take me away from here, from the shame and the dishonour!—Oh, what have I done? My God, my God!   [*Weeps*

JEAN. So that's your tune now, is it?—What've you done? The same as many another before you!

MISS JULIE [*screams convulsively*]. And now you despise me!—I'm falling, I'm falling!

JEAN. Fall down to me, and I'll lift you up again.

MISS JULIE. What terrible power drew me to you? Was it the lure of the weak to the strong? Or of someone falling to someone rising! Or was it love? Was that love? Do you know what love is?

JEAN. Me? You bet I do! Do you think this was my first time?

MISS JULIE. You say and think such awful things.

JEAN. It's what I've learnt; that's the way I am. Don't be nervous now, and stop acting the lady, we're birds of a feather now!— There, there, my girl, come here and I'll give you a glass of something special.

Opens the table drawer and takes out the bottle of wine; fills two used glasses.

MISS JULIE. Where did you get that wine from?

JEAN. The cellar.

MISS JULIE. My father's burgundy!

JEAN. Isn't it good enough for his son-in-law?

MISS JULIE. And I drink beer!

JEAN. That only goes to show your taste is worse than mine.

MISS JULIE. Thief!

JEAN. Are you going to tell?

MISS JULIE. Oh, my God! Accomplice to a sneak-thief! Was I drunk? Or have I spent the whole night dreaming? Midsummer Night! The night of innocent games...

JEAN. Innocent? Hm!

MISS JULIE [*paces up and down*]. Is there anyone anywhere as miserable as I am just now?

JEAN. Miserable? You? After such a conquest? Think of Kristin in there. Don't you think she's got feelings, too?

MISS JULIE. I thought so just now, but not any more. No, a servant's a servant...

JEAN. And a whore's a whore!

MISS JULIE [*on her knees, with her hands clasped*]. Oh, God in heaven, take my miserable life! Take me away from this filth into which I'm sinking. Save me! Save me!

JEAN. I can't deny I feel sorry for you. When I lay in the onion bed and saw you in the rose garden, then— — —I'll say it now— — — I had the same dirty thoughts that all boys have.

MISS JULIE. And you, who wanted to die for me!

JEAN. In the oat-bin? That was just talk.

MISS JULIE. A lie, you mean!

JEAN [*beginning to get sleepy*]. More or less! I read it in the paper once about a chimney-sweep who lay down in a wood-chest with some lilacs, because he'd had a paternity order brought against him— — —

MISS JULIE. So, that's your type...

JEAN. Well, what was I supposed to say? Women always fall for pretty stories!

MISS JULIE. Swine!

JEAN. *Merde!**

MISS JULIE. And now you've seen the hawk's back— — —

JEAN. Not its *back*, exactly— — —

MISS JULIE. And I was to be the first branch— — —

JEAN. But the branch was rotten— — —

MISS JULIE. I was to be the signboard of your hotel— — —

JEAN. And I the hotel— — —

MISS JULIE. Sit behind your desk, attract your customers, fiddle your bills— — —

JEAN. I'd do that myself— — —

MISS JULIE. That any human soul can be so foul!

JEAN. Wash it, then!

MISS JULIE. Lackey, servant, stand up when I speak to you!

JEAN. Lackey's whore, servant's tart, shut your mouth and get out of here! How dare you go and call me crude? No one of my sort has ever behaved as crudely as you have this evening. Do you think any of the girls around here would approach a man the way you did? Have you ever seen a girl of my class offer herself like that? I've only seen the like among animals and prostitutes.*

MISS JULIE [*crushed*]. That's right; hit me; trample on me; I've deserved no better. I'm a miserable wretch; but help me! Help me out of this, if there is a way.

JEAN [*more gently*]. I'll not deny myself a share in the honour of having seduced you; but do you believe a man like me would've dared to even look at you if you'd not extended the invitation yourself? I'm still amazed— — —

MISS JULIE. And proud— — —

JEAN. Why not? Though I must confess the conquest was altogether too easy to be really intoxicating.

MISS JULIE. Hit me again!

JEAN [*gets up*]. No. Forgive me for what I've just said. I don't hit someone who's down, least of all a woman. I can't deny the pleasure I took in seeing that what had us blinded down there was only fool's gold, that the hawk's back was also only grey, that fine cheek merely powder, those polished nails had black edges, and your handkerchief was dirty even though it smelt of perfume. All the same, I'm sorry that what I was myself aspiring towards wasn't something higher or more worthwhile; I'm sorry to see you sunk so low that you're far beneath your cook. It's as if I was watching the flowers being lashed to pieces by the autumn rain and turning into mud.

MISS JULIE. You speak as though you were already above me.

JEAN. I am, too. You see, I could turn you into a countess, but you can never make me a count.

MISS JULIE. But I'm a count's child—that's something you can never be.

JEAN. True. But my children could be counts—if— — —

MISS JULIE. But you're a thief; I'm not.

JEAN. There are worse things than being a thief. A lot worse! And besides, when I serve in a house I consider myself part of the family, like one of the children, and nobody calls it stealing when they take the odd berry from a heavily laden bush. [*He starts to feel passionate again*] Miss Julie, you're a fine woman, far too good for the likes of me. You've been the victim of an intoxication, and you want to cover it up by pretending you love me. You don't, apart, perhaps, from falling for my looks—and in that case, your love's no better than mine.—But I can never be satisfied with just being your creature, and I can never win your love.

MISS JULIE. Are you so sure?

JEAN. You'd like to think there was a chance.—That I could truly love you, yes, without a doubt: you're beautiful, you're refined [*he approaches her and takes her hand*], educated, charming when you want to be, and once you've aroused a man the flame will surely never die. [*Puts his arm around her waist*] You're like mulled wine, strongly spiced, and a kiss from you— — —

> *He tries to lead her out; but she slowly frees herself.*

MISS JULIE. Let me go!—You won't win me like that!

JEAN. *How*, then, if not like that? Not by caresses and fine words; not by giving careful thought to our future, rescuing you from degradation! *How*, then?

MISS JULIE. How? How? I don't know.—I've no idea.—I detest you as I do rats, but I can't run away from you!

JEAN. Run away with me!

MISS JULIE [*straightens herself*]. Run away? Yes, we'll run away.— But I'm so tired. Give me some wine. [JEAN *pours the wine*. MISS JULIE *looks at her watch*] But first we must talk, we've still got a little time. [*Drains the glass; holds it out for more*

JEAN. Don't drink so much, you'll get drunk.

MISS JULIE. So what?

JEAN. So what? It's vulgar.—What were you going to say to me just now?

MISS JULIE. We'll run away. But first we'll talk, that's to say, I'll talk, for up to now, you've done all the talking. You've told me about your life, now I want to tell you about mine. Then we'll know all about each other before we set off together.

JEAN. Wait a moment. Forgive me, but you might come to regret telling me all your intimate secrets.

MISS JULIE. Aren't you my friend?

JEAN. Yes, sometimes. But don't rely on me.

MISS JULIE. You're only saying that.—Besides, everyone knows my secrets.—My mother was a commoner, from a very humble background, you see. She was brought up according to contemporary theories about equality, women's emancipation, and all that; and she had a decided aversion to marriage. When, therefore, my father proposed to her she maintained she'd never become his wife, though he might become her lover. He told her he had no desire to see the woman he loved enjoy less respect than himself. But consumed by passion and believing that she didn't care what the world thought, he accepted her conditions. Though now he was cut off from his social circle, and thrown back upon his domestic life, which could hardly satisfy him. Then I came into the world—against my mother's wishes, as far as I can tell. My mother decided to bring me up as a child of nature and, what's more, I was to learn everything a boy has to learn, so that I might serve to demonstrate that a woman was just as good as any man. I had to wear boy's clothes, and learn to handle horses, but not to go into the barn; I had to groom and harness them, learn about farming, and go hunting, even how to slaughter the animals. Ugh, that was horrible! And on the estate the men were put to women's work, and the women to men's—so that everything went to the dogs, and we became the laughing-stock of the neighbourhood. Finally, my father must have woken up from his bewitchment and fought back, for everything was now done his way. After that my parents got married, quietly. My mother fell ill—with what, I don't know—but she often had convulsions, and hid herself in the attic or the garden. Sometimes she stayed out all night. Then came the great fire which you've heard about. The house, the stables, and the barn burnt down, in very peculiar circumstances that gave rise to suspicions of arson, for the accident happened the day after the quarterly insurance expired, and the premiums, which my father had sent, were delayed by the negligence of the bearer, and therefore didn't arrive in time.

She fills her glass and drinks.

JEAN. Don't drink any more!

MISS JULIE. Oh, what does it matter!—We were left penniless and had to sleep in the carriages. My father didn't know where to find the money to rebuild the house, for he'd had to neglect his old friends. Then mother advised him to ask for a loan from one of her old friends, a brick merchant who lived nearby. Father borrowed the money, but wasn't allowed to pay any interest, which surprised him. And so the house was rebuilt. [*Drinks again*] Do you know who burned it down?

JEAN. Your mother.

MISS JULIE. Do you know who the brick merchant was?

JEAN. Your mother's lover?

MISS JULIE. Do you know whose the money was?

JEAN. Wait a moment—no, I don't.

MISS JULIE. My mother's!

JEAN. The Count's too, then, or was there a settlement?*

MISS JULIE. There was no settlement.—My mother had a little capital of her own, which she didn't want my father to administer. Therefore she invested it with her—friend.

JEAN. Who pinched it.

MISS JULIE. Exactly! He kept it.—All this came to my father's notice, but he was unable to open proceedings, repay his wife's lover, or prove that the money was his wife's.—He was on the verge of shooting himself.—They said he tried but failed. But he got back on his feet, and my mother was forced to pay for her actions. Just imagine what those five years were like for me. I loved my father, but I sided with my mother, because I didn't know the real circumstances. She taught me how to hate men—I'm sure you've heard how she hated men—and I swore to her I'd never be a slave to any man.

JEAN. But then you got engaged to that lawyer.

MISS JULIE. Just so he'd be my slave.

JEAN. And I suppose he didn't fancy that?

MISS JULIE. Oh, he was willing enough, but he didn't get the chance. I tired of him.

JEAN. I saw—in the stable.

MISS JULIE. What did you see?

JEAN. What I saw.—How he broke off the engagement.*

MISS JULIE. That's a lie! I was the one who broke it off! Did he tell you that? The little swine!

JEAN. Hardly a swine, I imagine. Do you hate men, Miss Julie?

MISS JULIE. Yes.—Most of the time. But sometimes—when this weakness comes over me—ugh!

JEAN. Then you hate me, too?

MISS JULIE. More than I can say! I'd like to have you put down like an animal...

JEAN. 'The offender shall be sentenced to two years' penal servitude and the animal is killed.'* Isn't that right?

MISS JULIE. Right!

JEAN. But there's no prosecuter here—and no animal. So what shall we do?

MISS JULIE. Leave.

JEAN. And torment each other to death?

MISS JULIE. No. Enjoy ourselves, for a couple of days, a week, for as long as it lasts, and then—die.

JEAN. Die? That's daft! Better the hotel than that!

MISS JULIE [*without hearing* JEAN].—by Lake Como, where the sun always shines, where the laurel trees are in flower at Christmas and the oranges glow like fire—

JEAN. Lake Como's a rainy hole, and the only oranges I saw were at the grocer's. But it's a good spot for tourists, full of villas for hire to loving couples—and that's a paying game. Know why?—Because they lease them for six months—and then leave after three weeks.

MISS JULIE [*naively*]. Three weeks? Why?

JEAN. They quarrel, of course. But they have to pay the rent all the same! Meanwhile, you can hire it out again. And so it goes on, over and over again. You can always bank on love—even though it doesn't last long!

MISS JULIE. You don't want to die with me?

JEAN. I don't want to die at all! For one thing, I like life; for another, I consider suicide a crime against the providence that gave us life.

MISS JULIE. *You* believe in God?

JEAN. Of course I do. And I go to church every other Sunday.— Frankly, I'm fed up with all this. I'm going to bed.

MISS JULIE. I see, and you think I'll rest content with that? Don't you know what a man owes a woman he's dishonoured?

JEAN [*opening his purse and throwing a silver coin on the table*]. Here! I always like to pay my debts!

MISS JULIE [*pretending not to notice the insult*]. Do you know what the law says. . .

JEAN. Unfortunately the law says nothing about a woman who seduces a man.

MISS JULIE. What else can we do but leave, get married, and part?

JEAN. And if I refuse to enter into this *mésalliance*?*

MISS JULIE. *Mésalliance*. . .

JEAN. Yes, on my part. I come from a finer line than you, remember. None of my ancestors committed arson.

MISS JULIE. How do you know?

JEAN. You can't prove otherwise. We've no family records—except with the police. But I've read up on your pedigree in that Peerage book.* Do you know who your earliest ancestor was? A miller who let the king spend the night with his wife during the Danish war. I've no such pedigree. I've no pedigree at all, in fact, but I could sire one!

MISS JULIE. This is what I get for opening my heart to a wretch like you, for sacrificing my family's honour...

JEAN. Dishonour! You see, I told you not to drink, it sets one talking. And one *shouldn't* talk!

MISS JULIE. Oh, how I regret it! How I regret it!—If you only loved me!

JEAN. For the last time—what do you want me to do? Start crying, jump over your riding whip, kiss you, lure you down to Lake Como for three weeks, and then... what am I supposed to do? What do you want? This is getting tiresome! But that's what happens when you get involved with women. Miss Julie! I can see you're miserable, I know you're suffering, but I simply can't understand you. We don't carry on like this. We don't hate each other. For us love's a game, when work allows; but we don't have all day and all night for it, like you do. I believe you're sick, and your mother was certainly mad. We've whole parishes gone mad with pietism, of course, but this is a kind of pietism* run wild.

MISS JULIE. Be kind to me, Jean. Treat me like a human being.

JEAN. All right, then behave like one! You spit on me, and won't let me wipe it off—on you.

MISS JULIE. Help me! Help me! Just tell me what I'm to do. Where am I to go?

JEAN. Jesus, if only I knew!

MISS JULIE. I've been mad, I've been crazy, but does that mean there's no way out?

JEAN. Stay here, and say nothing. No one knows.

MISS JULIE. Impossible! The servants know. And Kristin.

JEAN. Not for sure, and anyway, they'd never believe it.

MISS JULIE [*hesitating*]. But—it could happen again!

JEAN. That's true!

MISS JULIE. And the consequences?

JEAN [*frightened*]. Consequences!—What on earth have I been thinking of?—All right, there's only one solution.—You must leave! At once!—I can't come with you, for then all really would be lost. You must travel alone—away from here—anywhere!

MISS JULIE. Alone? Where?—I can't!

JEAN. You must! And before his Lordship returns, too. If you stay, we know what'll happen. Once you've erred the harm's already done and so you go on—then you grow bolder and bolder—and finally get found out. So go! Then write to his Lordship and tell him everything, except that it was me. He'll never guess that. He won't be all that keen to know either, I imagine.

MISS JULIE. I'll go, if you'll come with me!

JEAN. Are you mad, woman? Miss Julie run away with her servant! The day after tomorrow it'd be in all the papers, and his Lordship'd never survive that.

MISS JULIE. I can't go. I can't stay. Help me! I'm so tired, so dreadfully tired! Order me! Just set me in motion—I can't think on my own any more, I can't act!

JEAN. Now you see what a pathetic creature you are! Why do you puff yourselves up so, and stick your noses in the air as if you were the lords of creation? All right, I'll give you your orders. Go upstairs and get dressed. Get some money for the journey, and then come back down again!

MISS JULIE [*half aloud*]. Come with me!

JEAN. To your room?—Now you're being crazy* again. [*Hesitates a moment*] No. Go! At once!   [*Takes her hand and leads her out*

MISS JULIE [*as she leaves*]. Speak kindly to me, Jean!

JEAN. An order always sounds unkind. Now you know what they sound like.

JEAN *alone, heaves a sigh of relief; sits at the table; takes out a notebook and pen; does some sums aloud now and then; dumb mime, until* KRISTIN *enters, dressed for church; holding a starched white shirt front and a white tie.*

KRISTIN. Lord Jesus, what a mess! What on earth have you been up to?

JEAN. Oh, it was Miss Julie brought the servants in. You must've been right out. Didn't you hear anything?

KRISTIN. I've slept like a log.

JEAN. Dressed for church already?

KRISTIN. Of course! And you promised to come with me to communion today!

JEAN. So I did, yes. And you've the outfit there, I see. Come along, then!

Sits down; KRISTIN *begins to dress him in his white shirt-front and white tie.*

Pause.

JEAN [*sleepily*]. What's the lesson today?

KRISTIN. The beheading of John the Baptist, I suppose.*

JEAN. Oh my God, that's a long one.—Ouch, you're strangling me!—Oh, I'm so sleepy, so sleepy!

KRISTIN. Yes, what've you been doing, up all night? You're quite green in the face?

JEAN. I've been sitting here, talking with Miss Julie.

KRISTIN. She doesn't know what's proper, that one!

Pause.

JEAN. I say, Kristin.

KRISTIN. Well?

JEAN. It's pretty strange when you think about it.—Her, I mean.

KRISTIN. What's so strange?

JEAN. All of it!

Pause.

KRISTIN [*sees the half-empty glasses on the table*]. Have you been drinking together, too?

JEAN. Yes.

KRISTIN. For shame!—Look me in the eye!

JEAN. Yes.

KRISTIN. Is it possible? *Is* it possible?

JEAN [*after thinking a moment*]. Yes. It is.

KRISTIN. Ugh! I'd never have thought it! No, for shame! Shame on you!

JEAN. You're not jealous of her, are you?

KRISTIN. Not of her, no. If it'd been Klara or Sophie, I'd have scratched your eyes out!—But her now—no—I don't know why.—Oh, but it's disgusting!

JEAN. Are you angry with her, then?

KRISTIN. No, with you! That was wicked, really wicked! Poor girl!—No matter who knows, I'm not stopping here a moment longer, not in a house where we can't respect our masters.

JEAN. Why should we respect them?

KRISTIN. Yes, you're such a know-all, you tell me! You don't want to work for people who behave vulgar, do you? Well? That's disgracing yourself, if you ask me.

JEAN. Yes, but surely it helps to know they're no better than we are.

KRISTIN. Not to my mind, it doesn't. If they're no better than we are, there's no point us trying to be like them.—And think of the Count. Just think of him and all the misery he's had in his days. Lord Jesus! No, I'll not stay in this house a moment longer! And with someone like you! If it'd been that lawyer, now—someone better...

JEAN. And who might that be?

KRISTIN. Oh, yes! You're not bad in your way, but all the same, there's a difference between man and beast.—No, I'll not forget this! Miss Julie, who was so proud, so down on men, you'd never have believed she'd go and give herself like that; and to someone like you! She who nearly had that bitch of hers shot for running after the gatekeeper's mutt.—Yes, I'll say my piece!—But I'll stay here no longer. Come the 24th of October* and I'll be on my way!

JEAN. And then?

KRISTIN. Yes, since you've raised the subject, it's about time you looked around for something, seeing as we're going to get married.

JEAN. And what might that be? I can't get a position like this once I'm married.

KRISTIN. No, that's plain. You might well get a job as a doorkeeper, though, or look for a post as a caretaker in some government office or other. It might not pay very well, but it's secure, and there's a pension for wife and child...

JEAN [*grimaces*]. That's all very well, but dying for a wife and child is hardly my style, not yet awhile. I have to confess I was setting my sights a little higher.

KRISTIN. Your sights?—You've responsibilities, too. You think of them!

JEAN. Don't you start on about my responsibilities, I know what I have to do all right. [*Listens to sounds from without*] We've time enough to think about all this, though.—Go in now and get yourself ready, then we'll go to church.

KRISTIN. Who's that walking about upstairs?

JEAN. How should I know, unless it's Klara.

KRISTIN. Surely it can't be his Lordship, come home without any-one hearing?

JEAN [*afraid*]. The Count? No, that's impossible, he'd have rung by now!

KRISTIN [*leaving*]. Well, God help us! I've never known the like!

The sun has now risen and is lighting up the tops of the trees in the park; its rays move gradually until they fall at an angle through the window.
JEAN *goes to the door and makes a sign.*

MISS JULIE [*enters in travelling clothes with a small birdcage covered with a cloth, which she places on a chair*]. I'm ready now.

JEAN. Quiet! Kristin's awake.

MISS JULIE [*extremely nervous throughout what follows*]. Does she suspect anything?

JEAN. Not a thing. My God, what a sight you look!

MISS JULIE. What do you mean?

JEAN. You're as white as a corpse and—forgive me, but your face is dirty.

MISS JULIE. Let me wash, then. [*She goes to the wash basin and washes her face and hands*] There. Give me a towel!—Oh, there's the sun.

JEAN. Which breaks the troll's spell.*

MISS JULIE. Yes, we've been spellbound tonight, that's for sure.—But Jean, listen. Come with me, I've got the money now!

JEAN [*doubtfully*]. Enough?

MISS JULIE. Enough to begin with. Come with me, I can't go alone, not today. Just think—Midsummer day, on a stuffy train packed in with crowds of people, all gaping at me; standing about on station platforms when one simply longs to fly away— no, I can't, I can't! And then all those memories, childhood memories of Midsummer days with the church garlanded with birch leaves and lilac, dinner laid out on the great table, with relatives and friends; the afternoon in the park, with dancing and music, flowers and games. Oh, no matter how far you run, a whole baggage-waggon full of memories, remorse, and guilt follows on behind!

JEAN. I'll come with you. But now, at once, before it's too late. Now, this minute!

MISS JULIE. Right! Get dressed, then!   [*Picks up the birdcage*

JEAN. But no luggage. That would give us away.

MISS JULIE. No, nothing. Only what we can take in the compartment.

JEAN [*has taken his hat*]. What have you got there? What is it?

MISS JULIE. Only my siskin. I can't leave her!

JEAN. Oh God, look at that! Take a birdcage along with us? You're mad! Put that cage down!

MISS JULIE. My one memory from home; the only living creature that loves me now Diana's betrayed me! Don't be cruel! Let me take her with me!

JEAN. Put that cage down, I tell you!—And don't talk so loud.— Kristin'll hear us.

MISS JULIE. I won't leave it in anyone else's hands. I'd rather you killed her!

JEAN. Bring the little beast here, then, I'll soon wring its neck!

MISS JULIE. All right, but don't hurt her. Don't— — —no, I can't!

JEAN. Bring it here; I can!

MISS JULIE [*takes the bird out of the cage and kisses it*]. Oh, my little *Serine*, are you going to die now, and leave your mistress behind?

JEAN. Please don't make a scene; it's your life and happiness that are at stake. Here, quickly! [*Snatches the bird away from her; takes it to the chopping block and picks up the kitchen axe.* MISS JULIE *turns away*] You should have learnt how to slaughter chickens instead of pistol-shooting [*brings down the axe*], then you wouldn't faint at a drop of blood.

MISS JULIE [*screams*]. Kill me too! Kill me! You, who can slaughter an innocent creature without turning a hair. Oh, I hate and despise you; there's blood between us! I curse the moment I set eyes on you, I curse the moment I was conceived in my mother's womb!

JEAN. What's the good of cursing? Get going now!

MISS JULIE [*approaches the chopping block, as though drawn there against her will*]. No, I don't want to go just yet; I can't— — — I must see— — —Quiet! There's a carriage outside—[*Listens to the sounds outside while keeping her eyes fixed on the block and the axe*] Do you think I can't bear the sight of blood? Do you think I'm so weak?— — —Oh—I'd like to see your blood, your brains, on a chopping block—I'd like to see your sex,* swimming in a sea of blood, like that bird there—I do believe I could drink from your skull, I'd like to paddle my feet in your breast, I'd roast your heart and eat it whole!—You think I'm weak; you think I love you because my womb desired your seed; you think I want to carry your brood beneath my heart and nourish it with my blood—to bear your child and take your name—by the way, what is your surname?—I've never heard it—you probably haven't got one. I'd become 'Mrs Gatekeeper'—or 'Madame Rubbish Dump'—You dog, who wears my collar, you drudge with my crest upon your buttons—I share with my cook? Compete with my maid?—Oh! oh! oh!—You think I'm a coward and want to run away. No, I'm staying now—and let the storm break! My father'll come home— find his desk broken open—his money gone—Then he'll ring—on that bell—twice for his lackey—And then he'll send for the police—and I'll tell them everything. Everything! Oh, it'll be so good to end it all—if only it is the end—And then he'll have a stroke and die—And it'll be all up with us—quiet—peace—eternal rest—And then our coat of arms will be broken upon the coffin;* the Count's line will be extinguished and the lackey's race will continue in an orphanage—winning its laurels in the gutter and ending its days in gaol.

JEAN. There's your blue blood talking! Bravo, Miss Julie! Now just put a sock in that miller, will you?

KRISTIN *enters, dressed for church, carrying a hymn-book*.

MISS JULIE [*hastens across to her and falls into her arms, as though seeking protection*]. Help me, Kristin! That man—help me!

KRISTIN [*motionless and cold*]. What kind of a spectacle is this on a Sunday morning? [*Looks at the chopping block*] And what a mess! It's like a pigsty!—What's going on? Why all this screaming and shouting?

MISS JULIE. Kristin! You're a woman and my friend. Don't trust this swine!

JEAN [*crestfallen*]. While you ladies are talking, I'll go in and shave.

[*Slips out to the right*

MISS JULIE. You'll understand me; you'll listen to me!

KRISTIN. No, I don't and I won't. Such sluttishness is quite beyond me. Where are you going dressed like that? And him with his hat on?—Well?—

MISS JULIE. Listen to me, Kristin, just listen to me and I'll tell you everything— — —

KRISTIN. I don't want to know anything— — —

MISS JULIE. You must listen to me— — —

KRISTIN. What about? That nonsense with Jean? I don't care a jot about that; it's of no concern to me. But if you're thinking of fooling him into bunking off we'll soon put a stop to that!

MISS JULIE [*extremely nervous*]. Try and be calm now, Kristin, and listen to me. I can't stay here and nor can Jean—so we simply have to go...

KRISTIN. Hm, hm!

MISS JULIE [*brightening up*]. But look, I've just had an idea.—What if all three of us were to go—abroad—to Switzerland, and start a hotel together?—I've money, look—and Jean and I could run everything—and you, I thought, might look after the kitchen.—Wouldn't that be fun? Oh, do say yes!

Embraces KRISTIN, *and caresses her.*

KRISTIN [*coldly and thoughtfully*]. Hm, hm!

MISS JULIE [*tempo presto*]. You've never been abroad, Kristin—you should get away and see the world.—You've no idea what fun it is to travel by train—new people all the time—new countries—we'll pass through Hamburg and see the Zoo—you'll like that—and we'll go to the theatre and hear the opera—and when we get to Munich there'll be the museums—you know, with Rubens and Raphael* and all the great painters—you've heard of Munich, haven't you, where King Ludwig* used to live—you know, the mad one—and then we'll see his castles—some of them are just like the ones in fairy-tales—and from there it's not far to Switzerland—and the Alps, Kristin—just fancy the Alps, with snow on in the middle of the summer—oranges grow there, and laurel trees that are green all the year round— — —

JEAN *can be seen in the wings to the right, whetting his razor on a strop, which he is holding between his teeth and left hand; he listens with satisfaction to the conversation and now and then nods approvingly.*

MISS JULIE [*tempo prestissimo*].—and there we'll take over a hotel—and I'll sit in the office while Jean welcomes the guests—I'll go out shopping—write letters—oh, what a life it'll be, Kristin—trains whistling, buses arriving, bells ringing on every floor and in the restaurant—and I'll make out the bills—I can salt them, yes I can—you've no idea how timid tourists are when it comes to paying the bill!—And you—you'll sit like a queen in the kitchen.—You won't have to stand over the stove yourself, of course—and you'll be nicely and neatly dressed when you appear before the guests—and with your looks—I'm not flattering you, Kristin—one day you'll get hold of a husband, a rich Englishman, you'll see—they're so easy to [*slowing down*]—catch—and then we'll get rich—and build ourselves a villa on Lake Como—it rains a little there now and then, of course—but [*subsiding*] the sun must shine there too, sometimes— — —though it looks dark— — — and—then—otherwise, we can always come home again—back to [*pause*]— — —here—or somewhere else— — —

KRISTIN. Listen, Miss Julie, do you really believe all this?

MISS JULIE [*crushed*]. Believe it?

KRISTIN. Yes!

MISS JULIE [*tired*]. I don't know; I don't believe in anything any more. [*Collapses on to the bench; puts her head on the table between her arms*] Nothing! Nothing at all!

KRISTIN [*turns to the right, where* JEAN *is standing*]. So, you were thinking of running away!

JEAN [*crestfallen, puts his razor down on the table*]. Running away? That's a bit strong. You heard Miss Julie's plan, though. She may be tired now after a long night, but it might well work.

KRISTIN. Hark at him! Do you really think I'd cook for that...

JEAN [*sharply*]. Kindly speak with a little more respect; she's still your mistress. Understand?

KRISTIN. Mistress!

JEAN. Yes!

KRISTEN. Oh, listen to him! Just listen to him!

JEAN. Yes, listen, you might learn something, if you talked a little less! Miss Julie's your mistress, and what you despise in her, you ought to despise in yourself!

KRISTIN. I've always had a proper respect for myself so— — —

JEAN.—that you could despise others!—

KRISTIN.—so that I've never sunk below my own station. You tell me when his Lordship's cook has been with the groom or the pig man! Just you tell me!

JEAN. You're all right, you've got yourself a fine man.

KRISTIN. Oh yes, so fine he sells his lordship's oats from the stables— — —

JEAN. You can talk, you take a slice on the groceries and bribes from the butcher!

KRISTIN. What's that?

JEAN. And you say you've no respect for your masters any more! You, you, you!

KRISTIN. Are you coming to church, or aren't you? You could do with a good sermon after your exploits!

JEAN. No, I'm not going to church today; you can go alone and confess your own doings!

KRISTIN. Yes, I will, and I'll bring back enough forgiveness for you, too! Our saviour suffered and died on the cross for all our sins, and if we approach him in faith and with a penitent heart, he'll take all our sins upon himself.

JEAN. Even the groceries?*

MISS JULIE. Do you believe that, Kristin?

KRISTIN. It's my living faith, as sure as I stand here. My childhood faith, to which I've kept ever since, Miss Julie. And where there's sin in abundance, there His mercy abounds.

MISS JULIE. Ah, if only I had your faith! Oh, if. . .

KRISTIN. But you can't, you see, not without God's special grace, and that's not given to everyone— — —

MISS JULIE. To whom is it given, then?

KRISTIN. That's the great secret of grace, Miss Julie, God's no respecter of persons. There the last shall be first*—

MISS JULIE. Yes, but then He does respect the last?

KRISTIN [*continues*].—and it's easier for a camel to pass through the eye of a needle than for a rich man to enter the Kingdom of Heaven.* That's how it is, Miss Julie. Well, now I'm going— alone. And on the way past I'll tell the groom not to let any of the horses out in case someone should think of leaving before the Count comes home.—Goodbye!   [*Leaves*

JEAN. Damned bitch!—And all this for a siskin!—

MISS JULIE [*dully*]. Oh, never mind the siskin!—Do you see any way out of this? Any end to it all?

JEAN [*ponders*]. No!

MISS JULIE. What would you do in my place?

JEAN. In yours? Wait, now.—A woman of noble birth who'd— sunk? I don't know—or yes, maybe I do.

MISS JULIE [*takes the razor and makes a gesture*]. Like this?

JEAN. Yes.—But *I* wouldn't do it—mind, for there's a difference between us!

MISS JULIE. Because you're a man and I'm a woman? What difference does that make?

JEAN. Precisely that—the difference between a man and a woman.

MISS JULIE. I want to. But I can't.—My father couldn't either, that time he should have done it.

JEAN. No, he was right not to. He had to be revenged first.

MISS JULIE. And now my mother's taking her revenge again, through me.

JEAN. Have you never loved your father, Miss Julie?

MISS JULIE. Yes, very much. But I've hated him, too. I must have done so without realizing it. It was he who brought me up to feel contempt for my own sex, as a half-woman and half-man. Who's to blame for all this? My father, my mother, myself? Myself? But I have no self of my own? I haven't a thought I didn't get from my father, not an emotion I didn't get from my mother, and this last idea—that everyone's equal—I got from him, my fiancé—which is why I called him a swine! How can it be my own fault, then? Shift all the blame on to Jesus, as Kristin did?—No, I'm too proud for that, and too intelligent—thanks to my father's teachings—and all that about a rich man not getting into heaven, that's a lie— Kristin's got money in the savings-bank, she won't get in at any rate! Whose fault is it?—What's it matter to us whose fault it is; I'm still the one who'll have to bear the blame, suffer the consequences.

JEAN. Yes, but———

There are two shrill rings on the bell; MISS JULIE *jumps to her feet;* JEAN *changes his coat.*

JEAN. His Lordship's home!—What if Kristin———

Goes to the speaking tube; knocks and listens.

MISS JULIE. Has he been to his desk yet?

JEAN. This is Jean, sir! [*Listens. Note that the audience cannot hear what the* COUNT *says*] Yes, sir! [*Listens*] Yes, sir! At once! [*Listens*] At once, sir! [*Listens*]—Yes, sir, in half an hour!

MISS JULIE [*extremely anxious*]. What did he say? For God's sake, what did he say?

JEAN. He wants his boots and his coffee in half an hour.

MISS JULIE. In half an hour, then!—Oh, I'm so tired; I can't bring myself to do anything, I can't repent, can't run away, can't stay, can't live—can't die! Help me, now! Order me, and I'll obey like a dog! Do me this last service, save my honour, save his name! You know what I *ought* to do, but can't, just will me to do it. Order me!

JEAN. I don't know why—but now I can't either—I don't under-stand—it's just as if this coat made me—I can't order you—and now, since his Lordship spoke to me—then—I can't explain it properly—but—oh, it's this damned lackey sitting on my back!—I believe if his lordship came down now and ordered me to cut my throat, I'd do it on the spot.

MISS JULIE. Then let's pretend you're him, and I'm you!—You acted so well just now, when you went down on your knees—then you were the aristocrat—or—have you never been to the theatre and seen a hypnotist? [*Jean gestures assent*] He says to his subject, 'Take this broom!', and he takes it; he says, 'Sweep!', and it sweeps*— — —

JEAN. But then the subject has to be asleep.

MISS JULIE [*ecstatically*]. I'm already asleep—it's as if the whole room were full of smoke; you look like an iron stove, dressed all in black with a top hat—your eyes glow like coals in a dying fire—and your face is a white spot, like ashes—[*The sunlight has now fallen upon the floor, and is shining on* JEAN]—it's so nice and warm—[*She rubs her hands as though warming them before a fire*]—and so light—and so peaceful!

JEAN [*takes the razor and places it in her hand*]. Here's the broom! Go now, while it's still light—out to the barn—and. . .

[*Whispers in her ear*

MISS JULIE [*awake*]. Thank you. Now I'm going to rest. But just tell me one thing—that the first may also receive the gift of grace. Tell me, even if you don't believe it.

JEAN. The first? No, I can't!—But wait—Miss Julie—now I know!—You're no longer among the first—you're among—the last.

MISS JULIE. That's true—I'm among the very last; I am the last. Oh!—But now I can't go—Tell me to go, just one more time!

JEAN. No, I can't now either. I can't!

MISS JULIE. And the first shall be last.

JEAN. Don't think, don't think! You're taking all my strength away too, and making me a coward—What's that? I thought the bell moved!—No! Shall we stop it with paper?— —To be so afraid of a bell!—Yes, but it's not just a bell—there's somebody behind it— a hand sets it in motion—and something else sets that hand in motion—but if you stop your ears—just stop your ears! Yes, but then he'll go on ringing even louder—and keep on ringing until someone answers—and then it's too late! Then the police will come—and then. . .

> *Two loud rings on the bell.*

JEAN [*cringes, then straightens himself up*]. It's horrible! But there is no other way!—Go!

> [MISS JULIE *walks resolutely out through the door*
> *Curtain.*

THE DANCE OF DEATH I*
[*Dödsdansen*]

(1900)

CHARACTERS

Edgar, Captain in the artillery
Alice, his wife, an ex-actress
Kurt, Quarantine Master
Jenny
Old Woman
Sentry [a silent role]

SETTING

The interior of a round tower in a granite fortress.

Upstage, a large double entrance with glass doors through which can be seen a seashore with gun emplacements and the sea.

On either side of this entrance, a window with flowers and birds.

To the right of the entrance, an upright piano. Downstage of this a sewing-table and two armchairs.

To the left, mid-stage, a desk with a telegraph apparatus; farther downstage a whatnot with photographic portraits. Next to it, a chaise longue. Against the wall, a sideboard.

A ceiling lamp. On the wall by the piano hang two large laurel wreaths with ribbons, one on either side of a large photograph of a woman in theatrical costume.

By the doorway a free-standing clothes-tree with items of uniform, sabres, etc. Next to it, a secretaire.

To the left of the door hangs a mercury barometer.

It is a mild autumn evening. The doors of the fortress stand open and an artilleryman is seen at his post down by the shore battery. He is wearing a helmet with a crest. Now and then his sabre glitters in the red glow of the setting sun. The sea is dark and still.

The CAPTAIN *is sitting in an armchair by the sewing-table, fingering an extinguished cigar. He is dressed in a worn undress uniform with riding boots and spurs. He looks tired and bored.*

ALICE is seated in the armchair on the right, doing nothing. She looks tired and expectant.

CAPTAIN. Won't you play something for me?

ALICE [*indifferent, but not crossly*]. What shall I play?

CAPTAIN. What *you* like.

ALICE. You don't like my repertoire.

CAPTAIN. Nor you mine.

ALICE [*avoiding the subject*]. Do you want the doors open?

CAPTAIN. If you do. I'm warm.

ALICE. Let them be then!————[*Pause*] Why aren't you smoking?

CAPTAIN. Strong tobacco doesn't seem to agree with me these days.

ALICE [*almost aimiably*]. Smoke something milder, then. It's your only pleasure, you say.

CAPTAIN. Pleasure! What's that?

ALICE. Don't ask me. I know as little about it as you do.— — — Don't you want your whisky yet?

CAPTAIN. I'll wait a little.— — —What's for supper?

ALICE. How should I know? Ask Kristin.

CAPTAIN. Isn't it about time for mackerel? It is autumn, after all.

ALICE. Yes, it's autumn.

CAPTAIN. Outside and in! But notwithstanding the chill that comes with autumn, outside and in, a broiled mackerel with a slice of lemon and a glass of white burgundy is not wholly to be despised.

ALICE. How eloquent you've become!

CAPTAIN. Have we any burgundy left in the cellar?

ALICE. I wasn't aware we'd had a cellar for the past five years. . .

CAPTAIN. You never know anything. All the same, we'll have to lay some in for our silver wedding. . .

ALICE. Do you really mean to celebrate that?

CAPTAIN. Naturally!

ALICE. It would be more natural if we were to hide our misery, our twenty-five years of misery. . .

CAPTAIN. Miserable, my dear Alice, yes, it has been, but fun too, at times. And we'd better use what little time there is, for afterwards it's all over.

ALICE. All over? If only that were so!

CAPTAIN. It's *all* over! Apart from a barrowload full to wheel out and spread on the garden.

ALICE. All this fuss for a bit of garden!

CAPTAIN. Well, that's how it is; it's not my doing.

ALICE. *All* this fuss!

Pause.

ALICE. Has the post come?

CAPTAIN. Yes.

ALICE. With the butcher's bill?

CAPTAIN. Yes.

ALICE. How much was it?

CAPTAIN [*takes a piece of paper from his pocket and puts on his glasses, but immediately removes them*]. You read it. I can't see any more...

ALICE. What's the matter with your eyes?

CAPTAIN. Don't know.

ALICE. Old age.

CAPTAIN. Rubbish! Me?

ALICE. Well, not me!

CAPTAIN. Hm!

ALICE [*looks at the bill*]. Can you pay it?

CAPTAIN. Yes; but not now.

ALICE. Later, yes. A year from now, when you're retired on a small pension, and it's too late. Later, when you're ill again...

CAPTAIN. Ill? I've never been ill, just a little out of sorts, once! I'll live for another twenty years.

ALICE. The Doctor thought otherwise.

CAPTAIN. Doctor!

ALICE. Well, who else should know?

CAPTAIN. I'm not ill. I never have been, and I never will be, I'll just drop down dead, like an old soldier.

ALICE. Talking of the Doctor, you know he's giving a party this evening.

CAPTAIN [*upset*]. So what? We're not invited, because we don't mix with them, and we don't mix with them because we don't want to, and because I despise them both. They're scum!

ALICE. You say that about everyone.

CAPTAIN. Because everyone is scum!

ALICE. Except you!

CAPTAIN. Yes, because I've behaved decently whatever's come my way. So I'm not scum!

Pause.

ALICE. Do you want to play cards?

CAPTAIN. Might as well.

ALICE [*takes out a pack of cards from the drawer of the sewing-table and begins to shuffle it*]. Just imagine, he's got the regimental band. For a private party.

CAPTAIN [*angry*]. That's because he toadies to the Colonel in town. Toadies, see!—Now, if I'd done that!

ALICE [*deals*]. I used to be friends with Gerda, but she cheated me. . .

CAPTAIN. They're all cheats, every one of them!— — —What's trumps?

ALICE. Put your glasses on!

CAPTAIN. They don't help.— — —Well?

ALICE. Spades!

CAPTAIN [*displeased*] Spades?— — —

ALICE [*plays a card*]. Mmnn, that may be so, but they've turned the new officers' wives against us at any rate.

CAPTAIN [*plays and takes the trick*]. What does that matter? We never give any parties, so nobody'll notice. I can manage alone. . . I always have done.

ALICE. So can I. But the children! The children are growing up without any friends!

CAPTAIN. They can find their own in town.— — —My trick! Have you any trumps left?

ALICE. Yes, one. That was mine!

CAPTAIN. Six and eight make fifteen. . .

ALICE. Fourteen, fourteen!

CAPTAIN. Six and eight gives me fourteen. . . I think I've forgotten how to count as well. And two makes sixteen. . . [*Yawns*] Your deal.

ALICE. Are you tired?

CAPTAIN. Not in the least.

ALICE [*listening*]. You can hear the music all the way here. [*Pause*] Do you think Kurt's invited?

CAPTAIN. Well, he got here this morning, so he's had time to get out his tails, even though he's not had time to call on us.

ALICE. Quarantine Master? Is there going to be a quarantine here? *

CAPTAIN. Yes!. . .

ALICE. He is my cousin, after all, and we once shared the same name. . .

CAPTAIN. That's nothing to be proud of. . .

ALICE. Listen. . . [*sharply*] you leave my family alone, and I'll leave yours!

CAPTAIN. All right, all right! Are we going to start again?

ALICE. Is a quarantine officer a doctor?

CAPTAIN. No. Some sort of civilian, that's all, an administrator or a bookkeeper. Kurt never did amount to much.

ALICE. He was a poor wretch. . .

CAPTAIN. Who cost me money. . . And leaving his wife and children like that, that was infamous!

ALICE. Don't be so hard, Edgar.

CAPTAIN. Yes, it was!———And what's he been up to in America? Eh? I'm not exactly longing to see him. He was a nice enough lad, though; I used to enjoy arguing with him.

ALICE. Because he always gave in. . .

CAPTAIN [*haughtily*]. Gave in or not, at least he was someone a man could talk to. . . *No one* on this island understands a thing I say. . . it's a community of idiots. . .

ALICE. All the same, it's strange that Kurt should turn up just now, to our silver wedding. . . whether we celebrate it or not. . .

CAPTAIN. What's strange about that?. . . Oh, I see, yes, he was the one who brought us together, or married you off, as they used to say.

ALICE. Well, didn't he?

CAPTAIN. Oh, yes!. . . It was his idea. . . though whether it was such a good one I'll leave you to judge!

ALICE. A half-baked notion. . .

CAPTAIN. That we've had to pay for, not he.

ALICE. Yes, just think if I'd stayed in the theatre! All my friends are big stars now!

CAPTAIN [*gets up*]. Yes, yes, yes!————Now I'll have a whisky! [*Goes to the cupboard and mixes a whisky and soda, which he drinks standing*] There ought to be a rail here to put your foot on, then we could dream we were in Copenhagen, at the American Bar.

ALICE. We'll have one made, just to remind us of Copenhagen. Those were our best times, in spite of everything.

CAPTAIN [*drinks quickly*]. Yes! Do you remember Nimb's* *navarin aux pommes?** Mmm!

ALICE. No, but I remember the concerts at Tivoli.*

CAPTAIN. You've got such refined taste!

ALICE. You ought to be glad you've a wife with taste!

CAPTAIN. I am...

ALICE. Sometimes, when it helps to boast about her...

CAPTAIN [*drinks*]. They must be dancing at the Doctor's... I can hear the bass tuba's three-four time—Oompah—pah!

ALICE. I can hear the Alcazar waltz,* every note. Yes, it's some time since I danced a waltz...

CAPTAIN. Could you still manage it?

ALICE. Still?

CAPTAIN. We-ell? You're done with dancing, aren't you, like me?

ALICE. But I'm ten years younger than you!

CAPTAIN. Then we're the same age, for the lady is always ten years younger!

ALICE. You ought to be ashamed! Why, you're an old man; but I'm in my prime!

CAPTAIN. Oh yes, of course, you can be perfectly charming—to others, when you want to be.

ALICE. Can we light the lamp now?

CAPTAIN. Fine!

ALICE. Then ring.

> The CAPTAIN *walks heavily to the desk and rings.*

*

JENNY *enters right.*

CAPTAIN. Jenny, would you please light the lamp.

ALICE [*sharply*] Light the ceiling lamp!

JENNY [*sarcastically*]. Yes, my Lady!

She lights the ceiling lamp, while the CAPTAIN *watches her.*

ALICE [*curtly*]. Have you wiped the glass properly?

JENNY. It'll do!

ALICE. Do you call that an answer?

CAPTAIN. Alice... Listen...

ALICE [*to Jenny*]. Get out! I'll light it myself! It's probably best!

JENNY. I think so, too! [*Going*

ALICE [*getting up*]. Go!

JENNY [*pausing*]. I wonder what you'd say if I did?

ALICE *remains silent.* JENNY *leaves.*

*

The CAPTAIN *walks over and lights the lamp.*

ALICE [*uneasy*]. Do you think she will go?

CAPTAIN. Wouldn't surprise me, but we'll be stuck if she does...

ALICE. It's your fault, you spoil them!

CAPTAIN. Rubbish! You see how polite they always are to me.

ALICE. Because you crawl to them! Just as you crawl to all your subordinates—you're a bully with the soul of a slave.

CAPTAIN. Is that so?

ALICE. Yes, you crawl to your men and to your non-commissioned officers, but you can't get along with your equals and superiors.

CAPTAIN. Ouf!

ALICE. Just like all tyrants!— — —Do you think she'll leave?

CAPTAIN. Yes, if you don't go and talk nicely to her.

ALICE. Me?

CAPTAIN. If I did, you'd only say I was flirting with the maids.

ALICE. What if she does leave! Then I'll have to do everything myself, like last time, and ruin my hands.

CAPTAIN. And that won't be the end of it! If Jenny goes, so will Kristin, and then we'll never get anyone else to come out here, not to this island. The pilot on the steamer frightens off anyone who comes looking for work... And if he forgets, my corporals don't.

ALICE. Yes, your corporals, whom I have to feed in my kitchen because you daren't show them the door...

CAPTAIN. No, for they'd go, too, at the first opportunity———and then we'd have to close the whole gunshop.

ALICE. But it's ruining us!

CAPTAIN. That's why the officer corps intends to petition His Majesty for a maintenance grant...

ALICE. For whom?

CAPTAIN. The corporals!

ALICE [*laughs*]. You're crazy!

CAPTAIN. Yes, let's have a little laughter! It wouldn't go amiss.

ALICE. I'll soon have forgotten how to laugh...

CAPTAIN [*lights his cigar*]. That's something we should never forget... Life's boring enough as it is.

ALICE. It's certainly no fun!— — —Do you want to play some more?

CAPTAIN. No, it tires me.

Pause.

ALICE. You know, it does annoy me that my cousin, this new Quarantine Master of ours, should start by calling on our enemies.

CAPTAIN. Oh, what does it matter?

ALICE. Well, did you see in the paper that the list of arrivals had him down as a *rentier*?* In that case, he must have come into some money.

CAPTAIN. *Rentier*! We-ell! A rich relation; the first in this family, that's for sure!

ALICE. In yours, yes! We've had plenty of rich ones in mine.

CAPTAIN. If he's got money you can be sure he'll be stuck up, but I'll keep him in check all right. He won't get a look at my cards!

The telegraph apparatus begins to click.

ALICE. Who could that be?

CAPTAIN [*remains standing*]. Quiet a moment, please!

ALICE. Well, go and see, then.

CAPTAIN. I can hear; I can hear what they're saying!—It's the children!

He goes over to the apparatus and taps out a reply. The apparatus then responds. The CAPTAIN *replies again.*

ALICE. Well?

CAPTAIN. Wait a moment!— — —[*Taps the final signal*]— — —It was the children. They're at headquarters in town. Judith is out of sorts again, and off school.

ALICE. Again? What else did they say?

CAPTAIN. Money, of course!

ALICE. Why does Judith have to be in such a hurry? Next year would be soon enough to take her exams.

CAPTAIN. You tell her, and see if that helps!

ALICE. You should tell her yourself.

CAPTAIN. Haven't I just, time and again! But you know very well that children do just as they please.

ALICE. In this house, anyway!— — —[*The* CAPTAIN *yawns*] Do you have to yawn in front of your wife?

CAPTAIN. What am I supposed to do?— — —Haven't you noticed that we say the same thing every day? Just now, when you made the same old reply, 'In this house, anyway', I should have answered with my old, 'It's not just my house'. But since I've already given the same answer five hundred times already, I yawned instead. My yawn could mean I can't be bothered to reply, or 'You're right, my angel', or 'Let's leave it there'.

ALICE. You really are in a delightful mood tonight.

CAPTAIN. Isn't it time for dinner soon?

ALICE. Do you know the Doctor has ordered supper from town?— the Grand Hotel no less.

CAPTAIN. No! Then they'll be having grouse. You know, grouse is the finest of birds, but it's a barbarity to roast it in lard!...

ALICE. Ugh! Must you talk about food?

CAPTAIN. Wine then? I wonder what those barbarians drink with grouse?

ALICE. Shall I play for you?

CAPTAIN [*sitting down at the desk*]. The last resource! Yes, as long as you don't play one of your funeral marches or laments— — —it sounds so purposeful. And I can always fill in the words. 'Hear how miserable I am!' Miaow, miaow! 'Hear what a horrible husband I've got.' Brum, brum, brum! 'Oh, if only he would die!' Joyful roll of drums, fanfares, and finally the Alcazar waltz! *The Champagne Galop!** Talking of champagne, there should be two bottles left. Shall we get them up and pretend we've got company?

ALICE. No we shan't! They're mine; they were a present to me!

CAPTAIN. You always keep tabs on everything, you do!

ALICE. And you're always stingy, to your wife, at least!

CAPTAIN. Then I've run out of ideas.—Shall I dance for you?

ALICE. No, thanks. You're dancing days are over, remember.

CAPTAIN. You know, you ought to have a female companion.

ALICE. Thanks!—You ought to have a male.

CAPTAIN. Thanks! We've tried it, to our mutual dissatisfaction. But the interesting thing about that experiment was: as soon as a stranger entered the house, we were both so happy———to begin with. . .

ALICE. But afterwards!

CAPTAIN. Yes, don't let's talk about that.

There is a knock at the door.

ALICE. Who can that be at this hour?

CAPTAIN. Jenny doesn't usually knock.

ALICE. Go and open it, and don't shout 'Come in', like some worker in a shop.

CAPTAIN. You don't like anything that smacks of work, do you?

The knocking is repeated.

ALICE. Well, open it!

CAPTAIN [*opens and takes the visiting card which is handed to him*]. It's Kristin!—Has Jenny gone? [*Since the answer cannot be heard by the audience, he says to* ALICE] Jenny's gone.

ALICE. So I'm to be a maid again.

CAPTAIN. And I the hired man.

ALICE. Can't we take one of your men to help in the kitchen?

CAPTAIN. Not these days.

ALICE. But that card isn't Jenny's, surely?

CAPTAIN [*looks at the card with his glasses, and passes it to* ALICE]. You read it, I can't.

ALICE [*reads the card*]. Kurt! It's Kurt! Go and greet him!

CAPTAIN [*exits left*]. Kurt! Well, that is nice!

*

ALICE *arranges her hair, and seems to come alive.*

*

CAPTAIN [*enters from the left, with* KURT]. Here he is, the traitor! Come on in, old chap!   [*Embraces him*

ALICE [*to* KURT]. Welcome to my house, Kurt!

KURT. Thank you!— — —It's been a long time!

CAPTAIN. What is it? Fifteen years! And we've grown old...

ALICE. Oh, I don't know. Kurt hasn't changed a bit.

CAPTAIN. Sit down, sit down!—Now, first of all, what have you got planned? Have you been invited anywhere this evening?

KURT. Yes, to the Doctor's, but I haven't promised to go.

ALICE. Then you'll stay with your relatives?

KURT. That seems the natural thing; but the Doctor's my superior, as it were, and it might make for trouble later.

CAPTAIN. Nonsense! I've never been afraid of my superiors...

KURT. Afraid or not, there'll be trouble, all the same.

CAPTAIN. On this island, I'm the master! You get behind me, and no one'll dare touch you.

ALICE. That's enough now, Edgar. [*Takes* KURT'S *hand*] Never mind masters and superiors, you stay here with us. Everyone will think it's only right and proper.

KURT. Very well, then.—Especially as I seem to be so welcome.

CAPTAIN. Why shouldn't you be welcome?— — —We've no bones to pick... [KURT *cannot hide a certain lack of enthusiasm*] What could there be? You were a bit heedless once, but you were young; and I've forgotten it. I don't bear a grudge.

ALICE *looks pained. All three sit by the sewing-table.*

ALICE. So, you've been out in the great wide world?

KURT. Yes, and now I land up here with you...

CAPTAIN. Whom you married off twenty-five years ago.

KURT. It wasn't quite like that, but never mind. It's nice to see you've stuck together for twenty-five years...

CAPTAIN. Yes, we've rubbed along; sometimes it's been a bit up and down, but as you say, we're still together. And Alice has no cause for complaint; plenty of everything, money just pouring in. Perhaps you don't know I'm a famous writer, of textbooks...

KURT. Oh, yes, I remember when we went our separate ways, you'd just published a rifle manual. It was doing quite well, I believe. Is it still in use at staff college?

CAPTAIN. It's still in print, and remains the best there is, even though they've tried to replace it with an inferior one... which they use, of course, though it's completely worthless.

Painful silence.

KURT. You've been abroad, I hear?

ALICE. Yes, we've been to Copenhagen. Five times. Imagine!

CAPTAIN. Yes. You see, when I took Alice away from the theatre...

ALICE. Took?

CAPTAIN. Yes, I took you as a wife should be taken...

ALICE. How bold you've become!

CAPTAIN. But since it's been shoved down my throat that I ruined her brilliant career... hm!... I had to make up for it by promising to take my wife to Copenhagen... and that promise I've kept—

faithfully! Five times we've been there! Five! [*Holds up the five fingers of his left hand*]— — —Have *you* been to Copenhagen?

KURT [*smiles*]. No, I've mostly been in America...

CAPTAIN. America? That's a pretty dreadful place, isn't it? Nothing but rednecks!

KURT [*gloomily*]. Well, it's not Copenhagen.

ALICE. Have you... heard anything... from your children?

KURT. No.

ALICE. Forgive me, Kurt, but it was a bit thoughtless of you to leave them like that...

KURT. I didn't leave them, the court awarded custody to their mother— — —

CAPTAIN. Let's not talk about that now. It seems to me you were well out of that mess.

KURT [*to* ALICE]. How are your children?

ALICE. Fine, thanks. They're at school, in town; they're almost grown up.

CAPTAIN. Yes, they're smart kids. The boy's got a brilliant mind. Brilliant! He'll be on the General Staff...

ALICE. If they take him.

CAPTAIN. Him? A Defence Minister in the making!

KURT. Changing the subject— — —there's going to be a quarantine here— — —plague, cholera, and so forth. And as you know, the Doctor's to be my superior... What sort of man is he?

CAPTAIN. Man? He's no man! He's an ignorant scoundrel!

KURT [*to* ALICE]. Worse luck for me.

ALICE. He's not as bad as Edgar makes out, but I can't say I like him...

CAPTAIN. He's a scoundrel! And so are the rest of them—the customs officer, the postmaster, the telephone girl, the chemist, the— — —what's he called—head pilot—scoundrels all of them, which is why I have nothing to do with them.

KURT. Are you at odds with all of them?

CAPTAIN. Every one!

ALICE. Yes, it's true, one really *can't* associate with these people!

CAPTAIN. It's as if every tyrant in the country had been interned on this island.

ALICE [*ironically*]. True enough!

CAPTAIN. Hm! Is that a dig at me? I'm no tyrant, not in my own home at any rate.

ALICE. You be careful!

CAPTAIN [*to* KURT]. Don't you believe a word she says. I'm a very good husband, and this old lady's the best wife in the world.

ALICE. Something to drink, Kurt?

KURT. Thank you, not now.

CAPTAIN. Have you become...

KURT. Moderately, that's all.

CAPTAIN. American?*

KURT. Yes.

CAPTAIN. Immoderately for me; otherwise there's no point. A man should be able to hold his drink.

KURT. About these neighbours of ours on the island now. My work here will bring me into contact with them all... and it'll be tricky to find the right tack; you always get mixed up in other people's intrigues, whether you want to or not.

ALICE. You go call on them; you'll always come back to us, we're your real friends.

KURT. Isn't it horrible to sit here all alone surrounded by enemies, as you are?

ALICE. It's no fun, that's for sure.

CAPTAIN. It's not the least bit horrible! I've known nothing but enemies all my life, and rather than harm me, they've helped me on my way. When I come to die, I'll be able to say I don't owe anybody anything. I've never got anything for nothing. Everything I own, I've had to fight for.

ALICE. Yes, Edgar's path hasn't been strewn with roses...

CAPTAIN. Thorns, and stones, flints... nothing but my own strength. Do you know what I mean?

KURT. Yes, I learned the inadequacy of that ten years ago.

CAPTAIN. Then you're a poor sort.

ALICE [*to the* CAPTAIN]. Edgar!

CAPTAIN. Well, he is a poor sort if he doesn't trust in his own strength. Once the mechanism's done for, of course, there's hardly so much as a barrowload of muck to tip on the garden, but as long as it holds you have to kick and fight with your hands and feet for all your worth. That's my philosophy.

KURT [*smiles*]. You know, you're amusing to listen to. . .

CAPTAIN. Don't you think I'm right, though?

KURT. No, I don't.

CAPTAIN. Well, it's true, all the same.

During the last scene the wind has risen, and now one of the upstage doors slams to.

CAPTAIN [*gets up*]. The wind's getting up. I felt it coming.

Goes and closes the doors and taps the barometer.

ALICE [*to* KURT]. You'll stay to supper, won't you?

KURT. Yes, thank you.

ALICE. It'll be very simple, mind. Our maid has left.

KURT. That's fine by me.

ALICE. Dear Kurt, you're so unpretentious.

*

CAPTAIN [*by the barometer*]. You should see how the barometer's falling! I felt it in my bones.

ALICE [*aside to* KURT]. He's so nervous.

CAPTAIN. We ought to eat soon.

ALICE [*getting up*]. I'll just go and see to it. You two sit here and philosophize. [*Aside to* KURT] But don't contradict him or he'll lose his temper. And don't ask why he never became a major.

KURT *nods assent.* ALICE *moves towards the right.*

CAPTAIN [*sitting down by the sewing-table with* KURT]. See to it we get something good now, old girl.

ALICE. Give me some money, and I will.

CAPTAIN. Always money! [ALICE *exits*

*

CAPTAIN [*to* KURT]. Money, money, money! All day long purse in hand—I've finally come to believe I am one. Do you know that feeling?

KURT. Oh, yes. The only difference was, I used to think I was a wallet.

CAPTAIN [*laughs*]. Yes, you've had a taste of it too! Women! [*Laughs again*] You certainly got hold of a proper one!

KURT [*patiently*]. Let that rest, now.

CAPTAIN. A perfect jewel, that one!———Whereas when all's said and done, I've got hold of a good woman; she's all right, you know, when all's said and done.

KURT [*smiles good-humouredly*]. When all's said and done!

CAPTAIN. Don't you laugh!

KURT [*as before*]. When all's said and done!

CAPTAIN. Yes, she's been a faithful wife... an excellent mother, really exceptional... but [*glances at the door, right*] she's got the devil of a temper. You know, there've been times when I've cursed you for saddling me with her.

KURT [*good-humouredly*]. But I didn't. Listen, old chap...

CAPTAIN. Well, well, well, you talk a load of rubbish and forget things you don't want to remember. Don't take it amiss, now, I'm used to ordering people about and swearing at them, but you know me, you won't take offence, will you?

KURT. Not at all. But I didn't bring you together, quite the contrary.

CAPTAIN [*without letting himself be interrupted*]. All the same, don't you think life's odd?

KURT. I suppose it is.

CAPTAIN. And growing old; not much fun, but it's interesting. Well, I'm not old, but I'm *beginning* to feel it. Everyone you know dies off, it makes you feel so alone.

KURT. Lucky the man who has a wife to grow old with!

CAPTAIN. Lucky? Yes, I suppose so; after all, the children also flee the nest. You shouldn't have left yours like that.

KURT. But I didn't. They were taken from me...

CAPTAIN. Now, you mustn't get angry when I say that...

KURT. But it wasn't like that...

CAPTAIN. Well, whatever happened, at least it's forgotten now; you are all alone, though!

KURT. My dear fellow, one gets used to everything.

CAPTAIN. Can one... can one get used to... to being quite alone, too?

KURT. Well, look at me.

CAPTAIN. What have you been doing these fifteen years?

KURT. What a question! These fifteen years.

CAPTAIN. They say you've come into money, that you're rich.

KURT. I wouldn't say rich...

CAPTAIN. I'm not on the borrow...

KURT. If you were, I'd gladly...

CAPTAIN. Thanks very much, but I've my own cheque account.* You see [*glancing at the door, right*] we must want for nothing in this house; the day the money ran out... she'd be off.

KURT. Oh, no!

CAPTAIN. No? I know it!—Can you imagine, she always waits until I'm out of money just for the pleasure of showing me that I don't look after my family.

KURT. But you've a large income, I remember you said.

CAPTAIN. Of course I've a large income— — —it's just not large enough.

KURT. Then it can't be that large, not by the usual standards...

CAPTAIN. Life is odd, and so are we.

The telegraph starts tapping.

KURT. What's that?

CAPTAIN. Only a time signal.

KURT. Haven't you got a telephone?

CAPTAIN. Yes, in the kitchen; but we use the telegraph—the operators repeat everything we say.

KURT. It must be a pretty awful life for you all out here by the sea.

CAPTAIN. Yes, it's quite terrible! Life is terrible! And you who believe in a life after this, do you suppose we'll find peace then?

KURT. I suppose there'll be storms and strife there too.

CAPTAIN. There, too—if there is any 'there'! Far better annihilation.

KURT. Do you think annihilation's possible without pain?

CAPTAIN. I shall simply drop down dead, without pain.

KURT. You're sure of that, are you?

CAPTAIN. Yes, I am.

KURT. You don't seem very content with your existence?

CAPTAIN [*sighs*]. Content? The day I die, I'll be content.

KURT [*gets up*] You don't know that.— — —But tell me, what are you two up to in this house? What's going on here? The walls smell of poison*—one feels ill the moment one comes in. I'd rather leave now, if I hadn't promised Alice I'd stay. There are corpses under the floorboards; there's so much hatred here it's hard to breathe.

The CAPTAIN *crumples up and stares vacantly ahead.*

KURT. What's the matter? Edgar! [*The* CAPTAIN *does not move.* KURT *slaps him on the shoulder*] Edgar!

CAPTAIN [*comes to himself*]. Did you say something? [*Looks around*] I thought it was... Alice... Oh, it's you.—Listen...

[*Relapses into torpor again*

KURT. This is horrible! [*Goes to the door right, which he opens*] Alice!

*

ALICE [*enters, wearing an apron*]. What is it?

KURT. I don't know. Look at him!

ALICE [*calmly*]. He goes off like that sometimes.— — —I'll play something, that'll soon wake him up!

KURT. No, don't do that! Don't!— — —Let me see!— — —Can he hear? Can he see?

ALICE. When he's like this he can neither hear nor see.

KURT. And you say that so calmly!... Alice, what's going on in this house?

ALICE. Ask that one there!

KURT. That one?— — —But he's your husband!

ALICE. For me he's a stranger, as much a stranger as he was twenty-five years ago. I know nothing about this man... except that...

KURT. Stop! He can hear you!

ALICE. He can hear nothing now!

A bugle sounds outside.

CAPTAIN [*jumps to his feet; takes his sabre and military cape*]. Excuse me! I must just inspect the sentries. [*Exits through the rear doors*

*

KURT. Is he ill?

ALICE. I don't know.

KURT. Is he out of his mind?

ALICE. I don't know.

KURT. Does he drink?

ALICE. Not as much as he boasts he does!

KURT. Sit down and tell me; but calmly and the truth.

ALICE [*sits down*]. What shall I say?—That I've spent a lifetime in this tower, a prisoner, watched over by a man I've always hated, and now hate so boundlessly that the day he died I'd laugh aloud for joy.

KURT. Why haven't you separated?

ALICE. Good question! We broke off our engagement twice, since then not a day has passed that we haven't tried to part... but we're welded together and can't break free. Once we lived apart—in the same house—for five years. Now only death can part us; we know that, and so we wait for him as our deliverer.

KURT. Why do you live so alone?

ALICE. Because he isolates me. First he eradicated all my brothers and sisters from the house—he calls it 'eradicating' himself—then my friends and other...

KURT. But *his* relations? Have you eradicated them?

ALICE. Yes, they almost killed me, once they'd taken my honour and my reputation.—In the end I had to keep in touch with the outside world through that telegraph—the telephone was no good, those girls always listened,—I've taught myself how to use the telegraph, but he doesn't know that. You mustn't tell him, or he'd kill me.

KURT. This is horrible! Horrible!— — —But why does he blame me for your marriage? Let me tell you what really happened. — — —Edgar and I were friends. He fell in love with you at first sight. He came and asked me to act as go-between. I said 'No' right from the start. And—my dear Alice, I knew how cruel and tyrannical you could be. So I warned him— — —and when he kept on at me I told him to go and get your brother to plead for him.

ALICE. I believe you; but he's been fooling himself all these years— you'll never get him to change his mind now.

KURT. Let him blame me, then, if it'll make him feel any better.

ALICE. That's asking too much...

KURT. Oh, I'm used to it... but what does hurt me is his saying I've abandoned my children. That's quite untrue...

ALICE. That's what he's like; he says what he fancies, and then believes it. But he seems to really like you, because you don't contradict him, I suppose... Do try and bear with us... I think you've come at a fortunate moment for us; for me it's nothing but an act of providence... Kurt! You mustn't tire of us, because we really are the most unhappy people in the whole world.　　　　　　　　　　　　　　　　　　　　*[Weeps*

KURT. I've seen *one* marriage at close quarters... and that was dreadful. But this is almost worse!

ALICE. Do you think so?

KURT. Yes.

ALICE. Whose fault is it?

KURT. Alice! The moment you stop asking whose fault it is, you'll feel a whole lot better. Try and take it as a fact, a trial that must be endured...

ALICE. I can't! It's too much! [*Gets up*] It's hopeless!

KURT. You poor things!... Do you know why you hate each other?

ALICE. No! It's a quite groundless hatred, without cause, without purpose, but also without end. Can you guess why he fears death so much? He's afraid I'll remarry.

KURT. Then he does love you!

ALICE. Probably. But that doesn't stop him from hating me.

KURT [*as if to himself*]. They call it love-hate, it comes from hell! — — —Does he like you to play for him?

ALICE. Yes, but only horrible tunes... this ghastly 'Entry of the Boyars',* for example. When he hears that, he becomes possessed and wants to dance.

KURT. Does he dance?

ALICE. Yes, he's really very funny sometimes.

KURT. One thing... forgive me asking. Where are the children?

ALICE. Maybe you don't know that two of them died?

KURT. You've been through that, too?

ALICE. What haven't I been through?

KURT. But the other two?

ALICE. In town. They couldn't stay at home. He set them against me...

KURT. And you against him.

ALICE. Of course. Then it came to taking sides, canvassing, bribery... and so in order not to destroy the children, we had to send them away. What should have bound us together divided us, what should have been a blessing became a curse... yes, sometimes I believe our whole family's cursed.

KURT. After the fall, yes; that's how it is.

ALICE [*with a poisonous look and a sharp tone*]. What fall?

KURT. Adam and Eve's.

ALICE. Oh, I thought you meant something else! [*Embarrassed silence.* ALICE *clasps her hands together*] Kurt! We're cousins, you've been my friend since childhood. I haven't always treated you as I should. But now I've been punished, and you've had your revenge.

KURT. Not revenge! This isn't revenge. Hush!

ALICE. Do you remember one Sunday, when you were engaged? I'd invited you both to dinner.

KURT. Don't!

ALICE. I must talk; forgive me!— — —Well... when you arrived, for dinner, we weren't at home, and you had to go away again.

KURT. You'd been invited out yourselves, what does that matter now?

ALICE. Kurt! When I invited you to eat with us just now... I thought there was something in the larder! [*Hides her face in her hands*] And there isn't, not even a crust of bread!— — —

KURT [*weeps*]. Poor, poor Alice!

ALICE. But when *he* comes back and wants something to eat, and there isn't anything... he'll get angry. You've never seen him angry!— — —Oh God, what a humiliation!

KURT. Won't you let me go out and get something?

ALICE. There's nothing to be had anywhere on the island.

KURT. Not for my sake, but for his and yours... let me think up something, anything... when he comes back we must make a joke of it... I'll suggest we have a drink, meanwhile I'll think of something... Get him in a good humour; play for him, it doesn't matter what... Sit down at the piano and be ready.

ALICE. Look at my hands. Are they fit to play with? I've had to polish the brass and wipe the glasses, lay the fire and clean the house...

KURT. But you've got two servants!

ALICE. That's what we have to say, because he's an officer... but they're always leaving, one after the other, so sometimes we've none at all... most of the time!— — —How am I going to get out of this business about supper? Oh, if only the house'd catch fire...

KURT. Alice! Don't say such things!

ALICE. If only the sea would rise and swallow us up!

KURT. No, no, no; I can't listen to you!

ALICE. What will he say; what will he say?— — —Don't go, Kurt, don't leave me!

KURT. No, Alice. . . I *won't* go!. . .

ALICE. Yes, but when you have gone. . .

KURT. Has he ever hit you?

ALICE. Me? Oh, no; he knows I'd leave him if he did that! One must have some pride!

> *Outside shouts of 'Halt! Who goes there?' 'Friend'.*

KURT [*gets up*]. Is that him?

ALICE [*frightened*]. Yes!

> *Pause.*

KURT. What on earth shall we do?

ALICE. I don't know, I don't know!

*

CAPTAIN [*enters upstage; in high spirits*]. There! Now I'm free! — — —Well, has she poured her heart out? A miserable life hers, eh?

KURT. What's the weather like out there?

CAPTAIN. A fair old storm!— — —[*Jokingly, opening one of the doors slightly*] Baron Bluebeard* with the maiden in his tower; and outside the sentry marches up and down with his sabre drawn, to guard the fair virgin. . . and along come her brothers, but there goes the sentry, look! Left, right! He's a good sentry! Look at him! Meli-tam-tam-ta, meli-ta-lia-ley!* Shall we dance the sword dance?* Kurt should see that.

KURT. No, let's have the 'Entry of the Boyars' instead.

CAPTAIN. Oh, you know that one, do you?— — —Alice in your apron, come and play. Come, I said!

> ALICE *crosses reluctantly to the piano.*

CAPTAIN [*pinches her arm*]. You've been telling lies about me.

ALICE. Me?

KURT *turns away.* ALICE *plays 'The Entry of the Boyars', while the* CAPTAIN *performs a kind of Hungarian dance behind the desk, his spurs jangling. Then he slumps to the floor, unnoticed by* KURT *and* ALICE, *who continues to play the piece to the end.*

ALICE [*without turning round*]. Shall we take it again?

Silence.

ALICE [*turns round and sees the* CAPTAIN *lying unconscious, concealed from the audience by the desk*]. Good God!

She stands with her arms crossed over her breast, and gives a sigh as of thankfulness and relief.

KURT [*turns round; hurries over to the* CAPTAIN]. What's happened? What is it?

ALICE [*in great suspense*]. Is he dead?

KURT. I don't know! Help me!

ALICE [*does not move*]. I can't touch him... is he dead?

KURT. No! He's alive!

ALICE *sighs.* KURT *helps the* CAPTAIN, *who has regained consciousness, to a chair.*

*

CAPTAIN. What happened? [*Silence*] What happened?

KURT. You fell.

CAPTAIN. What was it?

KURT. You fell on the floor. Is something the matter?

CAPTAIN. With me? Nothing at all! Not that I'm aware of. What are you two gawping at?

KURT. You're ill!

CAPTAIN. Nonsense! Go on playing, Alice... Ah! There it is again!

[*Clutches his head*

ALICE. You see, you are ill!

CAPTAIN. Don't shout! A little giddy, that's all!

KURT. We must get a doctor! I'll go and telephone...

CAPTAIN. I don't want any doctor!

KURT. You must! We must call him, for our sake; or we'll be held responsible.

CAPTAIN. I'll throw him out if he comes!... I'll shoot him down!— — —Ah! There it is again!   [*Clutches his head*

KURT [*goes to the door, right*]. I'm going to telephone.   [*Exits*

*

ALICE *takes off her apron.*

CAPTAIN. Will you give me a glass of water?

ALICE. I suppose I must.   [*Gives him a glass of water*

CAPTAIN. How sweet of you!

ALICE. Are you ill?

CAPTAIN. Forgive me for not being well.

ALICE. Are you going to nurse yourself, then?

CAPTAIN. I don't suppose you want to!

ALICE. You can be sure of that!

CAPTAIN. The moment you've been waiting for has come at last.

ALICE. Yes, the moment you believed would never come.

CAPTAIN. Don't be angry with me!

*

KURT [*enters right*]. This is appalling...

ALICE. What did he say?

KURT. He rang off, just like that!

ALICE [*to the* CAPTAIN]. That's what you get for all your arrogance.

CAPTAIN. I think I'm getting worse!— — —Try to get a doctor from town!

ALICE [*goes to the telegraph*]. I'll have to telegraph, then.

CAPTAIN [*half rises, amazed*]. Can—you—telegraph?

ALICE [*telegraphing*]. Yes, I can.

CAPTAIN. So?— — —Go on, then!— — —So false! [*To* KURT] Come and sit beside me. [KURT *sits beside the* CAPTAIN] Hold my hand. It's as though I'm sitting but falling, too. Does that make sense? Down, somehow; it's strange.

KURT. Have you had an attack like this before?

CAPTAIN. Never!————

KURT. While we're waiting for a reply from town, I'm going to have a word with the Doctor here. Has he attended you before?

CAPTAIN. He has.

KURT. Then he'll know your history————

> *Moves towards the door, left.*

ALICE. We'll get an answer shortly. This is kind of you, Kurt. But come back soon.

KURT. As soon as I can!   [*Exits*

*

CAPTAIN. Kurt is kind. And so changed.

ALICE. Yes, and for the better. All the same, I pity him for getting mixed up in our troubles, now of all times.

CAPTAIN. And wishing us well, too!————I wonder how things are with him, though. Did you notice he didn't want to talk about himself?

ALICE. Yes. But I don't think anyone asked him either.

CAPTAIN. Imagine, his life!————And ours! Is everyone's life like this, I wonder?

ALICE. Perhaps, though they don't talk about it, like we do.

CAPTAIN. I've sometimes thought that misery attracts misery; and the happy shun unhappiness. Perhaps that's why we see nothing but misery.

ALICE. Have you known any happy people?

CAPTAIN. Let me think... No!... Yes... the Ekmarks!

ALICE. What are you talking about? That operation she had last year...

CAPTAIN. Yes, that's true. I don't know, then... Yes, the von Kraffts.

ALICE. Oh, yes! A really idyllic life, that family—rich, respected, nice children, good marriages—until they were fifty. Then along comes that cousin of theirs, commits a crime and ends up in prison; that soon put a stop to their happiness. Their good name was dragged through all the papers... after the Krafft murder it was impossible for the once respected family to show its face in public; the children had to leave school— — — dear God!

CAPTAIN. I wonder what's wrong with me.

ALICE. What do you think?

CAPTAIN. My heart, or my head. It's as though my soul wanted to escape and dissolve in a cloud of smoke.

ALICE. Do you feel like eating?

CAPTAIN. Yes. Where's supper got to?

ALICE [*walks uneasily across the room*]. I'll ask Jenny.

CAPTAIN. She's left.

ALICE. Yes. Of course.

CAPTAIN. Ring for Kristin to get me some fresh water.

ALICE [*rings*]. Imagine... [*Rings again*] She doesn't hear.

CAPTAIN. Go and see... what if she's left too?

ALICE [*goes to the door left and opens it*]. What's this? Her trunk's in the corridor, packed.

CAPTAIN. Then she's left.

ALICE. This is hell!

Starts weeping; falls to her knees and lays her head on a chair, sobbing.

CAPTAIN. Everything at once!... And of course Kurt had to come and see the mess we're in. Oh, if there's a humiliation left, let it come now, right now!

ALICE. You know what I think? Kurt's gone, and he's never coming back.

CAPTAIN. That would be just like him.

ALICE. Yes, we're cursed...

CAPTAIN. What's that mean?

ALICE. Don't you see how everyone shuns us?

CAPTAIN. I don't give a damn! [*The telegraph starts tapping*] There's the answer. Quiet, I'm listening!— — —No one's got the time. Excuses!— — —The scum!

ALICE. That's what you get for despising your doctors... and neglecting to pay them.

CAPTAIN. That's not true...

ALICE. Even when you could, you didn't want to pay because you despised their work, just as you despised my work and everyone else's!— — —They don't want to come! And the telephone's been cut off because you didn't think that worth anything either. Nothing's worth anything except your rifles and cannons!

CAPTAIN. Don't stand there babbling...

ALICE. Everything comes full circle!

CAPTAIN. That's just superstition... an old wives' tale.

ALICE. You'll see!— — —Do you know we owe Kristin six months' wages?

CAPTAIN. She's stolen that much!

ALICE. But I've had to borrow from her too.

CAPTAIN. I can believe it.

ALICE. How ungrateful you are! You know it was so the children could go to town.

CAPTAIN. Kurt timed things perfectly. A scoundrel, like the rest of them. And a coward. Daren't say he'd had enough, and that it'd be more fun at the Doctor's ball. Expected a lousy meal here, I suppose.— — —Just like him, the bastard!

*

KURT [*enters hastily, left*]. Well, my dear Edgar! This is how it is! — — —The Doctor knows all about your heart...

CAPTAIN. Heart?

KURT. Yes, you've had a bad heart for some time, a hardening...

CAPTAIN. Stony heart?*

KURT. And...

CAPTAIN. Is it dangerous?

KURT. Yes, that's to say...

CAPTAIN. It *is* dangerous!

KURT. Yes.

CAPTAIN. Death?

KURT. You must be very careful. First: no more cigars! [*The* CAPTAIN *throws away his cigar*] Then: no more whisky!— — —And then: to bed!

CAPTAIN. No, not that! Not bed! Then it's all over! You never get up again. I'll sleep on the sofa tonight. What else did he say?

KURT. He was very friendly, he says he'll come at once if you ask him.

CAPTAIN. Friendly, was he, the hypocrite? I don't want to see him.— — —Can I eat?

KURT. Not tonight. And the next few days, nothing but milk.

CAPTAIN. Milk? I can't stand the stuff!

KURT. Well, you'll have to learn.

CAPTAIN. No, I'm too old to learn.— — —[*Clutches his head*] Ah! There it is again! [*He remains seated, staring ahead*

ALICE [*to* KURT]. What did the Doctor say?

KURT. That he *may* die.

ALICE. Thank God!

KURT. Take care, Alice! Take care!— — —Now go and get a pillow and a blanket and I'll put him to bed here, on the sofa. Then I'll sit up with him all night.

ALICE. What about me?

KURT. You go to bed. Your presence seems to make him worse.

ALICE. Command, and I'll obey. I know you want what's best for both of us. [*Exiting left*

KURT. Both of you, remember. I'm not taking sides.

[*He picks up the carafe of water and goes out right*

*

The wind can be heard blowing outside; then the outer doors at the rear blow open and an OLD WOMAN, *of poor and unpleasant appearance, peers in.*

CAPTAIN [*wakes up, rises, looks around*]. So, they've left me, the wretches! [*Catches sight of the* OLD WOMAN, *and is frightened*] Who's that? What do you want?

OLD WOMAN. I only wanted to shut the door, sir.

CAPTAIN. Why? What for?

OLD WOMAN. Because it blew open, just as I was going past.

CAPTAIN. You were going to steal something!

OLD WOMAN. There's not much to take, so Kristin says.

CAPTAIN. Kristin!

OLD WOMAN. Good night, sir, sleep well!

[*She closes the door and leaves*

*

ALICE *enters with pillows and a blanket.*

CAPTAIN. Who was that at the door? Was there someone?

ALICE. Yes, old Maja from the poorhouse, she was just passing by.

CAPTAIN. Are you sure?

ALICE. Are you frightened?

CAPTAIN. Frightened? Me? Of course not!

ALICE. Since you don't want to go to bed, you can lie here.

CAPTAIN [*goes and lies down on the sofa*]. Yes, I'll lie here.

He wants to take Alice's hand, but she draws it away. KURT *enters with the water carafe.*

CAPTAIN. Kurt, don't leave me!

KURT. I'm staying with you all night. Alice is going to bed.

CAPTAIN. Goodnight then, Alice.

ALICE [*to* KURT]. Goodnight, Kurt.

KURT. Goodnight.

*

KURT *takes a chair and sits down by the* CAPTAIN'S *bed.*

KURT. Don't you want to take off your boots?

CAPTAIN. No! A soldier must always be ready for action.

KURT. Are you expecting a battle, then?

CAPTAIN. Perhaps.— — —[*He sits up in bed*] Kurt, you're the only person I've ever confided in. Listen!— — —If I die tonight... look after my children.

KURT. I will.

CAPTAIN. Thank you. I trust you.

KURT. Can you explain why you trust me?

CAPTAIN. We haven't been friends—I don't believe in friendship, anyway. And our two families were born enemies, they've always been at war...

KURT. And yet you trust me?

CAPTAIN. Yes. I don't know why.

Silence.

*

CAPTAIN: Do you think I'm going to die?

KURT. Like everyone else. You're no exception.

CAPTAIN. Are you bitter?

KURT. Yes!... Are you afraid of dying? The wheelbarrow and the garden plot.

CAPTAIN. What if it isn't the end?

KURT. Many don't think it is.

CAPTAIN. What then?

KURT. Endless surprises, I imagine.

CAPTAIN. But no one knows for sure.

KURT. No, that's just it. So one must be prepared for everything.

CAPTAIN. Surely you're not so childish as to believe in—hell?

KURT. Don't you, when you're in the midst of it?

CAPTAIN. I was only speaking metaphorically.

KURT. What you've described was no metaphor, poetic or otherwise.

*

Silence.

CAPTAIN. If you only knew what agonies I'm suffering.

KURT. Physical?

CAPTAIN. No, not physical.

KURT. Then they must be spiritual; there's no third kind.

Pause.

CAPTAIN [*raises himself in the bed*]. I don't want to die!

KURT. A little while ago you were longing for annihilation.

CAPTAIN. Yes, if it's painless.

KURT. But it isn't.

CAPTAIN. Is this annihilation, then?

KURT. The beginning of it.

*

CAPTAIN. Goodnight.

KURT. Goodnight.

Curtain.

The same setting, but the lamp is about to go out. A cloudy morning is visible through the windows and the glass panes of the doors at the rear. A rough sea. A SENTRY *stands by the battery as before. The* CAPTAIN *is lying on the chaise longue; he is sleeping.* KURT *is sitting on a chair alongside him, pale and exhausted.*

ALICE [*enters from the left*]. Is he asleep?

KURT. Yes, since what should have been sunrise.

ALICE. How was the night?

KURT. He slept off and on, but he talked a lot too.

ALICE. What about?

KURT. He's been arguing about religion like a schoolboy who claims to have just solved the mysteries of the universe. Finally, towards morning, he discovered the immortality of the soul.

ALICE. To his own glorification.

KURT. Precisely.— — —He really is the most arrogant person I've ever come across. '*I* am, therefore God exists'.

ALICE. Now you see!— — —Look at those boots. He'd have trampled the world flat with them if he'd had the chance. Those boots have trampled over everyone and everything, stepping on everybody's toes and walking all over me.— — —You great bear, you've got your bullet now!

KURT. He'd be comic if he weren't tragic, and for all his pettiness there's something grand about him. Haven't you one good word to say for him?

ALICE [*sitting down*]. Yes, so long as he doesn't hear it; an encouraging word and he goes mad with pride.

KURT. He can't hear anything. He's had some morphine.

ALICE. He came from a poor home, there were many brothers and sisters. From an early age he had to support the family by giving lessons because his father was a good-for-nothing, or worse. It must be hard for a young man to have to forego all the pleasures of youth and slave for a pack of ungrateful kids he didn't even bring into the world. I was only a little girl when I first saw him, a young man who went about without a coat even though it was winter and bitterly cold— — —his little sisters all had duffel-coats— — — I found that noble and couldn't help but admire him even though his ugliness repelled me. He's extraordinarily ugly, isn't he?

KURT. Yes, he looks quite hideous sometimes. When we quarrelled, that's when I really used to notice it; and then, when he wasn't present, his image would grow and take on terrifying dimensions. He literally haunted me.

ALICE. Imagine what it's been like for me, then!— — —His years as a junior officer must have been a martyrdom, though. But now and then some wealthy people used to help him. Not that he'd ever admit it—he's always taken everything he ever got as his due, without a word of thanks.

KURT. We're supposed to be speaking well of him.

ALICE. After he's dead! Anyway— — —I don't remember anything else.

KURT. Has he been cruel, would you say?

ALICE. Yes—and yet he can be both kind and tender.—As an enemy he's simply terrible.

KURT. Why didn't he become a major?

ALICE. Isn't that obvious? They didn't want someone over them who'd already proved a tyrant under them. But don't ever mention a word of this. He says he didn't want to become a major.— — — Did he say anything about the children?

KURT. Yes, he longed to see Judith.*

ALICE. I can well believe it. Do you know who Judith is? His spitting image, trained by him to torment me. Just think, my own daughter... has actually raised her hand against me.

KURT. No, that's going too far!

ALICE. Shhh! He's moving!— — —Supposing he heard!— — — He's cunning, too.

KURT. He really is waking up.

ALICE. Doesn't he look like a troll? I'm afraid of him!

Silence.

CAPTAIN [*stirs, wakes, raises himself, and looks around*]. It's morning. At last!— — —

KURT. How are you feeling now?

CAPTAIN. Bad!

KURT. Do you want a doctor?

CAPTAIN. No!— — —I want to see Judith. My child!

KURT. Don't you think you ought to put your affairs in order, before, or if something should happen?

CAPTAIN. What do you mean? What should happen?

KURT. What happens to us all.

CAPTAIN. Oh, rubbish! I'll not die that easily, believe you me. Don't start celebrating just yet, Alice!

KURT. Think of your children! Make your will, so that your wife may at least keep the furniture!

CAPTAIN. Going to inherit me while I'm still alive, is she?

KURT. No! But if anything should happen, she oughtn't to be thrown out in the street. Someone who's cleaned, dusted, and polished these things for twenty-five years has some right to them, surely! Shall I get a lawyer?

CAPTAIN. No!

KURT. You're a cruel man, crueller than I thought.

CAPTAIN. Here it comes again!

[*He falls back unconscious on the bed*

*

ALICE [*going to the right*]. There are people in the kitchen, I have to go!

KURT. Yes, do! There's not much to be done here.

[ALICE *leaves*

*

CAPTAIN [*regaining consciousness*]. Well Kurt, how are you going to run this quarantine station?

KURT. Oh, I'll manage.

CAPTAIN. No, I'm the commandant on this island, so you'll have to deal with me. Don't forget that.

KURT. Have you ever seen a quarantine in action?

CAPTAIN. Have I? Yes, before you were born! And I'll give you some advice: don't put the disinfection ovens too near the shore.

KURT. I thought they were supposed to be as close to the water as possible...

CAPTAIN. That shows how much you know about your business: water's the element for germs, they thrive in it.

KURT. But salt water's essential for washing away the impurities.

CAPTAIN. Idiot!— — —Well, as soon as you've found somewhere to live you must bring your children to join you.

KURT. Do you think they'll agree to that?

CAPTAIN. Of course, if you're any kind of a man. It would make a good impression on people here to see you doing your duty in that respect, too...

KURT. I've always done my duty in that respect.

CAPTAIN [*raising his voice*]. ... in that respect where you are most at fault.

KURT. Haven't I told you...

CAPTAIN [*going straight on*]. ... Because a man doesn't desert his children like that...

KURT. Oh, carry on!

CAPTAIN. As your relative, an elder relative, I feel I have a certain right to tell you the truth, even if it is painful... And you mustn't take it amiss...

KURT. Are you hungry?

CAPTAIN. Yes, I am!— — —

KURT. Would you like something light?

CAPTAIN. No, something substantial.

KURT. That would finish you!

CAPTAIN. Isn't it enough to be ill, must one starve, too?

KURT. That's the way it is.

CAPTAIN. And no drinking or smoking. It's scarcely worth living.

KURT. Death demands sacrifices, otherwise he comes at once.

*

ALICE [*enters with some bouquets of flowers, telegrams and letters*]. These are for you!   [*Throws the flowers on the desk*

CAPTAIN. For me?— — —May I see them?— — —

ALICE. Yes, they're only from the non-commissioned officers, the band, and your corporals.

CAPTAIN. You're jealous!

ALICE. Hardly! If they were laurel wreaths. . . that would be different, but you'll never get any of those.

CAPTAIN. Hm!. . . Here's a telegram from the Colonel. . . Read it, Kurt. The Colonel's a gentleman, at any rate— — —even if he is a bit of an idiot!. . . This one's from. . . what does it say? It's from Judith!— — —Please would you telegraph her to come by the next boat!— — —This one. . . Yes!—One's not without friends after all, and it's nice of them to think about an invalid, who's deserving beyond his station, a man without fear and beyond reproach!

ALICE. I don't understand: are they congratulating you on being ill?

CAPTAIN. Hyena!

ALICE [*to* KURT]. Yes, we had a doctor here who was so hated that when he left the island they gave a banquet for him—after he'd left!

CAPTAIN. Put the flowers in vases. . . I'm not a credulous man, and people are scum, but this simple homage, by God, it's genuine. . . it can't be anything but genuine.

ALICE. Fool!

KURT [*reading a telegram*]. Judith says she can't come because the steamer's delayed by the storm.

CAPTAIN. Is that all?

KURT. Er, no!—There's a postscript.

CAPTAIN. Out with it!

KURT. Well, she asks you not to drink so much.

CAPTAIN. Impertinence!—There's children for you! My own beloved daughter... my Judith! My idol!

ALICE. And your spitting image!

CAPTAIN. That's life for you, the best it has to offer! Oh, to hell with it!

ALICE. Now you're reaping what you sowed. You turned her against her mother; now she's turning against you. And you say there is no God!

CAPTAIN [*to* KURT]. What does the Colonel say?

KURT. He grants you leave forthwith.

CAPTAIN. Leave? I haven't requested any.

ALICE. No, but I have.

CAPTAIN. I won't accept it.

ALICE. The orders have already been signed.

CAPTAIN. I don't care!

ALICE. You see, Kurt, here's a man for whom no laws exist, no rules apply, no authority matters... He stands above everything and everyone; the universe has been created for his private use; the sun and moon revolve merely to carry his praises to the stars; that's my husband! This insignificant captain who couldn't even become a major, whose puffed-up pride makes him the laughing-stock of those he supposes fear him; this lily-livered brute who's afraid of the dark and believes in barometers right down to and including the final curtain: a barrowload of muck, and second-rate muck at that!

CAPTAIN [*fans himself complacently with a bouquet of flowers, without listening to* ALICE]. Have you asked Kurt to breakfast?

ALICE. No.

CAPTAIN. Then make it two, two really good chateaubriands, right away.

ALICE. Two?

CAPTAIN. I'm having one too.

ALICE. But there are three of us!

CAPTAIN. Oh, you want one too, do you? All right, make it three then.

ALICE. And where am I to get hold of them? Yesterday evening you invited Kurt to supper, and there wasn't a crust of bread in the house; Kurt has had to sit up all night with you on an empty stomach without even a cup of coffee, because there isn't any, and our credit's run out.

CAPTAIN [*to* KURT]. She's mad at me because I didn't die yesterday.

ALICE. No, because you didn't die twenty-five years ago, because you didn't die before I was born!

CAPTAIN [*to* KURT]. Listen to her!———That's your match-making for you, my dear Kurt. Well, it certainly wasn't made in heaven.

> KURT *and* ALICE *exchange meaningful glances.*

CAPTAIN [*gets up and goes towards the door*]. However! Say what you will, I'm going on duty now. [*Puts on an old-fashioned artillery helmet with crest; fastens his sabre about his waist, and puts on his military cape*] If anyone wants me, I'm at the battery.

> KURT *and* ALICE *try to stop him, but in vain.*

CAPTAIN. Out of my way! [*Exits*

ALICE. Yes, go! You always do, when the going gets tough you turn your back and let your wife cover your retreat, you tosspot, braggart, liar! Ugh!

*

KURT. This is bottomless!

ALICE. You don't know the half of it yet!

KURT. Worse than this?

ALICE. Only I'm ashamed to...

KURT. Where's he going now? And where does he find the strength?

ALICE. You may well ask! Oh, now he'll go down to the noncoms and thank them for their flowers... and then he'll eat and drink with them and slander his fellow officers... If you knew how often he's been threatened with dismissal! It's only sympathy for his family that's kept him his post. And he thinks it's because they're afraid of his superiority. And those poor officers' wives who've gone out of their way to help us, why, he hates and abuses them!

KURT. I must confess, I came out here to the sea to find some peace and quiet... I'd no idea how things were between you...

ALICE. Poor Kurt!— — —How will you manage for food?

KURT. Oh, I can go to the Doctor's; but you? Please let me arrange something for you.

ALICE. As long as he doesn't find out, if he did he'd kill me!

KURT [*looking out through the window*]. Look, he's standing out on the ramparts. Never mind the wind!

ALICE. One can't but pity him... that he has to be the way he is.

KURT. You're both to be pitied!... But what's to be done?

ALICE. I don't know.— — —Some bills came, too, but he didn't notice them...

KURT. It can be a blessing not to see, sometimes.

ALICE [*at the window*]. He's opened his cape. He's letting the wind beat upon his chest. Now he wants to die!

KURT. I don't think he does, for just now, when he felt his life was slipping away, he clung tightly to mine and began to root around in my affairs, as if he wanted to creep into my skin and live my life.

ALICE. That's him precisely, a vampire*— — —seizing hold of other people's destinies, sucking excitement out of other people's lives, ordering and arranging for others, because his own life is quite devoid of interest. And remember this, Kurt: never let him into your family affairs, never let him get to know your friends, for he'll take them away from you and make them his... He's a real magician where that's concerned!— — —If he ever meets your children, you'll soon find they're *his* nearest and dearest, he'll soon be telling them what to do, and bring them up the way he wants, but above all *not* as you would.

KURT. Alice, he wasn't responsible for having my children taken from me at the time of my divorce, was he?

ALICE. Since it's done and gone: yes, he was!

KURT. I suspected it, but never knew for sure! So it was him!

ALICE. When you confided in him and sent him to talk things over with your wife, he started to flirt with her, and told her what to do to get custody of the children.

KURT. Oh, God!— — —Oh, God in heaven!

ALICE. There's another side of him for you!

Silence.

KURT. Do you know, last night— — —when he thought he was going to die— — —he made me promise to look after his children.

ALICE. But surely you won't revenge yourself on my children?

KURT. By keeping my promise? Of course! I'll look after your children.

ALICE. That really is the worst revenge you can take, for there's nothing he loathes more than magnanimity.

KURT. Then I may have my revenge, without taking revenge!

ALICE. I love it when justice and revenge are one, and it delights me to see evil punished.

KURT. Are you still at that stage?

ALICE. That's where I'll always be! The day I forgive or love an enemy I'd be a hypocrite!

KURT. Alice! Sometimes it's best to bite your tongue or look the other way: it's called tolerance. And we all need that.

ALICE. I don't! My life is open and above board. I've always put all my cards on the table.

KURT. That's saying a lot.

ALICE. No, too little! What about all the undeserved suffering I've been through at this man's hands, a man I've never loved...

KURT. Why did you marry him?

ALICE. Who knows?... Because he took me. Seduced me. I don't know. And then, I wanted to make my way in society...

KURT. So you left the theatre.

ALICE. Which people frowned on.—But he cheated me, you know. He promised me a good life... a beautiful home. And I found nothing but debts— — —the only gold was on his uniform, and even that wasn't real. He cheated me!

KURT. Wait a moment! When a young man falls in love, he always looks ahead with high hopes... He must be forgiven if these hopes aren't always realized. I've the same sort of deception on my conscience but I don't regard myself as a cheat.— — —What are you looking at out there?

ALICE. I'm looking to see if he's fallen.

KURT. Has he?

ALICE. No, unfortunately! He always cheats me!

KURT. Well, I'll go and see the Doctor and the authorities.

ALICE [*sitting down beside the window*]. You go, Kurt dear. I'll sit here and wait. How I've learned to wait!

Interval.

The same setting as before in daylight. The SENTRY *is on duty at the battery as before.* ALICE *is seated in the armchair, right. She is grey-haired.*

KURT [*enters from the left, having knocked*]. Good morning, Alice.

ALICE. Good morning, my dear. Sit down.

KURT [*sitting in the armchair to the left*]. The steamer's coming in.

ALICE. Then I know what to expect, if he's on it.

KURT. He is. I could see the glint of his helmet... What's he been doing in town?

ALICE. I can figure it out. He put on his parade uniform so he was going to see the Colonel; and he took his best gloves, that means he's been paying calls.

KURT. Did you notice how quiet he was yesterday? Since he gave up drinking he's become another person, calm, reserved, considerate...

ALICE. I know. If that man had always been sober, he'd have been a danger to humanity. Perhaps it's a good thing for us all that he made himself ridiculous and harmless with his whisky.

KURT. The genie in the bottle has chastened him!— — —But have you noticed that ever since death set its mark on him he's acquired a kind of dignity that somehow elevates him? Perhaps his new faith in immortality has given him a new view of life.

ALICE. Don't fool yourself! He's up to no good. And don't believe what he says, he's a premeditated liar and a born intriguer— — —

KURT [*regards* ALICE]. Alice! What's this? Your hair has turned grey in two nights!

ALICE. No, my dear, it's been like that for a long time; I've simply stopped dyeing it now my husband's as good as dead. Twenty-five years in a fortress— — —Do you know this used to be a prison once?

KURT. A prison! Yes, you can almost tell by the walls.

ALICE. And my complexion! Even the children had the pallor of prison here.

KURT. It's hard to imagine small children playing within these walls.

ALICE. They didn't play much. And the two who died wilted from lack of light.

KURT. What do you think will happen now?

ALICE. The decisive blow, against *both* of us. I saw a familiar glint in his eye when you read that telegram from Judith. It should have been directed at her, of course, but she's bulletproof, so his hatred descended on you.

KURT. What do you suppose he means to do to me?

ALICE. That's hard to say, but he's got a remarkable genius for nosing out other people's secrets, pure luck perhaps... and you must have noticed how he spent the whole of yesterday battening on your work, sucking an interest in life out of your existence, devouring your children alive... I know him, Kurt. He's a cannibal. His own life is passing away, or has already passed...

KURT. I've also got the impression that he's already on the other side. His face has a kind of phosphorescence, as if he'd begun to decompose... and his eyes flare like will-o'-the-wisps over graves or swamps... Here he comes! Tell me, has it occurred to you he might be jealous?

ALICE. No, he's too proud for that.— — —'Show me the man I should be jealous of!' His own words.

KURT. So much the better. Even his faults have a certain merit! — — —Should I go and meet him, at any rate?

ALICE. No, don't be polite, or he'll think you're up to something. And when he starts lying, pretend to believe him; I'm good at translating his lies; with my lexicon I can always get at the truth— — —Something dreadful's going to happen, I can feel it— — —but Kurt, don't lose your self-control!— — —In our long war my one advantage lay in being sober and so keeping my wits about me... Whisky was always his downfall!... Now we'll see.

*

The CAPTAIN *enters left, in parade uniform, helmet, military cape and white gloves. He is calm and dignified but pale and hollow-eyed. He stumbles towards a chair, right, and sits down in his helmet and cape, at a distance from* ALICE *and* KURT.

CAPTAIN. Good morning!—Forgive me for sitting down like this, but I'm a bit tired.

ALICE *and* KURT. Good morning!

ALICE. How are you?

CAPTAIN. Fine! Just a bit tired...

ALICE. What news from town?

CAPTAIN. Oh, this and that. Among other things, I've been to the Doctor, and he said there's nothing wrong with me; I can live another twenty years, if I take care of myself.

ALICE [*to* KURT]. Now he's lying. [*To the* CAPTAIN] That is good news, dear.

CAPTAIN. Yes, so it is!

A silence during which the CAPTAIN *looks at* ALICE *and* KURT *as though expecting them to speak.*

ALICE [*to* KURT]. Don't say anything. Let him speak first, then he'll show his hand.

CAPTAIN [*to* ALICE]. Did you say something?

ALICE. No, nothing at all!

CAPTAIN [*slowly*]. Listen, Kurt.

ALICE [*to* KURT]. Here it comes now.

CAPTAIN. I—I was in town, as you know. [KURT *nods assent*] I—er—met a few people... among them... a young cadet [*pausing*] in the artillery. [*Pause, during which* KURT *shows his unease*] Since———we're short of cadets here I arranged with the Colonel for him to come out here.———That ought to please you, particularly when I tell you that it... was... your own son!

ALICE [*to* KURT]. The vampire! You see!

KURT. Under normal circumstances that would please a father, but in my situation it is merely painful.

CAPTAIN. I don't understand.

KURT. You don't need to; it's enough that I don't want it.

CAPTAIN. Really! Is that so?— — —Then you ought to know that the young man has been ordered to report here, and from now on he's under my command.

KURT. Then I'll have him apply for a transfer to another regiment.

CAPTAIN. You can't, you've no rights over your son.

KURT. No rights?

CAPTAIN. No, the court has awarded them to his mother.

KURT. Then I'll get in touch with the mother.

CAPTAIN. There's no need.

KURT. No need?

CAPTAIN. No, I've already done so. Ha!

> KURT *starts to rise, but slumps back again*.

ALICE [*to* KURT]. Now he must die!

KURT. He really is a cannibal!

*

CAPTAIN. So much for *that*! [*Straight at* ALICE *and* KURT] Did you two say something?

ALICE. No! Are you hard of hearing?

CAPTAIN. A little.— — —But if you move closer, I'll tell you something, in confidence.

ALICE. There's no need. Anyway, it might be good for both of us to have a witness.

CAPTAIN. Quite right! It's always good to have a witness.— — — But first, is the will in order?

ALICE [*hands over a document*]. The solicitor drafted it himself.

CAPTAIN. In your favour!— — —Good! [*Reads the document, and then tears it carefully into pieces, which he throws on the floor*] So much for that! Ha!

ALICE [*to* KURT]. Have you ever seen another human being like him?

KURT. He's not a human being!

*

CAPTAIN. Oh, Alice! There's something else I had to tell you— — —

ALICE [*uneasy*]. Go ahead!

CAPTAIN [*calmly as before*]. In view of your long-expressed desire to bring this miserable life and unhappy marriage to an end, and given the complete lack of affection you have shown your husband and children, and furthermore in view of the negligence with which you have managed our domestic economy, I have, during my visit to town, been to court and filed a petition for divorce.

ALICE. Oh? On what grounds?

CAPTAIN [*calmly as before*]. Apart from the grounds already mentioned, I have some purely personal ones. Now that it has been established that I may live another twenty years, I've decided to exchange this present unhappy state of matrimony for one that suits me better; I intend to unite my destiny with a woman who will bring my home not only devotion to her husband but also youth and—shall we say—a little beauty?

ALICE [*removes her ring, and throws it at the* CAPTAIN]. There you are!

CAPTAIN [*picking up the ring and putting it in his breast pocket*]. She throws away her ring. Will the witness please note that?

ALICE [*rising in agitation*]. And you intend to throw me out and take another woman into my house?

CAPTAIN. Yes!

ALICE. Right, then. It's time for some plain speaking!— — —Kurt, you're my cousin, this man is guilty of trying to murder his wife!

KURT. Murder?

ALICE. Yes, he pushed me into the sea!

CAPTAIN. Without witnesses!

ALICE. He's lying! Judith saw it!

CAPTAIN. So what?

ALICE. She can testify!

CAPTAIN. No, she can't. She says she saw nothing.

ALICE. You've taught the child to lie!

CAPTAIN. I didn't need to. You'd already taught her.

ALICE. Did you see Judith?

CAPTAIN. Yes!...

ALICE. Oh, God! Oh, God!

*

CAPTAIN. The fortress has capitulated! The enemy is granted the freedom to withdraw and ten minutes in which to do it. [*Places his watch on the table*] Ten minutes! By my watch!

> *Remains standing; puts his hand to his heart.*

ALICE [*goes up to the* CAPTAIN *and takes his arm*]. What is it?

CAPTAIN. I don't know!

ALICE. Do you want something? A drink?

CAPTAIN. Whisky? No, I don't want to die. Alice!— — —[*Draws himself up*] Don't touch me!— — —Ten minutes, or the garrison will be put to the sword. [*He draws his sabre*] Ten minutes!

> [*Goes out through the rear doors*

*

KURT. Who is this man?

ALICE. He's not a man, he's a demon!

KURT. What does he want with my son?

ALICE. He wants him as a hostage so he can control you; he wants to isolate you from the island's authorities... Do you know that people here call this island 'Little Hell'?

KURT. No, I didn't.— — —Alice, you're the first woman I've ever felt sorry for, all the others seemed to me to deserve what they got.

ALICE. Don't abandon me now, Kurt, don't leave me or he'll beat me!— — —Like he's done for twenty-five years... in front of the children, too... he's even pushed me into the sea...

KURT. That does it! I can't take any more! I came here without any malice, forgetting how he used to humiliate me and blacken my name. I even forgave him when you told me he was the one who'd taken my children away from me— — —because he was sick and dying. . . but now that he wants to rob me of my son, he must die, he—or I.

ALICE. Good! Don't surrender the fortress! Blow it up, and him with it, even if we have to go with him! I'll fix the gunpowder!

KURT. I wasn't angry when I came here, and I thought of running away when I felt your hatred infecting me; but now I feel called upon to hate this man as I've always hated evil!— — —What can we do?

ALICE. I've learnt my tactics from him. Drum up his enemies and look for allies!

KURT. Fancy him tracking down my wife like that! Why didn't those two meet twenty-five years ago? Their battles would have made the earth tremble.

ALICE. But now they have—two kindred spirits—and they must be parted. I think I know his weak spot, I've long suspected it. . .

KURT. Who's his worst enemy on the island?

ALICE. The Ordnance Officer.

KURT. Can he be trusted?

ALICE. Yes!— — —And he *knows* what I—I know it, too, you see— — —He knows what the Sergeant Major and the Captain have been up to together.

KURT. Up to?. . . What do you mean?

ALICE. Embezzlement!

KURT. That's appalling! No, I don't want anything to do with this. . .

ALICE [*laughs*]. What a man! Can't you strike at an enemy?

KURT. I could, once; but not any more.

ALICE. Why?

KURT. Because I've discovered. . . that in the end justice is always done.

ALICE. Wait for it? Until he's taken your son from you? Look at my grey hair. . . yes, and feel how thick it still is too!. . . He intends to remarry, so I'm free—to do the same!—I am free! And in ten minutes he'll be sitting down there, under arrest; down there [*stamps on the floor*], down there. . . and I'll dance on his head,

I'll dance the 'Entry of the Boyars'... [*She performs a few dance steps with her hands on her hips*] Ha, ha, ha, ha! And I'll play the piano so he hears it! [*Hammers on the keys*] Oh, the tower will open its gates, and the sentry with the drawn sword will no longer stand guard over me, but over him... Meli-tam-tam-ta, meli-ta-lia-lay! Him, him, him, over him!

KURT [*has been watching her, fascinated and aroused*]. Alice! Are you a devil too?

ALICE [*jumps up onto a chair and takes down the laurel wreaths*]. I'll wear these as I march away... my triumphant laurels with their gaily waving ribbons! A bit dusty, but eternally green!—Like my youth!—I'm not old, Kurt!

KURT [*with blazing eyes*]. You are a devil!

ALICE. In Little Hell!— — —Listen, I must make myself beautiful... [*Lets down her hair*]—a couple of minutes to change my dress... two more to go to the Ordnance Officer... and then: up goes the fortress, sky-high!

KURT [*as before*]. You are a devil!

ALICE. That's what you always used to say when we were children, too. Do you remember when we were children and got engaged? [*Laughs*] You were shy, of course...

KURT [*seriously*]. Alice!

ALICE. Yes, you were. It suited you, too. You see, there are bold women who like shy men, and they say— — —there are shy men who like bold women!— — —You liked me a little in those days, didn't you?

KURT. I don't know where I am!

ALICE. With an actress, who is rather free in her ways, but who is otherwise an excellent woman! Yes! But now I'm free, free, free!— — —Turn your back while I change my blouse!

She unbuttons her blouse. KURT *rushes over to her, seizes her in his arms, lifts her high in the air, and bites her throat, so that she screams. Then he throws her from him onto the chaise longue and rushes out to the left.*

Curtain.

The same, in the evening. The SENTRY *at the battery is still visible through the upstage windows. The laurel wreaths are hanging over the back of a chair. The ceiling lamp is lit. Soft music.*

The CAPTAIN, *pale, hollow-eyed, and grizzled, wearing a worn undress uniform with riding boots, is sitting at the sewing-table, playing patience. He is wearing spectacles.*

The interval music continues after the curtain rises until the next character appears.

The CAPTAIN *lays out his cards, but now and then gives a start, and looks up, listening anxiously.*

He seems unable to get his game to come out; becomes impatient and sweeps the cards together. Then he goes over to the window left, opens it, and throws the pack of cards out. The window remains open, rattling on its hooks.

He goes to the cupboard; is frightened by the noise the window makes, and turns to see what it is. Takes out three dark, square-sided whisky bottles, looks at them carefully—and throws them out of the window. Then he takes out some cigar boxes, sniffs inside one, and throws them out of the window.

He then takes off his glasses, wipes them, and tests how he sees with them. Then he throws them out of the window; stumbles about among the furniture as if he does not see well, and lights a candelabra containing six candles that stands on the secretaire. Sees the laurel wreaths, picks them up, and goes towards the window, but turns. He takes the cloth decorating the piano and wraps it carefully round the wreaths; takes some pins from the desk, fastens the corners and then lays the bundle on a chair.

He goes over to the piano, strikes the keys with his fist; shuts the lid, locks it, and throws the key out of the window. Then he lights the candles on the piano. Goes to the whatnot, takes his wife's portrait, looks at it, and tears it to pieces, which he throws on the floor. The window rattles on its hooks and he is once again frightened.

Then, once he has calmed down, he takes the photographs of his son and daughter, kisses them quickly, and puts them in his breast pocket. He sweeps the other photographs to the floor, and kicks them into a heap with his boot.

Then he sits down, tired, at the desk and feels his heart. He lights the candles on the desk and sighs; stares in front of him as if he were seeing unpleasant visions.— — —Gets up, and goes to the secretaire. Opens the flap, takes out a bundle of letters fastened with blue silk ribbons, and throws them into the stove. Closes the secretaire.

The telegraph suddenly taps a single stroke, then falls silent. The CAPTAIN *starts in mortal fear and remains standing, with his hand on his heart, listening. But when he hears nothing further from the telegraph, he listens towards the door, left. He goes over to it, opens it, takes a step inside, and comes out with a cat on his arm, which he strokes along its back. Then he goes out, right. At this point the music ceases.*

*

ALICE *enters from the rear, dressed for walking, with black hair, hat, gloves, the image of a coquette. She looks around in amazement at the many candles.* KURT *enters from the left, nervous.*

ALICE. It looks like Christmas Eve in here.

KURT. Well?

ALICE [*extends her hand for him to kiss*]. Thank me!

KURT *kisses her hand unwillingly.*

ALICE. Six witnesses, four of them unshakeable. The matter has been reported and the reply is coming here, by telegraph—here into the heart of the fortress!

KURT. I see.

ALICE. Say 'thank you', not 'I see'!

KURT. Why has he lit so many candles?

ALICE. Because he's afraid of the dark, of course!... Look at the telegraph. Doesn't it look like the handle on a coffee-mill? I grind, I grind, and the beans crunch like teeth being pulled...

KURT. What's he been doing in this room?

ALICE. It looks as though he was thinking of going. Down there, that's where you're going!

KURT. Alice, don't! It's all so dreadful... he used to be my friend when we were young, and he was often kind to me when things were hard... I feel sorry for him.

ALICE. And me? Who did nothing wrong and yet had to sacrifice my career for that monster.

KURT. That career of yours. Was it really so brilliant?

ALICE [*furious*]. What's that? Do you know who I am, who I was?

KURT. All right, all right!

ALICE. Are you starting, too... already?

KURT. Already?

ALICE *throws her arms round* KURT'S *neck, and kisses him.*

ALICE. You're biting me!

KURT [*beside himself*]. Yes, I want to bite your neck, and suck your blood like a lynx. You've aroused the beast in me. For years I've sought to kill it by self-denial and self-sacrifice. When I came here I thought myself a little better than you two, but now I'm the vilest of us all. Since I saw you in all your horrible nakedness, since my passion blinded me, I know the full force of evil. What's ugly becomes beautiful and what's good seems ugly and weak!— — — Come here and I'll choke you— — —with a kiss!

He embraces her.

ALICE [*shows her left hand*]. See the mark of the chain you broke. I was a slave. Now I'm free...

KURT. But I shall bind you...

ALICE. You?

KURT. Yes, me!

ALICE. I thought for a moment you were...

KURT. Pious?

ALICE. Well, you talked about the Fall...

KURT. Did I?

ALICE. And I thought you'd come here to preach...

KURT. Did you?— — —In an hour we'll be in town. Then you'll see who I am...

ALICE. We'll go to the theatre tonight, and let everyone see us. If I run away, the shame will be his; do you understand?

KURT. I'm beginning to. It's not enough with prison...

ALICE. No, it's not! He must be shamed as well.

KURT. A strange world! You behave shamefully, and he has to bear the shame.

ALICE. Since that's the way the world is—stupid!

KURT. It's as though these prison walls had soaked in the evil of every criminal who's been imprisoned here; one only needs to breathe to catch it. While you were thinking about the theatre and supper, I was thinking about my son!

ALICE [*strikes him across the mouth with her glove*]. You old fool!

KURT *raises his hand to strike* ALICE.

ALICE [*recoils*]. *Tout beau!* *

KURT. Forgive me!

ALICE. On your knees, then! [KURT *goes down on his knees*] On your face! [KURT *puts his forehead to the floor*] Kiss my foot! [KURT *kisses her foot*] Never do that again!— — —Get up!

KURT [*gets up*]. What have I come to? Where am I?

ALICE. You know quite well!

KURT. I almost believe. . . I'm in hell!

*

CAPTAIN [*enters from the right, dejected, supporting himself on a stick*]. May I speak with Kurt? Alone!

ALICE. What about? Our safe-conduct?

CAPTAIN [*sits down by the sewing-table*]. Kurt, will you please sit with me a little while? And Alice, would you grant us a moment's. . . peace?

ALICE. What's this, then?— — —New signals! [*To* KURT] All right, sit down. [KURT *sits unwillingly*] And listen to the wisdom of old age!— — —If there's a telegram. . . then call me!

[*Exits left*

*

CAPTAIN [*with dignity, after a pause*]. Do you understand the purpose of a life like mine? Like ours?

KURT. No. As little as I understand my own.

CAPTAIN. This mess. What does it all mean?

KURT. In my better moments I've believed that was the meaning—that we shouldn't understand and yet submit...

CAPTAIN. Submit? With no fixed point outside myself, I can't submit.

KURT. Correct. But as a mathematician you should surely be able to find that unknown point when you have some given data to go on...

CAPTAIN. I have looked for it, but—I haven't found it.

KURT. Then your calculations have been at fault; start again.

CAPTAIN. I will!— — —Tell me, where did you find such resignation?

KURT. I've none left. Don't overestimate me.

CAPTAIN. As you may have noticed, for me the art of living has meant blotting out the past. That's to say: cross out and go on! Long ago I made myself a sack into which I stuffed all my humiliations. And when it was full, I threw it in the sea.—I don't believe anyone has suffered as many humiliations as I have. But when I crossed them out and went on, they ceased to exist.

KURT. I've noticed how you invented a life for yourself and those around you.

CAPTAIN. How else could I have lived? How could I have endured?   [*Clutches at his heart*

KURT. How are you feeling?

CAPTAIN. Bad! [*Pause*] There comes a moment when the ability to invent, as you call it, ends. And then reality is revealed in all its nakedness!— — —It's terrifying! [*His jaw sags and he now speaks with an old man's tear-laden voice*] You see, my dear friend... [*Controls himself, and speaks with his normal voice*] Forgive me... but when I was in town just now, and met the Doctor [*again with a tear-laden voice*], he said I was done for... [*with his normal voice*] and that I couldn't live much longer.

KURT. Did he say *that*?

CAPTAIN [*tearfully*]. Yes, that's what he said.

KURT. Then it wasn't true?

CAPTAIN. What? Oh that... No, it wasn't true.

Pause.

KURT. Was the rest of it a lie, too?

CAPTAIN. What, my dear fellow?

KURT. That my son was ordered here as a cadet?

CAPTAIN. I've not heard anything about that.

KURT. You know, your ability to cross out the past is quite incredible.

CAPTAIN. I don't understand what you're on about, old boy.

KURT. Then you are done for.

CAPTAIN. Yes, there's not a lot left.

KURT. Look, maybe you haven't insulted your wife by filing for a divorce?

CAPTAIN. Divorce? No, that's new to me.

KURT [*gets up*]. Then you admit you've been lying?

CAPTAIN. You use such strong words, old boy. We all need a little indulgence.

KURT. So you've found that out, have you?

CAPTAIN [*firmly, in a clear voice*]. Yes, I have!— — —So forgive me, Kurt! Forgive me everything!

KURT. Brave words.—But I've nothing to forgive you. And I'm not the man you think I am, not any more. And least of all worthy to accept your confessions.

CAPTAIN [*in a clear voice*]. Life was always so strange! So difficult, so vindictive, right from childhood... and people were so evil that I became evil too... [KURT *walks about uneasily, and looks at the telegraph apparatus*] What are you looking at?

KURT. Is it possible to switch that thing off?

CAPTAIN. Not easily.

KURT [*with increasing unease*]. Who is Sergeant Major Östberg?

CAPTAIN. An honest enough fellow—a bit of a dealer, of course.

KURT. Who is the Ordnance Officer?

CAPTAIN. Oh, he's got it in for me, right enough, but I've nothing really against him.

KURT [*looks out through the window, where a lantern can be seen moving about*]. What's that lantern doing down by the battery?

CAPTAIN. Lantern?

KURT. Yes, and people moving about.

CAPTAIN. Probably what we call a 'helping hand'.

KURT. What's that?

CAPTAIN. A few squaddies with a red-cap. Some poor devil's going to be arrested, I suppose.

KURT. Oh!

Pause.

CAPTAIN. Now that you know Alice, what do you think of her?

KURT. I can't say. . . I just don't understand people, not at all. She's as much an enigma as you are—as I am myself. I'm getting to the age when it's wise to admit that I neither know nor understand anything.—But when I see someone do something I want to know why.— — —Why did you push her in the sea?

CAPTAIN. I don't know. She was standing there on the jetty and it just seemed the obvious thing.

KURT. Have you never regretted it?

CAPTAIN. Never!

KURT. That's strange!

CAPTAIN. Yes, it is, isn't it? So strange that I don't actually believe I did such a thing.

KURT. Has it never occurred to you that she might get her revenge?

CAPTAIN. She's done that all right! And as far as I'm concerned that's just as natural.

KURT. How did you come to be so cynically resigned, and so quickly?

CAPTAIN. Since I looked death in the eyes, life has presented itself from another angle.— — —Listen, if you had to judge between Alice and me, who would you say was in the right?

KURT. Neither! But I pity you both profoundly. Perhaps you a little more.

CAPTAIN. Give me your hand, Kurt!

KURT [*holds out one hand and puts the other on the* CAPTAIN*'s shoulder*]. Old friend!

*

ALICE [*enters left, carrying a parasol*]. My, my, what affection! There's friendship for you!— — —Hasn't the telegram come?

KURT [*coldly*]. No.

ALICE. This delay's making me impatient; and when I get impatient I hurry things along!— — —Watch now, Kurt, I'm going to finish him off. This'll do for him!— — —First I load—I know the drill, you see, the famous rifle-manual that didn't even sell five thousand copies— — —then I take aim: fire! [*She aims with the parasol.*] How is your new wife? That young, beautiful, unknown girl? You don't know. But I know how my lover is! [*Puts her arms around* KURT*'s neck and kisses him; he pushes her away*] He's fine, but still a little shy.— — —You swine, I never loved you, you were too vain to be jealous, you never saw how I led you by the nose!

The CAPTAIN *draws his sabre and rushes at her, hewing wildly, but only succeeds in hitting the furniture.*

ALICE. Help! Help!　　　　　　　　　　[KURT *stands motionless*

CAPTAIN [*falls, with his sabre in his hand*]. Judith! Avenge me!

ALICE. Hurrah! He's dead!

　　　　　　　　KURT *moves towards the rear entrance.*

CAPTAIN [*gets up*]. Not yet! [*Sheathes his sabre and goes and sits in the armchair by the sewing-table.*] Judith! Judith!

ALICE [*goes towards* KURT]. Now I'm going—with you!

KURT [*pushes her away so that she falls to her knees*]. Go to the hell, from whence you came!—Goodbye! For ever!

　　　　　　　　　Starts to leave.

CAPTAIN. Don't leave me, Kurt, she'll kill me!

ALICE. Kurt! Don't desert me, don't desert us!

KURT. Goodbye!　　　　　　　　　　　　　　　　[*Goes

*

ALICE [*changes tack*]. What a wretch! There's a friend for you!

CAPTAIN [*gently*]. Forgive me Alice, and come here! Come quickly!

ALICE [*to the* CAPTAIN]. That's the biggest wretch and hypocrite I've met in all my life.—At least you're a man!

CAPTAIN. Alice, listen!— — —I can't live much longer!

ALICE. Really?

CAPTAIN. The Doctor told me.

ALICE. All the rest, was that untrue, too?

CAPTAIN. Yes!

ALICE [*beside herself*]. Oh, God! What have I done?— — —

CAPTAIN. It can all be put right.

ALICE. Not this!

CAPTAIN. There's nothing that can't be put right, as long as you cross it out and go on.

ALICE. But the telegram! The telegram!

CAPTAIN. What telegram?

ALICE [*on her knees beside the* CAPTAIN]. Are we damned? Did this have to happen? I've blown myself—us—sky high! Why did you have to make all that up? And why did this man have to come and tempt me?— — —We're lost! You, with your generous nature, would have forgiven everything!

CAPTAIN. What is it that's past forgiveness? What haven't I forgiven you?

ALICE. You're right. . . but this time there's no help.

CAPTAIN. Even though I know your fiendish powers of invention, I can't guess. . .

ALICE. Oh, if only I could get out of this! If I could, I'd take care of you. . . Edgar, I'd love you!

CAPTAIN. Just listen to that! What is all this?

ALICE. Can no one help us?. . . No, there's no one on earth who can do that!

CAPTAIN. Who could, then?

ALICE [*looks the* CAPTAIN *in the eyes*]. I don't know!— — —Oh think! What will become of the children when their name's dishonoured...

CAPTAIN. Have you dishonoured our name?

ALICE. Not me! Not me!— — —They'll have to leave school. And when they go out into the world, they'll be as lonely as we are, and just as evil! So you didn't meet Judith either?

CAPTAIN. No! But cross that out, too!

The telegraph starts tapping. ALICE *jumps up.*

ALICE [*screams*]. Now we're done for! Don't listen to it!

CAPTAIN [*calmly*]. My dearest child, I shan't listen, don't get upset— — —

ALICE [*stands beside the telegraph and raises herself on tiptoe so as to see out of the window*]. Don't listen! Don't listen!

CAPTAIN [*covering his ears*]. I'm holding my ears, Lisa, my child.

ALICE [*on her knees, with outstretched hands*]. Oh God! Help us!—It's the 'helping hand'... [*Weeps copiously*] Oh, God in heaven! [*She appears to move her lips, as if praying. The telegraph continues for a short while, and a long strip of paper has crept from it; then it falls silent.* ALICE *gets up, tears off the strip of paper and reads it in silence. Then she glances upwards before going over and kissing the* CAPTAIN] It's all right!—It was nothing!

She sits down in the other chair and cries violently into her handkerchief.

CAPTAIN. Now what are all these secrets?

ALICE. Don't ask! It's over now!

CAPTAIN. As you wish, my child.

ALICE. You wouldn't have spoken like that three days ago; what's come over you?

CAPTAIN. Well, you see, my dear, the first time I collapsed, I was for a moment on the other side of the grave. What I saw I've forgotten, but the impression remained.

ALICE. What was it?

CAPTAIN. The hope—of something better!

ALICE. Something better?

CAPTAIN. Yes. I've never really believed that this was life itself... this is death! Or something even worse...

ALICE. And we...

CAPTAIN. Have apparently been condemned to torment each other... or so it seems.

ALICE. Have we tormented each other enough?

CAPTAIN. Yes, I think so. And what havoc we've wreaked! [*Looks around*]— — —Shall we put the place in order? And clean up?

ALICE [*gets up*]. Yes, if we can.

CAPTAIN [*looks around the room*]. It won't be done in a day. Not this.

ALICE. In two, then! Many days!

CAPTAIN. Let's hope so!— — —

Pause.

CAPTAIN [*sits again*]. So you didn't escape this time. But you didn't get me put away either! [ALICE *is amazed*] Oh, I knew you wanted to have me put in prison; but I'll cross that out!— — —You've probably done worse things than that.— — —[ALICE *is speechless*] And I wasn't guilty of embezzlement!

ALICE. And now I'm to be your nurse?

CAPTAIN. If you wish.

ALICE. What else can I do?

CAPTAIN. I don't know.

ALICE [*sits down apathetically, in despair*]. This must be everlasting hell! Is there no end, then?

CAPTAIN. Yes, if we're patient. Perhaps when death comes, life begins.

ALICE. If only that were so!

Pause.

CAPTAIN. You think Kurt was a hypocrite, don't you?

ALICE. Of course I do!

CAPTAIN. I don't. But everyone who comes near us becomes evil, and then goes their way.— — —Kurt was weak, and evil is strong.

[*Pause*] How banal life is nowadays! In the old days one used to fight; now one merely shakes a fist.—I'm pretty sure that in three months we'll be celebrating our silver wedding... with Kurt as best man.*— — —And the Doctor and Gerda, too.— — —The Ordnance Officer will make a speech and the Sergeant Major'll lead the cheers. If I know the Colonel, he'll invite himself!—Yes, you can laugh! But don't you remember Adolf's silver wedding... that fellow in the Rifles? The bride had to wear her wedding ring on her right hand because in a tender moment the bridegroom had cut off her ring finger with a billhook. [ALICE *holds her handkerchief to her mouth to stifle a laugh*] Are you crying?—No, I believe you're laughing!—Yes, child, we laugh and we cry! Which is more proper? Don't ask me!— — —The other day I read in the paper that a man had been divorced seven times, consequently he'd married seven times as well... Finally, at the age of ninety, he ran off and remarried his first wife. There's love for you!— — — I've never been able to figure out whether life is serious or just a joke. When it's a joke it can be most painful, when it's serious it can be quite tranquil and pleasant.— — —And then, when you finally take it seriously, along comes someone and makes a fool of you. Like Kurt.— — —Do you want to celebrate our silver wedding? [ALICE *says nothing*] Say yes now.—They'll laugh at us, but what does that matter? We'll laugh, too. Or be serious, whichever seems best!

ALICE. All right!

CAPTAIN [*seriously*]. So, our silver wedding!— — —[*Gets up*] Cross out and go on!—All right then, let's go on!

Curtain.

A DREAM PLAY

[*Ett drömspel*]

(1901)

AUTHOR'S NOTE

In this dream play the author has, as in his former dream play, *To Damascus*,* attempted to imitate the inconsequent yet apparently logical form of a dream. Everything can happen, everything is possible and probable. Time and place do not exist; on an insignificant basis of reality the imagination spins and weaves new patterns: a blend of memories, experiences, spontaneous ideas, absurdities, and improvisations.

The characters split, double, multiply, evaporate, condense, disperse, and converge. But one consciousness holds sway over them all, that of the dreamer; for him there are no secrets, no incongruities, no scruples, no law. He neither acquits nor condemns, but merely relates, and, just as a dream is more often painful than happy, so a tone of melancholy and pity for all mortal beings runs through this uncertain tale. Sleep, the liberator, often seems a source of torment, but when the torture is at its worst the sufferer awakes and is reconciled with reality—which, however painful, is yet a mercy, compared with the torment of the dream.*

CHARACTERS*

The Voice of Indra

Indra's Daughter

Agnes

The Glazier

The Officer

The Father

The Mother

Lina

The Stage Doorkeeper

The Billposter

A Ballet Dancer

The Voice of Victoria

A Singer

The Prompter

The Policeman

The Lawyer

The One-Armed Clerk

The One-Eyed Clerk

Kristin

Three Doctoral Candidates

The Quarantine Master

The Dandy

The Coquette

Her 'Friend'

The Poet

He

She

The Retired Man

Three Maids

Edith

Edith's Mother

The Naval Officer

Alice

The Schoolmaster

A Schoolboy

A Newly Married Husband

A Newly Married Wife

The Blind Man

First Coal-Heaver

Second Coal-Heaver

The Gentleman

His Wife

The Chancellor of the University

The Dean of Theology

The Dean of Philosophy

The Dean of Medicine

The Dean of Law

Dancers, Members of the Opera Chorus, Children, Schoolboys, Sailors, All Right-Thinking People, etc.

PROLOGUE*

The backdrop represents banks of clouds resembling crumbling mountains of slate, with ruined castles and fortresses.

    The constellations Leo, Virgo, and Libra can be seen, with the planet Jupiter shining brightly among them.* INDRA'S DAUGHTER* is standing on the highest cloud.

INDRA'S VOICE [*from above*].
    Where are you, Daughter, where?

INDRA'S DAUGHTER.
    Here, Father, here!

INDRA'S VOICE.
    You have strayed, my child, beware, you are sinking...
    How did you come here?

INDRA'S DAUGHTER.
    Riding on a cloud I followed a lightning flash
    From the highest ether...
    But the cloud sank, and now I am downward bound...
    Tell me, oh holy father Indra, to what regions
    I have come? With air so close,
    So hard to breathe?

INDRA'S VOICE.
    You have left the second world and entered the third,*
    From Sukra,* the Morning Star,*
    You have travelled far and reached
    The vapour-laden atmosphere of Earth; mark there
    The seventh House of the Sun, called Libra,*
    Where the day star* hangs in the autumn balance
    When day and night weigh equal.*

INDRA'S DAUGHTER.
    The earth, you said. Is that this dark
    And heavy world there in the light of the moon?

INDRA'S VOICE.
    It is the densest and the heaviest
    Of all the spheres that wander in space.

INDRA'S DAUGHTER.

Does the sun never shine there?

INDRA'S VOICE.

Of course it does, but not always. . .

INDRA'S DAUGHTER.

The cloud is parting, now I can see. . .

INDRA'S VOICE.

What do you see, my child?

INDRA'S DAUGHTER.

I see. . . how beautiful it is. . . green forests,
Blue waters, white mountains, and yellow fields. . .

INDRA'S VOICE.

Yes, it is beautiful like all that Brahma* made. . .
But it was still more beautiful
In the dawn of time; then something happened,
A disturbance in its orbit, something else perhaps,
A revolt followed by a crime that had to be suppressed. . .

INDRA'S DAUGHTER.

Now I can hear sounds from down there. . .
What kind of creatures who dwell there?

INDRA'S VOICE.

Descend and see. . . I would not slander the Creator's children
But what you can hear is their language.

INDRA'S DAUGHTER.

It sounds like. . . it does not have a happy ring.

INDRA'S VOICE.

I can believe it! For their mother tongue
Is called Complaint. Yes! They are
A discontented and ungrateful race. . .

INDRA'S DAUGHTER.

Don't say that, now I can hear shouts of joy
And shots and thunder, look how the lightning flashes,
Now bells are ringing and fires blazing
And a thousand thousand voices
Sing praise and thanks to heaven. . .
You judge them too harshly, Father. . .

INDRA'S VOICE.
  Descend and see, listen and then return,
  And tell me if their complaints
  And lamentations are well-founded...

INDRA'S DAUGHTER.
  Then I shall go down, but come with me, Father!

INDRA'S VOICE.
  No, I cannot breathe that air...

INDRA'S DAUGHTER.
  The cloud is sinking, it's so close, I am choking...
  This is not air but smoke and water I am breathing...
  So heavy, it draws me down, down,
  I can already feel it turn and sway,
  This third world is surely not the best of worlds...

INDRA'S VOICE.
  Not the best, for sure, but nor is it the worst,
  Dust they call it, and it whirls like all the rest,
  So that at times its people dance dizzily,
  On the borderline between folly and insanity—
  Have courage, my child, it is but a trial.

INDRA'S DAUGHTER [*on her knees, as the cloud descends*].
  I am sinking!
                              Curtain.

The backdrop represents a forest of gigantic hollyhocks in flower; white, pink, purple, sulphur-yellow, and violet. Above them can be seen the gilded roof of a castle topped by a flower-bud resembling a crown.* At the base of the castle walls lie heaps of straw spread out over the stable manure.*

The wings, which remain the same throughout the play, are stylized wall paintings simultaneously representing a mixture of interiors, exteriors, and landscapes.

The GLAZIER *and the* DAUGHTER *enter.*

DAUGHTER. The castle keeps on growing out of the earth*... Do you see how much it has grown since last year?

GLAZIER [*to himself*]. I've never seen that castle before... nor heard of a castle that grows... but [*to the* DAUGHTER, *with firm conviction*] Yes, it has grown eight feet, but that's because they have given it some manure... if you look carefully, you can see it has sprouted a wing on the sunny side.

DAUGHTER. Shouldn't it flower soon? After all, we're past midsummer.

GLAZIER. Don't you see the flower up there?

DAUGHTER. Oh yes, yes, I do! [*Claps her hands*]— — —Tell me, Father, why do flowers grow out of dirt?

GLAZIER [*piously*]. Because they don't like the dirt, so they hasten up into the light, to flower and die.

DAUGHTER. Do you know who lives in that castle?

GLAZIER. I did once, but I've forgotten.

DAUGHTER. I believe there's a prisoner inside... someone who is waiting for me to set him free.

GLAZIER. But at what price?

DAUGHTER. One doesn't haggle over what has to be done. Let's go in to the castle!— — —

GLAZIER. Yes, let us go!

*

*They go towards the rear of the stage which slowly opens up towards the
sides, to reveal a simple, bare room with a table and a few chairs. An*
OFFICER *is sitting on one of the chairs, wearing a highly unusual
modern uniform. He is rocking in his chair and striking the table with
his sabre.*

DAUGHTER [*goes up to the* OFFICER *and gently takes the sabre from his
hand*]. Not like that! Not like that!

OFFICER. Oh, please, Agnes,* let me keep my sword!

DAUGHTER. No, you'll break the table! [*To the* GLAZIER] Father,
you go down to the harness room and put in that window pane.
We'll see each other later.   [*The* GLAZIER *leaves*

*

DAUGHTER. You are a prisoner in your own rooms; I have come to
set you free!

OFFICER. That is what I've been waiting for, I suppose, but I wasn't
sure you would want to.

DAUGHTER. The castle is strong, it has seven walls, but—we shall
manage!— — —Well, do you want to or not?

OFFICER. To be quite honest: I don't know, I shall suffer either way!
Every joy in life has to be paid for with double the sorrow. Sitting
here is hard, but were I to buy the pleasures of freedom I'd have to
pay for it twice over in suffering.—Agnes, I'd just as soon stay
here, as long as I can see you!

DAUGHTER. What do you see in me?

OFFICER. The harmony of the universe and its beauty—your form
has lines that are only to be found in the movement of the solar
system, in music at its most beautiful, or in the vibrations of
light.—You are a child of heaven...

DAUGHTER. So are you!

OFFICER. Then why should I have to tend horses? Clean out the
stables and shovel manure?

DAUGHTER. So that you will long to get away!

OFFICER. I do, I do, but it's so hard to work oneself free!

DAUGHTER. But it's our duty to seek freedom in the light!

OFFICER. Duty? Life has never recognized any duties to me!

DAUGHTER. You feel life has treated you badly?

OFFICER. Yes! It has been unjust. . .

*

Voices are now heard from behind a screen which is immediately drawn aside. The OFFICER *and the* DAUGHTER *look in that direction, and then freeze, holding their gestures and expressions.*

The MOTHER, *an invalid, is seated at a table. In front of her is a lighted tallow candle which she trims now and then with a pair of snuffers. On the table lie piles of newly sewn shirts which she is marking with marking-ink and a goose quill. To the left there is a brown wardrobe.*

The FATHER *hands her a silk shawl.*

FATHER [*gently*]. Don't you want it?

MOTHER. A silk shawl for me, my dear? What use is that when I shall die soon?

FATHER. Then you believe what the doctor says?

MOTHER. What he says, yes, but most of all I believe the voice that speaks here, within me.

FATHER [*sorrowfully*]. Then it really is serious?— — —And you think of your children, first and last!

MOTHER. But they were my whole life! My reason for being. . . my joy and my sorrow. . .

FATHER. Kristina, forgive me. . . everything!

MOTHER. For what? You must forgive me, my dear; we have tormented each other. And why? We don't know! We couldn't do otherwise!— — —However, here are the children's new shirts. See they change twice a week now, Wednesdays and Sundays, and that Lovisa washes them— — —all over, mind!— — — Are you going out?

FATHER. I have a meeting at eleven.

MOTHER. Ask Alfred to come in before you go.

FATHER [*points to the* OFFICER]. But, my dear, he's already here. Look!

MOTHER. My eyes are starting to go, too, imagine. . . Yes, it's getting dark. . . [*Trims the candle*] Alfred, come here!

*

The FATHER *goes out through the middle of the wall, nodding goodbye.*

*

The OFFICER *goes over to the* MOTHER.

MOTHER. Who is that girl?

OFFICER [*whispering*]. That is Agnes!

MOTHER. Oh, so that is Agnes, is it? Do you know what they say?— — —That she is the god Indra's daughter, who asked if she could come down here on earth to see what human life is really like— — —But don't say anything!— — —

OFFICER. A god's child, oh yes, she is!

MOTHER [*aloud*]. Alfred dear, I shall soon be leaving you and your brothers and sisters. . . There is just one thing I want you to remember, always.

OFFICER [*sadly*]. Yes, Mother.

MOTHER. Just one thing: Never quarrel with God!

OFFICER. What do you mean, Mother?

MOTHER. You mustn't go around feeling life has been unjust to you.

OFFICER. But when people do treat me unjustly. . .

MOTHER. You're thinking of the time you were unjustly punished for stealing a coin that later came to light!

OFFICER. Yes! And that injustice then warped my whole life. . .

MOTHER. I know. But just go over to that cupboard there. . .

OFFICER [*ashamed*]. So you know! It's. . .

MOTHER. *The Swiss Family Robinson* *. . . For which. . .

OFFICER. Don't go on!. . .

MOTHER. For which your brother was punished. . . and which *you* had torn up and hidden!

OFFICER. Fancy that cupboard still standing there after twenty years... We've moved so often, and my mother died ten years ago.

MOTHER. Well, what of it? You always have to question everything and ruin the best life has to offer you.— — —Ah, here's Lina.

*

LINA [*enters*]. It's very kind of you, Ma'am, but I can't go to the christening...

MOTHER. Why not, child?

LINA. I've nothing to wear.

MOTHER. You can borrow this shawl of mine.

LINA. Oh no, Ma'am, I couldn't do that!

MOTHER. I don't understand you. I shan't be going out again...

*

OFFICER. What will Father say? After all, it was a gift from him to you...

MOTHER. What small minds you all have...

*

FATHER [*sticking his head in*]. Are you going to lend my present to the maid?

MOTHER. Don't talk like that... remember I was once a servant, too... why must you hurt an innocent girl?

FATHER. Why must you hurt me, your husband...

MOTHER. Oh, this life! When you do a good deed, there is always someone who thinks it's bad... help one person, and you hurt another. Oh, this life!

She trims the candle so that it goes out. The stage grows dark and the screen is drawn across again.

*

DAUGHTER. Human beings are to be pitied!*

OFFICER. Do you think so?

DAUGHTER. Yes, life is hard, but love conquers all.* Come and see!
They cross towards the rear.

*

The backdrop is raised and a new one is to be seen representing an old, shabby party-wall. In the middle of the wall is a gate opening on to an alleyway, which leads to a bright green plot where a gigantic blue monkshood can be seen. To the left of the gate sits the STAGE DOOR-KEEPER, *a woman with a shawl over her head and shoulders, crocheting a bed cover patterned with stars. To the right is a cylindrical billboard which the* BILLPOSTER *is cleaning; beside him is a fishing net with a green handle. Farther to the right is a door with an airhole in the shape of a four-leaved clover.* To the left of the gate stands a slender lime tree with a coal-black trunk and several pale-green leaves. Next to it the air vent of a cellar.*

DAUGHTER [*goes up to the* DOORKEEPER]. Isn't the cover finished yet?

DOORKEEPER. No, my dear; twenty-six years is no time at all for something like this.

DAUGHTER. And your sweetheart never came back?

DOORKEEPER. No, but it wasn't his fault. He just *had* to leave... poor fellow; it's thirty years ago.

DAUGHTER [*to the* BILLPOSTER]. She was a ballet dancer, wasn't she? Up there, at the Opera?

BILLPOSTER. She was the best one there... but when *he* up and left, he seemed to take her dancing with him... she never got any more parts...

DAUGHTER. You all complain, at least with your eyes and voices...

BILLPOSTER. I don't complain that much... not now that I've got my net and a green fishing chest!

DAUGHTER. And that makes you happy?

BILLPOSTER. Oh yes, so happy, so... it was my childhood dream... and it's all come true, even though I am fifty now, of course...

DAUGHTER. Fifty years for a fishing net and chest...

BILLPOSTER. A *green* chest, a *green** one...

*

DAUGHTER [*to the* DOORKEEPER]. Give me the shawl now, then I can sit here and watch people passing by. But you must stand behind me and tell me about them.

Takes the shawl and sits down by the gate.

DOORKEEPER. Today's the last day before the opera closes... it's now they learn whether they're being kept on or not...

DAUGHTER. Those who aren't—what about them?

DOORKEEPER. Oh, Lord, that's really something... I always pull the shawl over my head...

DAUGHTER. Poor people!

DOORKEEPER. Look, here comes one now!— — —She hasn't been chosen... Look how she's crying...

*

The SINGER *enters from the right and rushes out through the gate, with a handkerchief to her eyes. She pauses a moment in the alley outside the gate and leans her head against the wall, then goes rapidly out.*

DAUGHTER. Human beings are to be pitied!— — —

DOORKEEPER. Look here, though; here's a happy man for you!

*

The OFFICER *enters down the alleyway wearing a frock coat and a top hat, and carrying a bouquet of roses, radiant and happy.*

DOORKEEPER. He is to marry Miss Victoria!— — —

OFFICER [*downstage; looks up and sings*]. Victoria!

DOORKEEPER. The young lady will be down soon.

OFFICER. Good, good! The carriage is waiting, the table set, and the champagne on ice... May I embrace you, ladies? [*He embraces the* DAUGHTER *and the* DOORKEEPER. *Sings*] Victoria!

WOMAN'S VOICE [*from above, sings*]. I am here!

OFFICER [*begins to stroll back and forth*]. All right! I'll wait!— — —

*

DAUGHTER. Do you know me?

OFFICER. No, I know only one woman... Victoria! For seven years I have walked here and waited for her... at noon when the sun reached the chimneytops and in the evening as darkness began to fall... Look at the asphalt here, and see the footprints of the faithful lover. Hurrah! She is mine! [*Sings*] Victoria! [*He gets no reply*] Well, she'll be dressing now. [*To the* BILLPOSTER] There's the net, I see! Everyone at the Opera is crazy about fishing nets... or rather fish. Because they can't sing, you see. Fish are dumb... What does one like that cost?

BILLPOSTER. It's rather expensive!

OFFICER [*singing*]. Victoria!— — —[*Shakes the lime tree*] Look, it's in leaf again! The eighth time!— — —[*Sings*] Victoria!— — — Now she's combing her fringe!— — —[*To the* DAUGHTER] Come on now, Madam, let me go up and fetch my bride!— — —

DOORKEEPER. No one's allowed on stage!

OFFICER. Seven years I've been walking up and down here! Seven times three hundred and sixty-five makes two thousand five hundred and fifty-five! [*Stops and pokes at the door with the four-leafed clover*]— — —And this door—I've seen it two thousand five hundred and fifty-five times and I still don't know where it leads! And this clover leaf to let in the light... light for whom?—Is there anyone in there? Does someone live there?

DOORKEEPER. I don't know. I've never seen it opened.— — —

OFFICER. It looks like a pantry door I saw when I was four and went out visiting with the maid one Sunday afternoon. To other families and other maids. But I never got beyond the kitchen, I just sat between the water butt and the salt tub; I've seen so many kitchens in my time, and the pantry was always by the entrance, with round holes and a clover leaf in the door.— — —But the Opera has no pantry because it doesn't have a kitchen. [*Sings*] Victoria!— — — But listen now, she can't get out some other way, can she?

DOORKEEPER. No, this is the only way out!

OFFICER. Good, then I can't miss her!

Members of the Company come pouring out of the Opera House, and are looked over by the OFFICER.

*

OFFICER. She must be here soon now!— — —You know, that flower out there, the blue monkshood. There was one like that when I was a child... Is it the same one, do you think?— — —I remember in a rectory garden, when I was seven... there are two doves, blue doves under that hood*... but that time a bee came and flew into the hood... then I thought: 'now I've got you!' And I pinched the flower together, but the bee stung me, right through it, and I cried... but then the parson's wife came and put some wet earth on it... Then we had wild strawberries and milk for supper!— — —I do believe it's already getting dark!—[*To the* BILL- POSTER] Where are you going?

BILLPOSTER. Home for supper.

OFFICER [*puts his hand to his eyes*]. Supper? At this time of day?— — — —Listen!— — —May I go in for a moment and telephone the Growing Castle?

DAUGHTER. What for?

OFFICER. I must tell the Glazier to put in double windows; it will soon be winter and I'm already freezing.

He goes into the DOORKEEPER'*s lodge.*

*

DAUGHTER. Who is Miss Victoria?

DOORKEEPER. The woman he loves!

DAUGHTER. Well put! It doesn't matter to him what she is to us or other people. It's what she is to *him* that matters!— — —

It grows suddenly dark.

DOORKEEPER [*lights a lamp*]. It's getting dark quickly today!

DAUGHTER. To the gods a year is as a minute!

DOORKEEPER. And to us on earth a minute can be as long as a year!

*

OFFICER [*comes out again. He looks dusty; his roses have withered*]. Hasn't she come yet?

DOORKEEPER. No!

OFFICER. She *will* come!——— *She's* sure to come! [*He strolls back and forth*]— — —But all the same, perhaps it would be wiser to cancel that lunch... since it's already evening!— — —Yes, I'll do that!   [*Goes in and telephones*

*

DOORKEEPER [*to the* DAUGHTER]. May I have my shawl now?

DAUGHTER. No, my friend, you rest a little longer; I'll take your place— — —I want to learn about people and life, so I can find out if it's as hard as they say it is.

DOORKEEPER. But you can't sleep at your post here, not for a moment, night or day...

DAUGHTER. Not even at night?

DOORKEEPER. Well, if you can with the bell-cord tied to your arm— — —there are night-watchmen on the stage, who are relieved every three hours...

DAUGHTER. But that must be torture...

DOORKEEPER. You may think so, but people like me are only too pleased to get a job like this. If you only knew how envied I am...

DAUGHTER. Envied? One is envied for being tortured?

DOORKEEPER. Yes! — — —But do you know what is worse than the long nights and the drudgery, the draughts, the cold, and the damp? Having all those unhappy people up there confide in you, as they do in me... They all come to me. Why? Maybe they read in the furrows of my face the runes that suffering carves, and that invites their confidences... Hidden in that shawl, my dear, are thirty years of anguish, mine and other people's!— — —

DAUGHTER. It's heavy, too, and it stings like nettles...

DOORKEEPER. Wear it if you like then... when it gets too heavy, call me, and I'll come and relieve you.

DAUGHTER. Goodbye! If you can bear it, then surely I can too!

DOORKEEPER. We shall see!— — —But be kind to my little friends and don't weary of their complaints.

She disappears down the alleyway. The stage is plunged into pitch darkness. Meanwhile the scenery is changed so that the lime tree loses its leaves. The blue monkshood has withered and when the light returns the greenery at the end of the path is an autumnal brown. The OFFICER *enters as the light comes up. He now has grey hair and a grey beard. His clothes are shabby, his collar soiled and limp. The bouquet of roses is so withered that only the stems remain. He wanders back and forth.*

OFFICER. All the signs are that summer is past—and autumn is at hand.—I can tell by the lime tree there, and the monkshood.— — —[*Paces back and forth*] But the autumn is *my* spring, because that's when the theatre opens again. And then she's bound to come! Dear lady, may I sit on this chair for a while?

DAUGHTER. You sit, my friend, I can stand.

OFFICER [*sits down*]. If only I could sleep a little, things would be better!... [*He falls asleep for a moment, then jumps up and starts to pace about again. He stops before the door with the clover leaf and pokes at it*] This door, it won't let me rest... what is there behind it? There must be something! [*Soft music in dance rhythm is heard from above*] So! Rehearsals have begun. [*The stage is now illuminated intermittently as if by the beam of a lighthouse*] What's this? [*In time with the flashes of light*] Light and dark; light and dark?

DAUGHTER [*imitates him*]. Day and night; day and night!— — —A merciful providence wants to shorten your waiting, and so the days take flight, pursuing the nights!

The light on stage becomes constant again. The BILLPOSTER *enters carrying his fishing net and billposting equipment.*

OFFICER. It's the Billposter, with his net... How was the fishing? Good?

BILLPOSTER. Oh, yes! The summer was warm and rather long... the net was pretty good, but not *quite* as I'd imagined it!

OFFICER [*accentuating the words*]. Not quite as I'd imagined it! — — —That's very well put! Nothing is ever as I'd imagined it!... because the idea is always greater than the deed—is superior to the object...

He walks up and down striking the bouquet of roses against the walls so that it loses its last leaves.

BILLPOSTER. Hasn't she come down yet?

OFFICER. No, not yet, but she'll come soon!— — —Do you know what's behind that door?

BILLPOSTER. No, I've never seen that door open.

OFFICER. I am going to telephone for a locksmith to come and open it.   [*He goes in to telephone*

The BILLPOSTER *pastes up a poster and then moves to exit right.*

DAUGHTER. What was wrong with the net?

BILLPOSTER. Wrong? Well, there wasn't anything wrong, not really... it just wasn't as I'd imagined it, and so the pleasure wasn't *that* great...

DAUGHTER. Just how had you imagined it?

BILLPOSTER. How?— — —I can't really say...

DAUGHTER. Let me tell you!— — —You had imagined it a little differently! Green, yes, but not *that* green!

BILLPOSTER. You do know, don't you! You know everything— that's why everyone comes to you with their worries!— — — Now if you'd only listen to me too, just this once...

DAUGHTER. Of course I will, gladly... Come in here and tell me everything...   [*She goes into her room*

The BILLPOSTER *stands outside the window, talking.*

*

It grows pitch dark again; then it gets lighter; and now the lime tree is in leaf once more and the monkshood is in flower. The sun is shining on the greenery at the end of the alley. The OFFICER *enters. He is now old and white haired, in tatters, with worn-out shoes. He is carrying the remains of the bouquet of roses. He walks back and forth, slowly like an old man. He reads the poster.*

*

A member of the corps de ballet enters from the right.

OFFICER. Has Miss Victoria gone?

BALLET DANCER. No, not yet.

OFFICER. Then I'll wait!—She'll be along soon, will she?

BALLET DANCER [*earnestly*]. Oh, yes, I'm sure she will.

OFFICER. Don't go now, then you'll be able to see what's behind this door. I have sent for the locksmith.

BALLET DANCER. It will be really interesting to see that door opened. That door and the growing castle. Do you know the growing castle?

OFFICER. Do I just?—Why, I was a prisoner there!

BALLET DANCER. No, was that you? But why did they have so many horses there?

OFFICER. It was a horse castle, of course. . .

BALLET DANCER [*hurt*]. How stupid of me, not to realize that!

*

A member of the opera chorus enters from the right.

OFFICER. Has Miss Victoria gone?

SINGER [*seriously*]. No, she hasn't gone! She never goes!

OFFICER. That is because she loves me!— — —But you mustn't go now, not before the locksmith comes. He's going to open this door.

SINGER. Oh, is the door to be opened? What fun!— — —I just want to ask the Doorkeeper something.

*

The PROMPTER *enters from the right.*

OFFICER. Has Miss Victoria gone?

PROMPTER. No, not as far as I know.

OFFICER. You see! Didn't I say she would wait for me!—Don't go, the door's going to be opened.

PROMPTER. Which door?

OFFICER. Is there more than one?

PROMPTER. Oh, I know—the one with the four-leafed clover!— — —Then I shall certainly stay.—I must just have a word with the Doorkeeper.

*

The BALLET DANCER, *the* SINGER, *and the* PROMPTER *form a group
beside the* BILLPOSTER *outside the* DOORKEEPER'S *window where they
speak to the* DAUGHTER *in turn. The* GLAZIER *enters via the gate.*

OFFICER. Are you the locksmith?

GLAZIER. No, the locksmith was out on call; but a glazier will do just
as well.

OFFICER. Yes, of course— — —of course. But have you brought
your diamond with you?

GLAZIER. Naturally! Whoever heard of a glazier without a diamond?*

OFFICER. That's true!—Let's get to work then!

*He claps his hands. They all gather in a circle around the door. Singers
from the chorus in* Die Meistersinger* *and dancers and extras in* Aida*
pour onstage from the right.

*

OFFICER. Locksmith—or Glazier—do your duty! [*The* GLAZIER
steps forward, with his diamond] Such moments as this are rare in
a man's life, therefore my friends, I beg you... consider carefully...

*

POLICEMAN [*approaches*]. In the name of the law I forbid the opening of this door!

OFFICER. Oh, God, the trouble there is when you try to do something new and important!— — —But we'll take this to court!
— — —To the lawyer, then! We'll see what the law has to say
about this!—To the lawyer!

*

*In full view of the audience the scene changes to a lawyer's office thus: the
gate remains and functions as the gate to the office railing which extends
right across the stage. The* DOORKEEPER'S *room remains as the*
LAWYER'S *nook containing his desk, but opens to the front of the stage;
the lime tree, stripped of leaves, is a hat-and-clothes stand. The poster
hoarding is covered with official notices and court papers. The door with
the four-leafed clover has now become a filing cabinet.*

The LAWYER *in white tie and tails is sitting to the left inside the gate at a desk covered with papers. His appearance bears witness to extreme suffering; his face is chalk-white and heavily lined, with purple shadows. He is ugly, and his face reflects all the kinds of crimes and vices in which his profession has necessarily involved him.*

Of his two CLERKS, *the first has only one arm and the other is one-eyed.*

The crowd that had gathered to see the opening of the door remain on stage, now as clients waiting to see the LAWYER. *They appear to have been standing there forever.*

The DAUGHTER *(wearing the shawl) and the* OFFICER *are the furthest downstage.*

LAWYER [*goes up to the* DAUGHTER]. May I have the shawl, my dear— — —I'll hang it in here until I light the stove; then I'll burn it with all its griefs and sorrows— — —

DAUGHTER. Not yet, my friend, I want it to be really full first, above all I want to gather up all your sufferings, all the confidences you have ever received about crimes, vices, false arrests, slanders, and libels...

LAWYER. Your shawl wouldn't suffice, my child. Look at these walls; isn't it as though the wallpaper is soiled with every kind of sin? Look at these papers where I record instances of injustice; look at *me*... Nobody who comes here ever smiles; nothing but angry looks, bared teeth, and clenched fists... And all of them squirt their malice, their envy, their suspicions over me... Look, my hands are black, and can never be washed clean, just look how cracked and bloody they are... I can never wear clothes for more than one or two days because they stink of other people's crimes... Sometimes I have the place fumigated with sulphur, but that doesn't help; I sleep in the next room, and dream of nothing but crimes— — —At the moment I have a murder case at court — — —but however terrible that may be, do you know what is even worse?— — —Separating husbands and wives!—Then it's as if the very earth and heaven itself cried out... cried treason against the origin of life, against the source of good, against love... And you know, after both parties have filled reams of paper with their mutual accusations and some kind soul takes one or other of them aside, tweaks him or her by the ear, and asks, in a friendly sort of way, 'What have you really got against your husband—or wife?'—then he—or she—just stands there, speechless, without the faintest idea! Once—well, it had something to do with a green salad, another time it was some word or other, mostly it's about nothing at all. But the pain, the suffering! Which I have to bear! — — —Take a look at me! And tell me if you think I could win a woman's love with this criminal's face? And do you think that anyone wants to be friends with a man who has to collect all the city's debts?— — —What is life if not misery?

DAUGHTER. Human beings are to be pitied!

LAWYER. So they are! And yet what people live on is a mystery to me. They marry on an income of two thousand crowns when they need four— — —then they borrow, of course, everyone does! And then they scrape along or muddle through until they die— — —always in debt! Who has to pay in the end, you tell me that?

DAUGHTER. He who feeds the birds!*

LAWYER. Yes! But if He who feeds the birds were to come down to His earth and see how we poor mortals fare, maybe He would feel some compassion. . .

DAUGHTER. Human beings are to be pitied!

LAWYER. Indeed they are!—[*To the* OFFICER] What do you want?

*

OFFICER. I only wanted to ask if Miss Victoria has gone!

LAWYER. No, she hasn't, you needn't worry.— — —Why do you keep poking away at my cupboard?

OFFICER. I thought the door was just like. . .

LAWYER. Oh no, oh no; no!

The sound of church bells is heard.

*

OFFICER. Is there a funeral in town?

LAWYER. No, they are conferring degrees, doctor's degrees. And I am just about to go and receive my doctorate in law! Perhaps you would like to graduate too and get a laurel wreath?

OFFICER. Yes, why not? It would make a change...

LAWYER. Then perhaps we should proceed at once to the ceremony?—Just go and change your clothes.

The OFFICER *leaves. The stage now grows dark and the following changes
occur: the barrier remains but now serves as the chancel rail in a church;
the poster hoarding becomes the number board listing the hymns; the lime
tree/coat-stand becomes a candelabra; the* LAWYER's *desk becomes the*
CHANCELLOR's *lectern; the door with the four-leafed clover now leads to
the vestry.*

The chorus from Die Meistersinger *become* HERALDS *carrying
sceptres while the* DANCERS *carry the laurel wreaths.*

The rest of the people become spectators.

*The backdrop is raised. The new one represents a single large organ
with a keyboard below, and the mirror above it.*

Music is heard. To the sides the DEANS *of the four faculties of*
PHILOSOPHY, THEOLOGY, MEDICINE, *and* LAW.*

After a moment the HERALDS *enter from the right followed by the*
DANCERS *holding their laurel wreaths before them at arm's length. Three*
CANDIDATES *enter one behind the other from the left, and are crowned by
the* DANCERS *before exiting right. The* LAWYER *steps forward to be
crowned with laurels.* *The* DANCERS *turn away, refusing to crown him,
and go out. The* LAWYER, *shaken, leans against a pillar. Everyone goes
out, leaving the* LAWYER *alone.*

*

DAUGHTER [*enters, with a white veil over her head and shoulders*].
Look, I've washed the shawl— — —But why are you standing
here? Didn't you get your wreath?

LAWYER. No, I wasn't worthy.

DAUGHTER. Why not? Because you spoke up for the poor, put in a
good word for the criminal, lightened the burden of the guilty,
won respite for the condemned... These poor people... they may
not be angels; but they are to be pitied.

LAWYER. Don't speak badly of mankind, I have to plead on their
behalf, after all...

DAUGHTER [*leaning against the organ*]. Why do they spit in the face
of anyone who wants to help them?

LAWYER. They don't know any better!

DAUGHTER. Let us enlighten them! You and I together! Will you?

LAWYER. They will not accept enlightenment!... Oh, if only the gods in heaven would hear our complaint— — —

DAUGHTER. It shall reach the throne itself!— — —[*Sits at the organ*] Do you know what I see in this mirror?— — —The world set to rights!— — —Yes, as it is, it's the wrong way round!— — —

LAWYER. How did it come to be the wrong way round?

DAUGHTER. When the copy was made...

LAWYER. That's it! The copy... I always did think it was a faulty copy... and when I began to recall what the original images were like,* I grew dissatisfied with everything... People called me hard to please and said I had bits of the devil's mirror in my eye,* and a whole lot more besides...

DAUGHTER. It is crazy, too! Just look at these four faculties!— — — So as to keep things as they are the government supports all four of them: theology, the doctrine of God, which is always attacked and ridiculed by philosophy, which claims to be wisdom itself. And medicine, which always questions the validity of philosophy, and doesn't consider theology a science but a superstition... And they all sit together in the same council which is supposed to teach the young respect—for the university. It's nothing but a madhouse! Heaven help whoever first sees sense!

LAWYER. That will be the theologians.—They start off reading philosophy, which teaches them that theology is nonsense; then they learn in theology that philosophy is nonsense! Madmen, eh?

DAUGHTER. And law, which serves everyone, except the servants!

LAWYER. Justice that destroys itself in seeking to be just!— — — Right, that so often fosters wrong!!!

DAUGHTER. What a mess you children of men have made of your lives! Yes, children!—Come, I'll give you a wreath— — —one that will become you more! [*Places a crown of thorns on his head*]* Now I'll play for you.

She sits at the organ and plays a Kyrie;* but instead of organ music human voices are heard.

CHILDREN'S VOICES. Eternal One! Eternal One!

The final note is prolonged.

WOMEN'S VOICES. Have mercy on us!

The final note is prolonged.

MALE VOICES [*tenors*]. Save us, for Thy mercy's sake!

The final note is prolonged.

MALE VOICES [*basses*]. Spare Thy children, O Lord, and be not wrathful against us!

*

ALL. Be merciful! Hear us! Have pity on us mortals!—Eternal One, why art Thou so far from us?— — —Out of the depths we call: 'Mercy, oh Eternal One! Place not too heavy a burden upon Thy children! Hear us! Hear us!'*

*

The stage grows dark. The DAUGHTER *stands up and goes over to the* LAWYER. *By lighting, the organ is transformed into Fingal's Cave.* The sea surges in under the basalt pillars, producing the combined sound of wind and waves.*

LAWYER. Where are we, sister?

DAUGHTER. What do you hear?

LAWYER. I hear the drops as they fall— — —

DAUGHTER. Those are the tears of people crying... What else do you hear?

LAWYER. A sighing... a wailing... a moaning...

DAUGHTER. Mankind's lament has reached this far... and no further. But why this eternal lamentation? Is there no joy in life at all?

LAWYER. Yes, the sweetest which is also the most bitter, love! Marriage and a home! The highest and the lowest!

DAUGHTER. Let me try it!

LAWYER. With me?

DAUGHTER. With you! You know the rocks, the stumbling-blocks, we can avoid them.

LAWYER. I am poor!

DAUGHTER. What does that matter, as long as we love each other? And a little beauty costs nothing.

LAWYER. But what if my likes are your dislikes?

DAUGHTER. Then we can compromise!

LAWYER. Suppose we grow tired of each other?

DAUGHTER. Then the child that comes will be a never-ending source of delight!

LAWYER. You want me, poor and ugly, despised, rejected?

DAUGHTER. Yes! Let us join our destinies!

LAWYER. So be it, then!

Curtain.

A very simple room adjoining the LAWYER'S *office. To the right a large canopied double bed; next to it a window.*

To the left an iron stove with pots and pans. KRISTIN *is busy pasting strips of paper around the edges of the inner windows.**

Upstage, an open door to the office, where a number of poor people can be seen waiting to be admitted.

KRISTIN. I'm pasting, I'm pasting!

DAUGHTER [*pale and worn, seated by the stove*]. You're shutting out the air. I'm suffocating!...

KRISTIN. Now there's only one little crack left!

DAUGHTER. Air, air, I can't breathe!

KRISTIN. I'm pasting, I'm pasting!

LAWYER [*in the doorway, with a document in his hand*]. That's right, Kristin; heat costs money!

DAUGHTER. Oh, it's as though you were gluing my mouth up!

LAWYER. Is the child asleep?

DAUGHTER. Yes, at last!

LAWYER [*mildly*]. Its crying frightens away my clients.

DAUGHTER [*friendly*]. What can we do about it?

LAWYER. Nothing!

DAUGHTER. We shall have to get a bigger apartment.

LAWYER. We have no money!

DAUGHTER. May I open the window; the air in here is stifling?

LAWYER. Then all the warmth will escape, and we shall freeze.

DAUGHTER. This is awful!— — —Can't we at least scrub the floor out there?

LAWYER. You haven't the strength, nor have I, and Kristin has to do the pasting; she must paste over every crack in the house, ceilings, floors, and walls.

DAUGHTER. I was prepared for poverty, but not for dirt!

LAWYER. Poverty is always dirty, more or less.

DAUGHTER. I never dreamt it would be like this!

LAWYER. It could be a whole lot worse. At least there's still some food in the pot.

DAUGHTER. Do you call that food?— — —

LAWYER. Cabbage is cheap, nourishing, and good.

DAUGHTER. If you happen to like cabbage. I can't stand it!

LAWYER. Why didn't you say so?

DAUGHTER. Because I loved you! I wanted to make a sacrifice!

LAWYER. Then I must sacrifice my love of cabbage for you. The sacrifice must be mutual—

DAUGHTER. Then what shall we eat? Fish? You hate fish.

LAWYER. And it's expensive!

DAUGHTER. This is much harder than I thought!

LAWYER [*friendly*]. You see how hard it is!— — —And the child, which should be our bond and blessing— — —is our undoing!

DAUGHTER. Dearest! I am dying in this air, in this room, with its window overlooking the yard and the child's endless crying, not a moment's sleep, and all those people out there with their complaining, squabbling, and accusations... If I stay here I shall die!

LAWYER. My poor little flower, with no light, no air...

DAUGHTER. And yet you say there are other people even worse off than we are.

LAWYER. I am among the most envied people in the neighbourhood!

DAUGHTER. Everything would be all right if only I could have a little beauty in our home.

LAWYER. I know what you have in mind—a flower, a heliotrope,* maybe. But they cost one crown fifty, that is six litres of milk or two pecks of potatoes.

DAUGHTER. I would gladly go without food if only I could have my flower.

LAWYER. There is one kind of beauty that doesn't cost anything, but for a man with a sense of beauty it's the worst possible torment when he doesn't find it in his home.

DAUGHTER. What is that?

LAWYER. If I tell you, you will be angry.

DAUGHTER. We have agreed never to be angry.

LAWYER. We have agreed... Everything will be all right, Agnes, as long as we avoid those sharp, hard tones... You know the ones I mean?—No, not yet you don't!

DAUGHTER. We shall never use them!

LAWYER. Never if I have anything to do with it.

DAUGHTER. So, now tell me!

LAWYER. Well, when I enter a house I look first to see if the curtain hangs straight on its rail... [*He goes over to the window and straightens the curtain*] If it hangs like a rope or a rag... I leave right away!———Then I glance at the chairs... if they are where they should be, I stay!... [*He puts a chair straight against the wall*]— Next I look at the candles... If they are crooked, then the whole house is awry. [*He straightens a candle on the bureau*] ———Now that, my dear, is the kind of beauty that doesn't cost anything!

DAUGHTER [*bowing her head*]. Not that sharp tone, Axel!

LAWYER. It wasn't sharp!

DAUGHTER. Yes it was!

LAWYER. Oh, for Christ's sake!...

DAUGHTER. What kind of language is that?

LAWYER. Forgive me, Agnes! But I have suffered from your untidyness as much as you suffer from dirt. And I haven't dared set things to right myself because then you get so angry, as if I was reproaching you... Ugh! Shall we stop now?

DAUGHTER. Being married is so hard... it is the hardest thing of all. I believe you have to be an angel.

LAWYER. So do I!

DAUGHTER. I think I am beginning to hate you after this!

LAWYER. Then heaven help us!———But let us beware of hatred. I promise I shall never mention your untidyness again... even though it is a torture to me.

DAUGHTER. And I shall eat cabbage, even though that torments me.

LAWYER. A life tormenting each other, then! One person's pleasure is the other's pain!

DAUGHTER. Human beings are to be pitied!

LAWYER. You see that now?

DAUGHTER. Yes. But in God's name let us avoid the rocks, now that we know them so well!

LAWYER. Let us do that!—After all, we are humane and enlightened people; we can forgive and forget.

DAUGHTER. Why, we can smile at such trifles!

LAWYER. If anyone can, we can!— — —You know, I read in the paper this morning. . . by the way—where is the paper?

DAUGHTER [*embarrassed*]. Which paper?

LAWYER [*harshly*]. Do I take more than one paper?

DAUGHTER. Now smile, and don't speak sharply. . . I used your paper to light the fire. . .

LAWYER [*violently*]. Oh, for Christ's sake!

DAUGHTER. Now smile!— — —I burned it because it ridiculed all that I hold sacred. . .

LAWYER. Which isn't sacred to me. Right!— — —[*Strikes one fist into his other hand, beside himself*] Oh, I shall smile, I shall smile so my hind teeth show. . . I shall be humane and sweep my opinions under the carpet, and say yes to everything, and creep around and play the hypocrite! So, you've burned my paper, have you? [*Rearranges the bed curtain*] You see! Now I'm tidying up again, and making you angry!— — —Agnes, this is simply impossible!

DAUGHTER. Yes, it is.

LAWYER. And yet we must carry on, not because of our vows, but for the sake of the child.

DAUGHTER. That's true. For the sake of the child! Oh!—Oh! — — —We must carry on!

LAWYER. And now I must attend to my clients. Listen, they're buzzing with impatience; they can't wait to tear each other apart, to have each other fined and imprisoned. . . lost souls. . .

DAUGHTER. Poor, poor people! And this pasting!

She bows her head in dumb despair.

KRISTIN. I'm pasting, I'm pasting!

The LAWYER *stands by the door, nervously fingering the doorhandle.*

DAUGHTER. Oh, how that handle squeaks; it's as though you were twisting a knife in my heart...

LAWYER. I'm twisting, I'm twisting...

DAUGHTER. Stop it!

LAWYER. I'm twisting...

DAUGHTER. No!

LAWYER. I'm...

*

OFFICER [*from the office, taking hold of the handle*].   Allow me!

LAWYER [*letting go of the handle*].   Go ahead! Since you are now a doctor!

OFFICER. The whole world is mine! All paths stand open to me, I have climbed Parnassus,* and won my laurels, immortality, honour, it is all mine!

LAWYER. What will you live on?

OFFICER. Live on?

LAWYER. Surely you need a home, clothes, some food?

OFFICER. Oh, that's no problem, not as long as you have someone who loves you.

LAWYER. I can imagine!— — —Indeed, I can!— — —Paste away, Kristin. Paste! Until they can't breathe!

[*He goes out backwards, nodding*

KRISTIN. I'm pasting, I'm pasting, until they can't breathe!

*

OFFICER. Well, are you coming?

DAUGHTER. At once! But where?

OFFICER. To Fairhaven! There it is summer, there the sun is shining and there are young people, children, and flowers; singing and dancing, parties and feasting!

DAUGHTER. Then that is where I want to go.

OFFICER. Come on, then!

*

LAWYER [*re-enters*]. Now—I am returning to my first hell— — — this was the second— — —and the worst! The greatest happiness is the greatest hell— — —Look, now she's gone and dropped hairpins on the floor again!...   [*He picks one up*

OFFICER. Imagine, now he's found the hairpins, too!

LAWYER. Too?— — —Look at this one! There are two prongs, but one pin. It is two and yet one. If I straighten it out, it is all one piece. If I bend it, it is two, but without ceasing to be one. That means: the two are one. But if I break it—like this! Then the two are two!   [*He snaps the hairpin in two and throws the pieces away*

OFFICER. He has seen it all!... But before you can break it, the prongs have to diverge. If they converge, it holds.

LAWYER. And if they are parallel—then they never meet—it neither holds nor breaks.

OFFICER. The hairpin is the most perfect of all created things. At once a straight line and two parallels.

LAWYER. A lock that closes when it is open.

OFFICER. Enclosing while open a plait of hair that remains open when it is enclosed...

LAWYER. Like this door: when I close it, I open the way out for you, Agnes!   [*Goes out and shuts the door*

*

DAUGHTER. Now what?

Change of scene: the bed with its hangings is transformed into a tent; the iron stove remains; the backcloth is raised and to the right we see in the foreground charred mountain sides with red heather and black and white stumps following a forest fire; red pigsties and outhouses. Below this an open-air gymnasium where people are exercising on machines that resemble instruments of torture.*

To the left, in the foreground, part of the open shed of the quarantine building* with its ovens; furnace walls and piping.

In the middle ground the water between two islands; in the background a beautiful wooded beach with jetties decorated with flags where white boats have been moored, some with their sails hoisted, some not. Small Italian-style villas,* pavilions, summer-houses, and marble statues can be seen along the shore, among the foliage.

The QUARANTINE MASTER, *dressed as a blackamoor, is walking along the beach.*

OFFICER [*steps forward and shakes his hand*]. Well, if it isn't Ordström!* Have you fetched up here?

QUARANTINE MASTER. Yes, here I am, you see!

OFFICER. Is this Fairhaven?

QUARANTINE MASTER. No, that's over there; this is Foulstrand.*

OFFICER. Then we've come wrong.

QUARANTINE MASTER. We?—Aren't you going to introduce me?

OFFICER. No, that wouldn't be proper. [*Low*] This is Indra's own daughter!

QUARANTINE MASTER. Indra's? I thought it was Varuna* himself!— — —Well, aren't you surprised at my black face?

OFFICER. My dear boy, I'm past fifty, nothing surprises me any more!—I assumed right away you were going to a fancy-dress ball this afternoon.

QUARANTINE MASTER. Correct! And you'll both come with me, I hope?

OFFICER. Of course; this place... well, it's not exactly appealing!... What kind of people live here?

QUARANTINE MASTER. Only the sick, the healthy live over there.

OFFICER. Nothing but poor people here, then?

QUARANTINE MASTER. No, old man, these are the rich! Look at that one on the rack over there. He's eaten too much *pâté-de-foie-gras* with truffles, and drunk so much burgundy his feet have got knots in them.

OFFICER. Knots?

QUARANTINE MASTER. That's right, feet like knotted wood! — — — And that one over there on the guillotine; he's drunk so much Hennessy* that his spine needs putting through the mangle.

OFFICER. That can't be much fun!

QUARANTINE MASTER. The fact is, everyone on this side has got some misfortune or other to hide. Take that one over there, for example.

An elderly DANDY *is wheeled on to the stage in a wheelchair, accompanied by a sixty-year-old* COQUETTE *dressed in the latest fashion and attended by her 'FRIEND', a man of forty.*

OFFICER. Why, it's the Major! Our old schoolfellow!

QUARANTINE MASTER. Don Juan! You see, he's still in love with that Spectre at his side. He doesn't see that she's grown old, that she's ugly, faithless, and cruel!

OFFICER. There's love for you! I'd never have believed that old libertine had it in him to love so deeply and so long.

QUARANTINE MASTER. That's putting it very nicely!

OFFICER. I have been in love myself, with Victoria— — —yes, I still haunt the corridor,* waiting for her— — —

QUARANTINE MASTER. So you're the one who walks the corridor, are you?

OFFICER. Yes, that's me!

QUARANTINE MASTER. Well, have you got the door opened yet?

OFFICER. No, we're still fighting the case— — —The Billposter's out with his fishing-net, of course, so the hearing has been delayed... in the meantime, the Glazier has fixed the windows in the castle, which has grown half a storey... It has been an unusually good year, this year— — —Warm and damp!

QUARANTINE MASTER. But you've still not had it as warm as I have in here!

OFFICER. How warm are your ovens then?

QUARANTINE MASTER. When we disinfect cholera suspects, we set them at sixty degrees centigrade.

OFFICER. Cholera? Is that loose again then?

QUARANTINE MASTER. Didn't you know?— — —

OFFICER. Yes, of course, but I so often forget what I know!

QUARANTINE MASTER. I often wish I could forget, especially about myself; that's why I'm so fond of masquerades, dressing up, and theatricals.

OFFICER. What have you been up to, then?

QUARANTINE MASTER. If I talk about it people say I'm boasting; if I keep quiet they call me a hypocrite.

OFFICER. Is that why you've blacked your face?

QUARANTINE MASTER. Yes. A little blacker than I really *am*!

OFFICER. Who is that coming now?

QUARANTINE MASTER. Oh, just some poet, going to have his mud-bath.*

The POET *enters, gazing at the sky, and carrying a pail filled with mud.*

OFFICER. But surely he should be bathing in light and air!

QUARANTINE MASTER. No, he spends so much time up there that he gets homesick for mud... And wallowing in the mire makes his skin tough, like a pig's. Then he doesn't feel the gadfly's sting.

OFFICER. This curious world of contradictions!

*

POET [*ecstatically*]. Of clay the god Ptah* created man on a potter's wheel, a lathe, [*sceptically*] or some other damned thing!— — — [*Ecstatically*] Of clay the sculptor creates his more or less immortal masterpieces [*sceptically*] which are usually nothing but junk! [*Ecstatically*] Of clay are formed these vessels so essential for the pantry, which are commonly called jars and plates, [*sceptically*] though really I don't give a damn what they're called! [*Ecstatically*] This is clay! In its liquid state they call it mud—*C'est mon affaire!** [*Calls*] Lina!

*

LINA *enters, carrying a bucket.*

POET. Lina, show yourself to Miss Agnes!—She knew you ten years ago when you were a young, happy, and, let us say, beautiful girl... Now look at her! Five children and a life of drudgery, squabbling, hunger, and blows! Look how her beauty has faded, how her joy has vanished even though she has fulfilled those duties which ought to have brought her the kind of inner contentment to be found in a perfectly formed face and the still glow of the eyes...

QUARANTINE MASTER [*putting his hand over the* POET'S *mouth*]. Shut up! Shut up!

POET. That's what they all say! But if you do remain silent, they insist you speak! How impossible people are!

*

DAUGHTER [*goes up to* LINA]. Tell me your troubles?

LINA. No, I daren't, it would only make things worse!

DAUGHTER. Who would be so cruel?

LINA. I daren't say anything, or they'll beat me!

POET. That's the way it is, sometimes. But I'll not keep quiet even if this blackamoor does want to knock my teeth out!— — — Let me tell you, injustice can and does occur.— — — Agnes, daughter of the gods! Do you hear that music and dancing up there on the hillside?—Well!— — —That is Lina's sister who has come home from the city where she went astray, if you know what I mean... Now they are killing the fatted calf* while Lina, who stayed at home, has to carry the swill and feed the pigs!— — —

DAUGHTER. They are rejoicing because the one who went astray has forsaken the path of evil, not just because she has come home. Remember that!

POET. But in that case why don't they have a dance and supper every evening for this blameless working-girl who has never gone astray?— — —They never do, though. When Lina does have any time off she has to go to church, where they reproach her for not being perfect. Is that just?

DAUGHTER. Your questions are so hard to answer, because... there are so many unforeseen circumstances...

POET. That's what the caliph, Haroun the Just,* thought too.— Sitting there calmly on his throne he never saw what life was like for those down below. In the end their complaints reached his exalted ear. So one fine day he stepped down, disguised himself, and walked unnoticed among the crowds to see the state of justice.

DAUGHTER. You surely don't think that I am Haroun the Just, do you?

OFFICER. Let's talk about something else.— — —We've got company!

A white boat shaped like a dragon with a light-blue silk sail on a gilded yard and a golden mast with a rose-red pennant glides forward across the sound from the left. At the helm, with their arms around each other's waists, sit HE *and* SHE.

OFFICER. Look at that, perfect happiness, utter bliss, the ecstasy of young love!

The stage grows lighter.

*

HE [*stands up in the boat and sings*].

> Hail to thee, fair bay
> Where I spent my youthful springs,
> Where I dreamt those early rosy dreams,
> Here you have me back again,
> But not alone as I was then!
> Groves and bays,
> Skies and sea,
> Greet her!
> My love, my bride!
> My sun, my life!

The flags on the jetties of Fairhaven salute them, white handkerchiefs wave from the villas and the shore, and a chord composed of harps and violins rings out across the sound.

POET. See how the light shines from them! Hear how the sea resounds with music!—Eros!*

OFFICER. It is Victoria!

QUARANTINE MASTER. Well, so what?

OFFICER. It is *his* Victoria, I have my own! And *mine* is mine and mine alone!— — —Hoist the quarantine flag now, and I'll haul in the net.

The QUARANTINE MASTER *waves a yellow flag. The* OFFICER *pulls on a line so that the boat turns towards Foulstrand.*

OFFICER. Hold hard there!

HE *and* SHE *become aware of the dreadful landscape and express their horror.*

QUARANTINE MASTER. All right, all right! It may be hard. But everyone from a contaminated area has to land here!

POET. How can you talk like that, how can you do such things to two people whom you've just seen joined in love? Don't touch them! Don't touch love; that is treason!— — —Alas! Everything beautiful must go down, down into the mire!

      HE *and* SHE *step ashore, rueful and ashamed.*

HE. What have we done?

QUARANTINE MASTER. You don't need to have done anything to happen upon life's little vexations!

SHE. Happiness and joy are all too brief!

HE. How long must we remain here?

QUARANTINE MASTER. Forty days and forty nights!*

SHE. Then we'd rather throw ourselves in the sea!

HE. Live here, among charred hills and pigsties?

POET. Love conquers all, even the fumes of sulphur and carbolic acid!*

*

QUARANTINE MASTER [*lights the oven; blue sulphurous fumes arise*]. I am lighting the sulphur. Please step inside!

SHE. Oh, my blue dress will lose its colour!

QUARANTINE MASTER. And turn white. Your red roses will turn white too.

HE. And your cheeks as well! In forty days!

SHE [*to the* OFFICER]. That will please you.

OFFICER. No, it won't.— — —Your happiness caused my grief, of course it did, but— — —it doesn't matter—I have my doctorate now and a tutor's position over there... Heigho, and this autumn I've got a place in a school... teaching boys the lessons I learnt in my childhood and all through my youth; now I am going to read the same lessons again throughout my manhood and finally in my old age, the same lessons: how much is two times two? How many times does two go into four?... Until I am pensioned off with nothing to do but wait around for my meals and the papers—until at last they cart me off to the crematorium and burn me up... Have you no pensioners out here? That must be the worst of all after two times two is four; going to school again when you've got your doctorate; asking the same questions until you die... [*An* ELDERLY MAN *walks past with his hands behind his back*] Look, there goes a pensioner, waiting to die; some Captain, probably, who never made it to Major, or a high-court clerk who never became a judge—many are called, but few are chosen*... He's waiting for his breakfast...

PENSIONER. No, for the paper! My morning paper!

OFFICER. And yet he's only fifty-four; he can go on for another twenty-five years, just waiting for his meals and his paper... Isn't that awful?

PENSIONER. What isn't? You just tell me that!

OFFICER. Yes do, if anyone can.—Now I must go and teach those boys that two times two is four. How many times does two go into four? [*He holds his head in despair*] And Victoria, whom I loved and for whom I therefore desired the greatest happiness here on earth... She has that happiness now, the greatest there is, and consequently I must suffer... suffer, suffer!

*

SHE. Do you think I can be happy, when I see you suffer? How can you believe that? Perhaps it will ease your pain to know that I shall be sitting here a prisoner for forty days and nights? Well, does it?

OFFICER. Yes, and no. I can't be happy while you suffer. Oh!

HE. And do you think my happiness can be built on your suffering?

OFFICER. We're to be pitied—all of us! Oh!

ALL [*raise their hands to heaven and give voice to a discordant cry of anguish*]. AH!

DAUGHTER. Eternal One, hear them! Life is evil! Human beings are to be pitied!

ALL [*as before*]. Ah!

＊

It grows pitch black on stage for a moment during which all those there either exit or change places. When the light rises again, Foulstrand and its shore are upstage, but in shadow. The water of the sound remains centre stage, and Fairhaven is downstage, both of them brightly lit.

Stage right the corner of the resort's assembly rooms with the windows open; inside couples dancing. On an empty box outside are three YOUNG MAIDSERVANTS, *their arms round each other's waists, watching the dancing. On the steps of the assembly rooms is a bench on which* UGLY EDITH *is sitting, bare-headed and miserable, with her mass of hair dishevelled. In front of her an open piano.*

To the left a yellow wooden house.

Outside it, two CHILDREN *in summer clothes are playing ball.*

In the foreground is a jetty with white boats and flagpoles with flags hoisted.—Out in the sound lies a white man-of-war, rigged brig-fashion, and with its gunports open.

But the whole landscape is in winter dress, with snow on the ground and on the leafless trees.

The DAUGHTER *and the* OFFICER *enter.*

＊

DAUGHTER. Here is the peace and happiness of holiday! All work has stopped; every day there is a party; people are dressed in their best clothes with music and dancing even in the morning. [*To the* MAIDS] Why don't you girls go in and dance?

MAIDS. Us?

OFFICER. But they are servants!

DAUGHTER. That is true!— — —But why is Edith sitting there instead of dancing?   [EDITH *hides her face in her hands*

OFFICER. Don't ask her that! She's been sitting there for three hours and no one has asked her to dance— — —

[*Goes into the yellow house, left*

DAUGHTER. What a cruel diversion!

*

MOTHER [*enters from the assembly rooms, wearing a low-cut dress; goes up to* EDITH]. Why don't you go in like I said?

EDITH. Because... I can't make myself cheap. I know I am ugly, so no one wants to dance with me, but you don't need to remind me of it!

She begins to play the piano. Bach's Toccata and Fugue, No. 10.*

The waltz from within the assembly rooms is heard, at first softly, then louder as if competing with the Bach Toccata. However, Edith overwhelms it and reduces it to silence. The GUESTS appear in the doorway and listen to her playing; everyone on stage stands listening reverently.

A NAVAL OFFICER [*takes* ALICE, *one of the dancers, round the waist and leads her down to the jetty*]. Come, quickly!

EDITH *breaks off, stands up, and watches them despairingly. She remains standing as if turned to stone.*

*

Now the wall of the yellow house is removed and we see three school benches with BOYS *on them, among them the* OFFICER. *In front of them stands the* SCHOOLMASTER *with spectacles, chalk, and cane.*

SCHOOLMASTER [*to the* OFFICER]. Now, my boy, can you tell me what two times two is? [*The* OFFICER *remains seated, painfully searching his memory without finding the answer*] Stand up when you're asked a question!

OFFICER [*stands up, tormented*]. Two— — —times two... Let me see.— — —That makes two two!

SCHOOLMASTER. I see! You haven't done your homework!

OFFICER [*ashamed*]. Yes, I have, but... I know what it is, but I just can't say it...

SCHOOLMASTER. You're trying to get out of it! You know, but you *can't* say it. Perhaps I can help you!

[*He pulls the* OFFICER'S *hair*

OFFICER. Oh, this is dreadful, really dreadful!

SCHOOLMASTER. Yes, dreadful, that's precisely what it is when a big boy like you has no ambition...

OFFICER. [*pained*]. A *big* boy, yes, I am big, much bigger than them; I'm grown up. I've finished school... [*as if waking up*] but I've a doctorate... What am I doing sitting here? Haven't I got my doctorate?

SCHOOLMASTER. Yes, of course, but you'll sit here and mature, you see, mature... Isn't that it?

OFFICER [*clasping his forehead*]. Yes, that's right, one must mature... Two times two... is two, and I can prove it by analogy, the highest form of proof. Listen, now!... One times one is one, so two times two must be two! For what applies to one must apply to the other!

SCHOOLMASTER. The proof is perfectly in accord with the laws of logic but the answer is wrong.

OFFICER. What is in accord with the laws of logic can't be wrong. Let us put it to the test. One into one goes once, therefore two into two goes twice.

SCHOOLMASTER. Absolutely correct by analogy. But in that case, how much is one times three?

OFFICER. Three!

SCHOOLMASTER. Consequently, two times three is also three!

OFFICER [*thoughtfully*]. No, that can't be right... it can't be... otherwise [*sitting down in despair*]... no, I'm still not mature!

SCHOOLMASTER. No, you are still far from mature...

OFFICER. But how long will I have to sit here, then?

SCHOOLMASTER. How long? Do you think that time and space exist?... Suppose that time exists, you ought to be able to say what time is. What is time?

OFFICER. Time?... [*Considers*] I can't say, but I know what it is. *Ergo** I know what two times two is, without being able to say it.— Can you tell me what time is, sir?

SCHOOLMASTER. Of course I can!

ALL THE BOYS. Then tell us!

SCHOOLMASTER. Time?— — —Let me see! [*Remains standing motionless with his finger to his nose*] While we are talking, time flies. Therefore time is something that flies while I talk!

A BOY [*getting up*]. You are talking now, and while you are talking, I'm flying, therefore I am time! [*Flees*

SCHOOLMASTER. According to the laws of logic that is perfectly correct!

OFFICER. But in that case the laws of logic are absurd, because Nils can't be time just because he flew away!

SCHOOLMASTER. That is also perfectly correct according to the laws of logic, although it remains quite absurd.

OFFICER. Then logic is absurd!

SCHOOLMASTER. It really looks that way. But if logic is absurd, then so is the whole world too... and in that case why the hell should I sit here teaching all of you such absurdities!— If someone will stand us a drink, we'll go for a swim!

OFFICER. This is a *posterius prius** or back-to-front world. People usually go swimming first and then have a drink. You old fogey!

SCHOOLMASTER. Don't be so arrogant, Doctor!

OFFICER. Captain, if you don't mind! I'm an officer, and I don't understand why I have to sit here being scolded among all these schoolboys...

SCHOOLMASTER [*raises his finger*]. We must mature!

*

QUARANTINE MASTER [*enters*]. The quarantine is beginning!

OFFICER. Oh, there you are! Can you imagine, that fellow's had me sitting on a school bench, even though I've got my doctorate!

QUARANTINE MASTER. Well, why don't you just leave?

OFFICER. You can talk! Leave? That's easier said than done!

SCHOOLMASTER. No, I should think not!—Just you try!

OFFICER [*to the* QUARANTINE MASTER]. Save me! Save me from his eyes!

QUARANTINE MASTER. Come on!— — —Come and help us dance ... we must dance before the plague breaks out. We really must!

OFFICER. So the brig is sailing?

QUARANTINE MASTER. Yes, the brig will sail first.— — — There will be tears, of course.

OFFICER. Always tears: when she comes and when she goes.— Let us go!   [*They go out*

    The SCHOOLMASTER *continues teaching in silence.*

*

The MAIDS, *who have been standing at the window of the assembly rooms watching the dance, move sadly towards the jetty;* EDITH, *who has been standing by the piano as if turned to stone, follows slowly after them.*

DAUGHTER [*to the* OFFICER]. Isn't there a single happy person in this paradise?

OFFICER. Yes, those two newlyweds! Listen to them!

*

The NEWLYWEDS *enter.*

HUSBAND [*to the* WIFE]. My bliss is so boundless I could die...

WIFE. Why die?

HUSBAND. Because in the midst of happiness there is always a seed of unhappiness; it consumes itself like fire—it can't burn forever, sooner or later it must die; and this presentiment of the end destroys my happiness when it is at its height.

WIFE. Then let us die together, now, at once!

HUSBAND. Die? Very well! For I'm afraid of happiness. It's deceitful! [*They go towards the sea*

*

DAUGHTER [*to the* OFFICER]. Life is evil! Human beings are to be pitied!

OFFICER. Do you see that man coming now. He's the most envied person in the whole place. [*The* BLIND MAN *is led in*] He owns these hundred Italian villas and all these bays and beaches, forests and inlets are his along with all the fish in the sea, the birds in the air, and the game in the woods.* These thousands of people are his tenants while the sun rises on his sea and sets on his lands. . .

DAUGHTER. And even he complains?

OFFICER. Yes, and with good reason, he can't see.

QUARANTINE MASTER. He is blind!— — —

DAUGHTER. And everyone envies him!

OFFICER. He is here to see the brig sail, with his son on board.

*

BLIND MAN. I may not be able to see, but I can hear. I can hear the fluke of the anchor clawing the sea bed, like a hook ripping up out of a fish through the gullet, along with its heart!— — —My son, my one and only child, is going away across the vast ocean; I can follow him only with my thoughts— — —now I can hear the chain grating— — —and—something fluttering and flapping like clothes on a washing line. . . wet handkerchiefs, perhaps— — — and a sighing or sobbing like people crying. . . the waves lapping against the hull perhaps, or maybe the girls on the shore— — — the abandoned ones. . . the inconsolable— — —I once asked a child why the sea was salty, and straight away the child, who had a father at sea, replied: 'the sea is salty because sailors cry so much.'— 'And why do sailors cry so much?', I asked. 'Oh,' said the child, 'because they always have to go away.— — —That's why they always dry their handkerchiefs up on the masts!'— — — 'And why do people cry when they feel sad?' I continued.—'Oh,' he said, 'that's because they have to wash the glass in their eyes, so they can see better!'— — —

The brig has set sail and glides away; the GIRLS *on the shore wave their handkerchiefs and, alternately, dry their tears. Now the signal 'Yes' is hoisted on the foremast, a red ball on a white ground.* ALICE *waves jubilantly in reply.*

DAUGHTER [*to the* OFFICER]. What does that flag mean?

OFFICER. It means 'Yes'. It is the lieutenant's 'Yes' in red, his heart's blood drawn across the blue cloth of the sky.

DAUGHTER. What does 'no' look like then?

OFFICER. Blue, as blue as the tainted blood in blue veins...* but have you seen how radiant Alice is?

DAUGHTER. And how Edith is weeping!— — —

BLIND MAN. Meeting and parting!—Parting and meeting!—That is what life is.—I met his mother. And then she left me.—I still had my son; now he has gone.

DAUGHTER. But he will surely come back.— — —

BLIND MAN. Who is that? I've heard that voice before, in my dreams, in my youth, when the summer holidays began, when I was newly married, when my child was born; every time life smiled at me I heard that voice, like the soft whisper of the southern wind, like the sound of a harp from on high, just as I imagine the angel's greeting on Christmas night*...

*

The LAWYER *enters, goes over to the* BLIND MAN, *and whispers.*

BLIND MAN. Is that so?

LAWYER. Yes, it is. [*Goes up to the* DAUGHTER]— — —You have seen most things now, but you still haven't experienced the worst thing of all.

DAUGHTER. What can that be?

LAWYER. Repetition!*— — —Doing the same thing over and over again!!— — —Going back over everything! Having to learn your lesson again and again!— — —Come!

DAUGHTER. Where?

LAWYER. Back to your duties!

DAUGHTER. What are they?

LAWYER. Everything you loathe! Everything you don't want to do, but must! It means giving up things, doing without, denying yourself, leaving things behind... everything unpleasant, repulsive, and painful...

DAUGHTER. Are there no pleasant duties?

LAWYER. They become pleasant when you have performed them ...

DAUGHTER. When they no longer exist.— — —So duty is always unpleasant! What is pleasant, then?

LAWYER. Sin is pleasant.

DAUGHTER. Sin?

LAWYER. Which must be punished, yes!—If I have had a pleasant day and evening, I suffer the pangs of hell and a bad conscience the following day.

DAUGHTER. How strange!

LAWYER. Yes, I wake up in the morning with a headache; and then the repetition begins—a repetition that perverts the past, however. Everything that was beautiful, pleasant, and witty yesterday evening appears in recollection as ugly, vile, and stupid. Pleasure turns sour, it seems, and happiness dissolves. What people call success always brings about the next misfortune. My successes have been my ruin. You see, people have an instinctive horror of other people's good fortune; they think it is unjust of fate to favour one man, and so they try to restore the balance by placing obstacles in his way. To have talent is highly dangerous, you can easily starve to death.— — — However, return to your duties, or I shall file for divorce, and then we shall have to go through each stage in turn, one, two, three!*

DAUGHTER. Return? To the iron stove and the cabbage and the baby clothes...

LAWYER. That's right! Today is washing day, all the handkerchiefs have to be washed...

DAUGHTER. Oh, must I go through all that again?

LAWYER. That is what life amounts to, doing the same thing over and over again... look at the schoolmaster in there... Yesterday he was given a doctorate, a laurel crown, and a twenty-one gun salute, he climbed Parnassus and was embraced by the King... And today he's starting back at school again, asking how much two times two are, and he will go on doing that until he dies... However, come back now, to your home!

DAUGHTER. I would rather die!

LAWYER. Die? That isn't allowed! In the first place, suicide is so dishonourable that even one's corpse is defiled, and then— — —it excludes us from grace— — —it is a mortal sin!

DAUGHTER. It's not easy to be a human being!

*

ALL. True!

*

DAUGHTER. I will not return to that dirt and degradation with you!— — —I want to go back to where I came from, but— — — first the door has to be opened so I may know the secret... I want the door opened!

LAWYER. Then you must retrace your steps, go back the way you came, and undergo all the horrors of a trial, all the repetitions, reiterations, and recapitulations...

DAUGHTER. So be it, but first I must go alone into the wilderness to find myself again! We shall meet again! [*To the* POET] Follow me!

Distant cries of anguish and lamentation are heard from the rear.

DAUGHTER. What was that?

LAWYER. The lost souls of Foulstrand.

DAUGHTER. What makes them cry so loudly today?

LAWYER. Because the sun is shining here, because there is music, and dancing, and young people. That makes their suffering so much worse.

DAUGHTER. We must set them free!

LAWYER. Try it! Once someone did try to set people free, but they hanged Him on a cross.

DAUGHTER. Who did?

LAWYER. All right-thinking people.

DAUGHTER. Who are they?

LAWYER. Don't you know all the right-thinking? Then you soon will!

DAUGHTER. Were they the ones who refused you your degree?

LAWYER. Yes!

DAUGHTER. Then I do know them!

A beach by the Mediterranean. In the foreground to the left there is a white wall over which orange trees in fruit are visible. In the background villas and a Casino with a terrace. To the right, a huge pile of coal and two wheelbarrows. Upstage right, a strip of blue sea.*

Two COAL-HEAVERS, *naked to the waist, their faces, hands, and the exposed parts of their bodies blackened, are sitting on their wheelbarrows in despair.*

The DAUGHTER *and the* LAWYER *enter from the rear.*

DAUGHTER. This is paradise!

FIRST COAL-HEAVER. This is hell!

SECOND COAL-HEAVER. A hundred and twenty in the shade!

FIRST COAL-HEAVER. Shall we go for a swim?

SECOND COAL-HEAVER. We can't. The police will come! No bathing here, not for the likes of us.

FIRST COAL-HEAVER. What about picking one of those oranges?

SECOND COAL-HEAVER. No, the police will come!

FIRST COAL-HEAVER. But I can't work in this heat; I'm packing it in.

SECOND COAL-HEAVER. Then the police will come and arrest you!— — —[*Pause.*] Besides, you'll have no food...

FIRST COAL-HEAVER. No food?— — —We who work the most eat the least; while the rich, who do nothing, get the most!— — — Wouldn't it be fair to say—without going too far, now—that that's not right?—What does the daughter of the gods over there have to say about it?

＊

DAUGHTER. I don't know what to say!— — —But tell me, what have you done to be so black and have so hard a lot?

FIRST COAL-HEAVER. What have we done? We were born poor and our parents weren't up to much— — —We got punished once or twice too, maybe.

DAUGHTER. Punished?

FIRST COAL-HEAVER. Yes; those who didn't get punished are sitting up there in the Casino eating eight-course dinners with wine.

DAUGHTER [*to the* LAWYER]. Can this be true?

LAWYER. By and large, yes.— — —

DAUGHTER. Do you mean that at some time or other everyone deserves to go to prison?

LAWYER. Yes.

DAUGHTER. You too?

LAWYER. Yes!

＊

DAUGHTER. Is it true that these poor men aren't allowed to swim in the sea here?

LAWYER. Yes; not even with their clothes on. Only those who try to drown themselves get away without paying. But they no doubt get a good drubbing down at the police station.

DAUGHTER. Isn't there somewhere out of town where they can bathe?

LAWYER. No, all the land's been fenced off.

DAUGHTER. I mean out in the country, where it belongs to everyone.

LAWYER. It all belongs to someone, everywhere's taken!

DAUGHTER. Even the sea, the great, open...

LAWYER. Everywhere! You can't go out in a boat or land anywhere without getting permission and having to pay. Marvellous, isn't it?

DAUGHTER. This is no paradise!

LAWYER. No, I can promise you that!

DAUGHTER. Why don't people do something to improve things?

— — —

LAWYER. Oh, they do, but everyone who tries to improve the world ends up in prison or the madhouse...

DAUGHTER. Who puts them in prison?

LAWYER. All the right-thinking people, all those honourable...

DAUGHTER. Who puts them in the madhouse?

LAWYER. Their own despair, when they see how hopeless their efforts are.

DAUGHTER. Has it never occurred to anyone that there might be some hidden reason why things are the way they are?

LAWYER. Oh yes, those who are well-off always think like that.

DAUGHTER. That things are all right as they are?— — —

*

FIRST COAL-HEAVER. And yet society rests on us; without coal everything would come to a standstill or go out, your kitchen stove, the fire in your fireplace, and the machine in the factory as well as all the lights in the streets, in the shops, and in your homes: darkness and cold would engulf you... that is why we sweat like hell bringing you the black coal... What do you give us in return?

LAWYER [*to the* DAUGHTER]. Help them!— — —[*Pause*] I know there can't be complete equality, but do things have to be so unequal?

*

The GENTLEMAN *and the* LADY *cross the stage.*

LADY. Are you going to join us for a game of cards?

GENTLEMAN. No, I must take a little walk so I can work up a bit of an appetite.

*

FIRST COAL-HEAVER. A *bit* of an appetite...

SECOND COAL-HEAVER. A *bit*...?

The CHILDREN *enter and scream in terror at the sight of the blackened workers.*

*

FIRST COAL-HEAVER. One look at us and they scream! They scream...

SECOND COAL-HEAVER. God damn it!— — —It's about time we brought out the scaffolds and cut this rotten body about a bit...

FIRST COAL-HEAVER. Yes, damn it, that's what I say too! Ugh!

*

LAWYER [*to the* DAUGHTER]. Crazy, isn't it? People aren't so bad... it's just...

DAUGHTER. Just...?

LAWYER. The way things are run...

DAUGHTER [*hides her face and leaves*]. This is no paradise!

COAL-HEAVERS. No, it isn't. It is hell!

Curtain.

Fingal's cave. Long green billows roll slowly into the cavern; downstage a red bell-buoy rocks upon the waves, although it makes no sound except where indicated. The music of the winds. The music of the waves. The DAUGHTER *and the* POET *on stage.*

POET. Where have you brought me?

DAUGHTER. Far from the murmur and misery of mankind, to the ocean's farthest reach, to this cave that we call the Ear of Indra because they say that here the Lord of Heaven listens to mankind's complaints.

POET. Here? How?

DAUGHTER. Don't you see how this cave is shaped like a seashell? Of course you do! Don't you know that your ear is shaped like a shell? You do, but you haven't given it a thought! [*She picks up a shell from the shore*] As a child, did you never hold a shell to your ear and hear... hear your blood singing in your heart, your thoughts murmuring in your brain, the parting of a thousand little worn-out tissues in the fabric of your body... If that is what you can hear in this tiny shell, then imagine what can be heard in one this great!— — —

POET [*listening*]. I hear nothing but the sighing of the wind...

DAUGHTER. Then I shall interpret it for you. Listen! The lamentation of the winds!   [*Recites to soft music*

> Born under the clouds of heaven
> We were chased by the bolts of Indra
> Down to the dusty fields of earth...
> The mulch of meadows soiled our feet,
> The dust of the highways,
> The smoke of the cities,
> Foul human breath,
> The smell of food and wine—
> All this we had to bear...
> Out over the wide sea we soared
> To air our lungs,

To shake our wings
And bathe our feet!
Indra, Lord of Heaven,
Hear us!
Hear when we sigh.
The earth is not clean.
Life is not good.
Men are not evil,
Nor are they good.
They live as they can,
One day at a time.
Sons of dust in dust they wander,
Born of dust
To dust they return.*
They were given feet to trudge,
Not wings to fly.
They grow dusty,
Is the fault theirs
Or Yours?

*

POET. I heard this once before...

DAUGHTER. Hush! The winds are still singing!

*

[*Recites to soft music*

We the winds, children of the air,
Carry the laments of mankind.
If you heard us
In the chimney on autumn evenings
In the stove pipe's vent,
In the cracks of the window,
When the rain wept upon the tiles,
Or on a winter evening
In snowy forests
Or upon the storm-swept sea,
If you heard moaning and sighing
In sails and rigging...

It is we, the winds,
Children of the air,
Who from the human breasts
Through which we passed
Learnt these notes of suffering...
In sickrooms, on battlefields,
And most of all in nurseries
Where the newborn cry,
Complain and scream
At the pain of being born.

It is we, we the winds
Who whine and cry
Woe! woe! woe!

*

POET. It seems to me that once before...

DAUGHTER. Hush! The waves are singing!

[*Recites to soft music*

It is we, we the waves—
Who rock the winds
To rest!
Green cradles are we,
Wet are we and salt;
Like tongues of fire;
Wet flames are we
Quenching, burning
Cleansing, bathing,
Breeding, bearing,
We, we the waves,
Who rock the winds
To rest!

*

DAUGHTER. False waves and faithless; everything that is not burned
on earth is drowned—in the waves.—Look here![*Points to a heap of
flotsam*] Look what the sea has plundered and destroyed!———All
that remains of these sunken ships is their figureheads———and

their names: *Justice*, *Friendship*, *Golden Peace*, and *Hope*—this is all that remains of Hope!— — — Treacherous Hope!— — — Gunwales, rowlocks, and bailers! And look: the lifebuoy— — —it saved itself, but let those in distress go down!

POET [*picking among the wreckage*]. Is that the nameplate of the *Justice*? That was the ship which left Fairhaven, with the Blind Man's son on board. So it has sunk! And with Alice's sweetheart on board, Edith's hopeless love!

DAUGHTER. The Blind Man? Fairhaven? I must have dreamt all that. And Alice's sweetheart, ugly Edith, Foulstrand and the quarantine, sulphur and carbolic acid, the graduation ceremony in the church, the Lawyer's office, the corridor and Victoria, the Growing Castle and the Officer... I dreamt it all...

POET. I put it into poetry once!

DAUGHTER. Then you know what poetry is...

POET. Then I know what dreams are... — — —What is poetry?

DAUGHTER. Not reality, but more than reality... not dreams, but waking dreams...

POET. And people believe we poets only play... invent and make believe.

DAUGHTER. That is just as well, my friend, otherwise the world would be laid waste for lack of encouragement. Everyone would lie on their backs and gaze at the sky; no one would turn their hands to plough or spade, plane or pick.

POET. And you say that, you, Indra's daughter, who half belong up there— — —

DAUGHTER. You are right to reproach me; I have been down here too long, bathing in mud as you do... My thoughts can no longer fly; clay on my wings... earth on my feet... and I... [*Raises her arms*] I am sinking, sinking... Help me, Father, God of Heaven! [*Silence*] I can no longer hear what he says. The ether no longer carries the sound from His lips to the shell of my ear— — —the silver thread has parted... Alas! I am earthbound!

POET. Do you intend to ascend again... soon?

DAUGHTER. As soon as I have burned this mortal coil away... for all the ocean's water cannot cleanse me. Why do you ask?

POET. Because. . . I have a prayer. . . a petition. . .

DAUGHTER. What kind of petition. . .

POET. A petition from mankind to the ruler of the world, drawn up by a dreamer.

DAUGHTER. To be presented by. . .

POET. Indra's daughter. . .

DAUGHTER. Can you recite your poem?

POET. Yes.

DAUGHTER. Go on then!

POET. It is better if you do it.

DAUGHTER. Where am I to read it?

POET. In my thoughts, or here!　　　　[*Hands her a scroll of paper*

DAUGHTER [*takes the paper, but recites from memory*]. Very well, then I shall speak it.

*

'Why were you born in pain,
Why do you torment your mother,
Child of man, when you would give her
The joy of motherhood,
The joy beyond all other joys?
Why do you wake to life,
Why do you greet the light
With a cry of anger and of pain?
Why don't you smile at life,
Child of man, when the gift of life
Should be joy itself?
Why are we born like beasts,
We children of the gods and men?
Our spirit craved another garment
Than this one of blood and dirt!
Must God's own image cut its teeth. . .'

— — —Hush! You presume too much. . . the creature
should not censure its creator!
No one has yet solved the riddle of life!— — —

'And so begins our wandering
Over thistles, thorns, and stones;
Walk upon a beaten path
And it is at once forbidden you;
Pick a flower and straight away
You find it belongs to someone else;
If your way is through a field
And you have to go directly,
You trample on another's crops;
Others trample then on yours,
To make the difference less.
Every pleasure you enjoy
Brings sorrow to all others,
But your sorrow gives no one joy,
Because sorrow is heaped upon sorrow.
So goes the journey until your death.
And you become another's breath!'

— — —

—Is this the way for the son of dust
To approach the Almighty?

POET.　　How shall the son of dust find
Words bright, pure, and light enough
To rise from the earth...
Child of God, will you translate
Our lament into language
The Immortals understand?

DAUGHTER. I will.

POET [*gesturing towards the buoy*]. What is that floating there?
A buoy?

DAUGHTER. Yes.

POET. It is like a lung with a windpipe.

DAUGHTER. It is the watchman of the sea; when danger threatens, it
sings.

POET. The sea seems to be rising and the waves are beginning to
roar...

DAUGHTER. You are right.

POET. Oh! But what is that?—A ship... beyond the reef!

DAUGHTER. What ship can it be?

POET. I believe it is the ghost ship.

DAUGHTER. What is that?

POET. *The Flying Dutchman.**

DAUGHTER. Him? Why is he punished so cruelly, why does he never come ashore?

POET. Because he had seven unfaithful wives.

DAUGHTER. Must *he* be punished for that?

POET. Yes. All right-thinking people condemned him...

DAUGHTER. Strange world!— — —How can he be freed from his curse, then?

POET. Be freed? One should beware of setting anyone free...

DAUGHTER. Why?

POET. Because... No, it isn't the *Dutchman*. It's an ordinary ship in distress!— — —Why isn't the buoy sounding now?— — —Look, the sea is rising, the waves are running high; soon we'll be trapped within this cave!— — —Now the ship's bell is ringing!—soon we'll have another figurehead... Scream, buoy, do your duty, watchman... [*The buoy sounds a four-part chord in fifths and sixths like a foghorn*]— — —The crew is waving to us... But we, too, shall perish!

DAUGHTER. Don't you want to be set free?

POET. Of course I do, but not now... and not by water!

*

THE CREW [*singing in four-parts*]. Christ Kyrie!

Christ Ky - ri -- e!

POET. They are calling now; and so is the sea! But no one hears!

THE CREW [*as before*]. Christ Kyrie!

DAUGHTER. Who is that coming there?

POET. Walking on the water? There is only One who walks on water.* It cannot be Peter, the rock, for he sank like a stone...*

> *A white glow can be seen out on the water.*

THE CREW. Christ Kyrie!

DAUGHTER. Is it He?

POET. It is He, the Crucified...

DAUGHTER. Why—tell me, why was He crucified?

POET. Because He wanted to set men free...

DAUGHTER. Who—I have forgotten—who crucified Him?

POET. All the right-thinking!

DAUGHTER. What a strange world!

POET. The sea is rising! Darkness is upon us... The storm is growing worse...

*

THE CREW cry out.

POET. The crew is crying out in terror because they have seen their redeemer... And now— — —they are jumping overboard, in fear of their saviour... [THE CREW *cry out again*] Now they are crying because they have to die. They cry when they are born and they cry again when they die.

> *The rising waves threaten to drown them in the cave.*

DAUGHTER. If only I were sure it is a ship...

POET. To tell you the truth... I don't think it is a ship... it is a two-storied house, with trees outside... and... a telephone tower*... a tower reaching up into the skies... It is the modern Tower of Babel,* sending its wires up there—to communicate with those above...

DAUGHTER. Child, human thoughts need no metal wires to transmit themselves;— — —The prayers of the devout make their way through every world... That is certainly no Tower of Babel, for if you would storm heaven, then storm it with your prayers!

POET. No, it is no house— — —no telephone tower— — —Don't you see?

DAUGHTER. What do you see?

POET. I see a snow-covered heath, a parade ground— — —the winter sun is shining behind a church on the hill, and the tower casts its long shadow over the snow— — —Now a troop of soldiers is marching across the heath; they are marching across the tower and up the spire; now they have reached the cross, but it seems to me that the first man to tread on the cock must die... they are almost there... the corporal is at their head... Ha! a cloud is darting across the heath, blotting out the sun, of course... now all of it has vanished... the cloud's water quenched the sun's fire!—The sun's rays created the dark image of the tower, but the cloud's dark image extinguished the tower's.— — —

During the above the scene has changed to the theatre corridor.

DAUGHTER [*to the* DOORKEEPER]. Has the Lord Chancellor arrived yet?

DOORKEEPER. No.

DAUGHTER. What about the Deans?

DOORKEEPER. No.

DAUGHTER. Then call them, at once, the door is to be opened...

DOORKEEPER. Is it so urgent?

DAUGHTER. Yes, it is! For people suspect that the solution to the riddle of existence* lies hidden in there.— — —So, call the Lord Chancellor and the Deans of the four faculties! [*The* DOORKEEPER *blows a whistle*] And don't forget the Glazier and his diamond, otherwise we shall get nowhere!

*

Singers, actors, and dancers enter left, as at the beginning of the play.

*

OFFICER [*enters upstage in frock coat and top hat, with a bouquet of roses in his hand, radiantly happy*]. Victoria!

DOORKEEPER. The young lady will be down in a minute.

OFFICER. Good, good! The carriage is waiting, the table set, and the champagne on ice... May I embrace you, madam? [*He embraces the* DOORKEEPER] Victoria!

A WOMAN'S VOICE FROM ABOVE [*sings*]. I am here!

OFFICER [*begins to wander back and forth*]. All right! I'll wait!

*

POET. I seem to have been through this before...

DAUGHTER. I too!

POET. Perhaps it was a dream?

DAUGHTER. Or a poem?

POET. Or a poem!

DAUGHTER. Then you know what poetry is!

POET. Then I know what dreams are!

DAUGHTER. It seems to me we have said these words before, somewhere else.

POET. Then you can soon work out what reality is.

DAUGHTER. Or dreaming!

POET. Or poetry!

*

The LORD CHANCELLOR *and the* DEANS *of* THEOLOGY, PHILOSOPHY, MEDICINE, *and* LAW *enter.*

LORD CHANCELLOR. It is this question of the door, of course.— What do you think about it as Dean of Theology?

DEAN OF THEOLOGY. I don't think, I believe... *Credo**...

DEAN OF PHILOSOPHY. I think...

DEAN OF MEDICINE. I examine...

DEAN OF LAW. I withhold judgement, until I have proper proof and witnesses.

LORD CHANCELLOR. Now they are going to start squabbling again!— — —Well, what do you believe, as Dean of Theology?

DEAN OF THEOLOGY. I believe this door must not be opened, because it conceals dangerous truths...

DEAN OF PHILOSOPHY. The truth is never dangerous!

DEAN OF MEDICINE. What is truth?*

DEAN OF LAW. Whatever can be proved with two witnesses.

DEAN OF THEOLOGY. Anything can be proved with two false witnesses*—by a law-twister!

DEAN OF PHILOSOPHY. Truth is wisdom, and wisdom, which is knowledge, is philosophy... Philosophy is the science of sciences, the knowledge of all knowledge, and all the other sciences are its servant.

DEAN OF MEDICINE. The only science is natural science; philosophy is not a science. It is merely empty speculation.

DEAN OF THEOLOGY. Bravo!

DEAN OF PHILOSOPHY [*to the* DEAN OF THEOLOGY]. You say bravo! And just what are you, may I ask? You are the sworn enemy of all learning, you are the antithesis of science, you are ignorance and darkness...

DEAN OF MEDICINE. Bravo!

DEAN OF THEOLOGY [*to the* DEAN OF MEDICINE]. You say bravo— you who can see no further than your nose in a magnifying glass, you who only believe what your treacherous senses tell you, your eye, for example, which may be long-sighted, short-sighted, blind, purblind, cross-eyed, one-eyed, colour-blind, red-blind, green-blind...

DEAN OF MEDICINE. Fool!

DEAN OF THEOLOGY. Donkey!

They fly at each other.

LORD CHANCELLOR. Quiet! One raven shouldn't hack the other's eyes out!

DEAN OF PHILOSOPHY. If I had to choose between those two, theology and medicine, I'd choose—neither!

DEAN OF LAW. And if I had to sit in judgement over you three, I'd find against—you all!— — —You can't agree on a single point, and never have been able to!—To the matter in hand, now My Lord Chancellor, what is your view of this door and its opening?

LORD CHANCELLOR. View? I don't have any views. I am merely appointed by the government to see that you don't break each other's arms and legs in council— — —while you are educating the young. Views? No, I am wary of them. I had a few once, but they were soon disproved; views are soon disproved—by one's opponent, of course!— — —Perhaps we might open the door now, even at the risk of it concealing dangerous truths?

DEAN OF LAW. What is truth? Where is truth?

DEAN OF THEOLOGY. I am the truth and the life...*

DEAN OF PHILOSOPHY. I am the knowledge of knowledge...

DEAN OF MEDICINE. I am exact knowledge...

DEAN OF LAW. I doubt!

They fly at each other.

DAUGHTER. Shame on you, you teachers of youth!

DEAN OF LAW. Lord Chancellor, as representative of the government and head of our faculty, punish this woman's presumption. She has cried shame on you, that is an insult, and she called you a teacher of youth in a sneering, ironic tone of voice, that is libellous!

DAUGHTER. Poor young people!

DEAN OF LAW. By pitying the young she is accusing us! Lord Chancellor, punish her presumption!

DAUGHTER. Yes, I accuse you, all of you, of sowing doubt and discord in the minds of the young.

DEAN OF LAW. Listen to her! She encourages the young to question our authority and then accuses us of sowing doubt. I appeal to all right-thinking people, is not that a criminal offence?

*

ALL RIGHT-THINKING PEOPLE. Yes, it is criminal!

DEAN OF LAW. All right-thinking people have condemned you!— Now go in peace with your gain.* Otherwise...

DAUGHTER. My gain?—Otherwise? Otherwise what?

DEAN OF LAW. Otherwise you will be stoned!

POET. Or crucified!

DAUGHTER. I am going. Follow me, and you will learn the answer to the riddle.

POET. What riddle?

DAUGHTER. What did he mean by 'my gain'?— — —

POET. Probably nothing. It's what we call talk. He was just talking.

DAUGHTER. But he hurt me deeply by saying that.

POET. That's why he said it.— — —People are like that.

*

ALL RIGHT-THINKING PEOPLE. Hurrah! The door is open!

*

LORD CHANCELLOR. What was hidden behind the door?

GLAZIER. I can't see anything.

LORD CHANCELLOR. *He* can't see anything! No, I can believe it! — — —Deans! What was hidden behind the door?

DEAN OF THEOLOGY. Nothing! That is the solution to the riddle of the universe!— — —In the beginning God created heaven and earth out of nothing.

DEAN OF PHILOSOPHY. Nothing will come of nothing.*

DEAN OF MEDICINE. Rubbish! That's all nothing!

DEAN OF LAW. I have my doubts!... There is a fraud here some-where. I appeal to all right-thinking people!

*

DAUGHTER [*to the* POET]. Who are these right-thinking people?

POET. If only one could say! It usually means just the one person. Today it's I and mine, tomorrow it's you and yours.—You are appointed to the post, or rather, you appoint yourself.

*

ALL THE RIGHT-THINKING. We have been deceived!

LORD CHANCELLOR. Who has deceived you?

ALL THE RIGHT-THINKING. The Daughter!

LORD CHANCELLOR [*to the* DAUGHTER]. Will you kindly tell us what you intended by opening this door?

DAUGHTER. No, my friends! If I told you, you wouldn't believe it!

DEAN OF MEDICINE. But there is nothing there!

DAUGHTER. Exactly!—But you still don't understand!

DEAN OF MEDICINE. What she says is nonsense!

ALL. Nonsense!

DAUGHTER [*to the* POET]. They are to be pitied!

POET. Are you serious?

DAUGHTER. I am always serious.

POET. Are the right-thinking to be pitied too?

DAUGHTER. They most of all, perhaps.

POET. The four faculties too?

DAUGHTER. They too, and by no means the least. Four heads, four minds on a single body. Who created such a monster?

ALL. She doesn't answer!

LORD CHANCELLOR. Then stone her!

DAUGHTER. I have answered.

LORD CHANCELLOR. Listen, she is answering.

ALL. Stone her! She is answering!

DAUGHTER. It's 'stone her' if she answers and 'stone her' if she doesn't!— — —[*To the* POET.] Come, seer, and—far away from here—I will tell you the riddle—but out in the wilderness, where no one can hear or see us. Because— — —

*

LAWYER [*comes forward, takes the* DAUGHTER *by the arm*]. Have you forgotten your duties?

DAUGHTER. God knows, I have not! But I have higher duties!

LAWYER. And your child?

DAUGHTER. My child! What more?

LAWYER. Your child is calling for you.

DAUGHTER. My child! Alas, I am earthbound!— — —And this torment in my breast, this anguish... what is it?

LAWYER. Don't you know?

DAUGHTER. No!

LAWYER. The pangs of conscience.

DAUGHTER. Is this the pangs of conscience?

LAWYER. Yes. They follow upon every neglected duty and every pleasure, however innocent—if there is such a thing as an innocent pleasure, which I rather doubt. They come every time you hurt those closest to you too.

DAUGHTER. And there is no cure?

LAWYER. Yes, but only one! To do one's duty without delay — — —

DAUGHTER. You look like a demon when you say that word 'duty'!—But suppose you have two duties to fulfil, as I have?

LAWYER. Then you must fulfil first one, and then the other.

DAUGHTER. The highest first... look after my child, then, and I shall fulfil *my* duty...

LAWYER. Your child suffers without you— — —can you bear to know someone is suffering on your account?

DAUGHTER. My soul just split in two... this is tearing me apart!

LAWYER. Life's little tribulations, you see.

DAUGHTER. Oh, how it tears me!

*

POET. If you only knew what destruction and grief I have caused by fulfilling my calling, my calling, mind you, which is the highest of all duties, then you wouldn't want to take me by the hand.

DAUGHTER. What do you mean?

POET. I had a father who placed all his hopes in me as his only son, someone who would carry on his business... But I ran away from commercial school... My father died of grief. My mother

intended me for the church... but I just couldn't bring myself...
she disowned me... I had a friend who saw me through hard
times... but he exploited those whose cause I pleaded in my
poems. To save my own soul I was forced to strike down my friend
and benefactor, and since then I have known no peace; people call
me infamous, scum of the earth, but it is no help my conscience
saying: 'You did the right thing', for the next moment that same
conscience says: 'You did wrong.' Such is life!

*

DAUGHTER. Come with me into the wilderness!

LAWYER. Your child!

DAUGHTER [*indicating all those present*]. Here are my children. Indi-
vidually each of them is kind and good, but they only have to come
together to start fighting. Then they turn into demons.— — —
Goodbye!

*Outside the castle. The same scenery as in Scene 1. But the earth at the
foot of the castle is now covered with flowers (blue monkshoods or
aconitum). On the roof of the castle, surmounting its glass lantern, is a
chrysanthemum bud ready to burst into bloom. The windows of the castle
are illuminated by candles. The* DAUGHTER *and the* POET.

*

DAUGHTER. The moment has almost come when, consumed by fire,
I shall rise again into the ether... This is what you call death, and
approach with so much fear.

POET. Fear of the unknown.

DAUGHTER. Which you know!

POET. Who knows it?

DAUGHTER. Everyone. Why don't you have faith in your prophets?

POET. Prophets have always been distrusted; why is that?—And 'if
God has spoken why do people not believe?'* His power to
persuade must surely be irresistible!

DAUGHTER. Have you always doubted?

POET. No. I have often felt certain, but after a while my certainty
would vanish as a dream does when one wakes up.

DAUGHTER. It's not easy to be a human being!

POET. You see that now, do you?

DAUGHTER. Yes.

POET. Listen! Wasn't it Indra who once sent his Son down to the earth to hear mankind's complaints?

DAUGHTER. Yes, it was. How was He received?

POET. To answer with a question, how did he accomplish his mission?

DAUGHTER. To answer with another... Wasn't man's lot better after His stay on earth? Answer truthfully.

POET. Better?—Yes, a little. A very little!— — —But instead of all these questions: won't you explain the riddle?

DAUGHTER. Yes. But what good will that do? You won't believe me.

POET. I want to believe you, for I know who you are.

DAUGHTER. Very well, I will tell you.

In the dawn of time* before the sun shone, Brahma, the divine primal force, allowed Maya,* the world mother, to seduce him, so that he might multiply himself. This contact between the divine element and the earthly element was heaven's fall from grace. The world, life, and mankind are therefore only phantoms, an illusion, a dream image— — —

POET. My dream!

DAUGHTER. A true dream!— — —But in order to be free of the earthly element, the decendants of Brahma seek self-denial and suffering... There you have suffering as the liberator... But this yearning for suffering conflicts with the desire for pleasure, or Love... do you understand what Love is yet, a supreme joy coupled to the most profound suffering, sweetest when it is most bitter? Do you understand now what woman is? Woman, through whom sin and death entered life?

POET. I understand!— — —And the end...?

DAUGHTER. You know that already... The strife between the pain of pleasure and the pleasure that suffering brings... the penitent's anguish and the voluptuary's joys...

POET. Strife, then?

DAUGHTER. Strife between opposites generates power, just as fire and water produce steam...

POET. But what of peace? Rest?

DAUGHTER. Hush! You must ask no more, and I may not answer!
— — —The altar is already adorned for the sacrifice— — — the flowers keep watch; the candles are lit... white sheets cover the windows... spruce-twigs lie in the doorway... *

POET. You say this so calmly, as though suffering did not exist for you.

DAUGHTER. Not exist?... I have suffered all your sufferings, but a hundredfold, because my perceptions were finer...

POET. Tell me your sorrows.

DAUGHTER. Poet, could you find the words to match your sorrows; could your words ever really express your thought?

POET. No, you are right. To myself, I always seemed like a deaf-mute, and whenever my songs caught the fancy of the crowd, they seemed only a cacophany to me—that is why I was always ashamed when people praised me, you see.

DAUGHTER. And yet you want me to? Look me in the eye!

POET. I can't endure your gaze...

DAUGHTER. How would you endure my words if I were to speak in my own language?— — —

POET. Tell me, though, before you go: what did you suffer most from here on earth?

DAUGHTER. From—just being alive; feeling my sight dimmed by these eyes, my hearing dulled by these ears, and my thoughts, my bright, airy thoughts bound in a labyrinth of fat. You have seen a brain, haven't you?... What twisting, crooked ways...

POET. Yes, that is why all right-thinking people have twisted minds.

DAUGHTER. Malicious, always malicious, but then you all are!
— — —

POET. How can one be otherwise?

DAUGHTER. Now I must shake the dust from my feet... the earth, the clay...

[*She takes off her shoes and places them in the fire*

*

DOORKEEPER [*enters, places her shawl in the fire*]. Perhaps I might burn up my shawl too? [*Exits*

OFFICER [*enters*]. And I my roses. Only the thorns remain! [*Exits*

BILLPOSTER [*enters*]. My posters can go, but my fishing net, never! [*Exits*

GLAZIER [*enters*]. The diamond? That opened the door? Farewell! [*Exits*

LAWYER [*enters*]. A report on the proceedings concerning the Pope's beard or the depletion in the sources of the Ganges*— [*Exits*

QUARANTINE MASTER [*enters*]. A small contribution, the black mask which made a blackamoor of me against my will. [*Exits*

VICTORIA [*enters*]. My beauty, my sorrow! [*Exits*

EDITH [*enters*]. My ugliness, my sorrow! [*Exits*

BLIND MAN [*enters, puts his hand in the fire*]. My hand for an eye! [*Exits*

Enter the DON JUAN *in a wheelchair together with the* COQUETTE *and the* 'FRIEND'.

DON JUAN. Hurry up, hurry up, life is short! [*All three exit*

*

POET. I read somewhere that when life approaches its end, everyone and everything passes quickly by in review... is this the end?

DAUGHTER. For me, yes. Farewell!

POET. A parting word!

DAUGHTER. No, I can't! Do you think your words could express our thoughts?

*

DEAN OF THEOLOGY [*enters in a fury*]. I have been repudiated by God, I am persecuted by men, abandoned by the government, and mocked by my colleagues! How can I have faith when no one else does?— — —How can I defend a God who doesn't defend his own? It's all nonsense!

[*Throws a book on the fire and goes out*

*

POET [*pulls the book from the fire*]. Do you know what it was?—A Book of Martyrs; a calendar with a martyr for every day in the year.

DAUGHTER. Martyr?

POET. Yes, someone who has been tortured and killed for his belief. Tell me why!

DAUGHTER. Do you think that everyone who is tortured suffers, and that everyone who is killed feels pain?—After all, suffering is redemption and death deliverance.

*

KRISTIN [*with her strips of paper*]. I'm pasting, I'm pasting until there's nothing left to paste...

POET. And if heaven itself cracked open, you would try to paste that back together again, too... Go away!

KRISTIN. Aren't there any double windows in the castle over there?

POET. No, Kristin, not in there.

KRISTIN [*leaves*]. I'll go then!

*

DAUGHTER.

Our parting is at hand, the end approaches;
Farewell you child of man, you dreamer,
You poet who understands best how to live;
Hovering on wings above the earth,
You dive at times into the mire
To graze against it, not fasten in it!
— — — — — — — — — — — — —
Now when I am about to leave... at the moment of parting

As one takes leave of a friend, a place,
How the loss of all one has loved rises up,
And regret for what one has destroyed...
Ah, now I know all the agony of living,
So this is what it means to be mortal— — —
One misses even what one has not valued,
One regrets even misdeeds never done...
One yearns to go, and yet one longs to stay...
So the heart's two halves are rent asunder,
As if wild horses were pulling it apart, torn to pieces
By contradiction, indecision, disharmony...
— — —

Farewell! Tell your brothers and sisters I shall remember them,
Where I now go, and their lament
I shall bear in your name to the throne.
For human beings are to be pitied!
                    Farewell!

*She goes into the castle. Music is heard. The backcloth is illuminated by
the burning castle, showing a wall of human faces, questioning, sorrowing,
despairing... As the castle burns, the bud on the roof bursts open into a
giant chrysanthemum.**

OPUS 3*

THE GHOST SONATA*
[*Spöksonaten*]

(1907)

CHARACTERS

The Old Man, Hummel, a Company Director
The Student, Arkenholz
The Milkmaid, a vision
The Caretaker's Wife
The Caretaker
The Dead Man, a consul
The Dark Lady, the daughter of the Dead Man and the Caretaker's Wife
The Colonel
The Mummy, the Colonel's wife
The Young Lady, his daughter, but actually the Old Man's daughter
The Posh Man, called Baron Skanskorg. Engaged to the Caretaker's daughter
Johansson, Hummel's servant
Bengtsson, the Colonel's manservant
The Fiancée, Hummel's former fiancée. A white-haired old lady
The Cook
The Maid
Beggars*

SCENE 1

The ground floor and first floor façade of a modern apartment building [c.1900]. But only one corner is visible ending, on the ground floor, in a round drawing-room and, on the first floor, in a balcony with a flagpole.

When the blinds are raised a white marble statue of a young woman is visible through the open window of the round drawing-room, surrounded by palms and brightly lit by sunlight. In the window to the left there are pots of hyacinths (blue, white, pink).

Hanging over the balustrade of the balcony at the corner of the first floor are a blue silk quilt and two white pillows. The windows to the left are covered in white sheets.*

It is a bright Sunday morning.

In the foreground, in front of the façade, there is a green bench.

To the right, in the foreground, a public drinking-fountain; to the left an advertising column.

To the rear, on the left, is the main entrance to the house, through which can be seen a staircase, with steps of white marble and a banister of mahogany and brass; on either side of the door tubs containing laurel bushes stand on the pavement.

The corner with the round drawing-room also looks on to a side street which leads towards the rear of the stage.

To the left of the entrance on the ground floor is a window with a gossip mirror.*

When the curtain rises the bells of several churches are audible in the distance.

The doors in the front of the house are open; the DARK LADY *is standing motionless on the steps.*

The CARETAKER'S WIFE *is sweeping the hallway; then she polishes the brass on the door; after that she waters the laurels.*

The OLD MAN *is sitting reading a newspaper in a wheelchair by the advertising column; his hair and beard are white, and he wears glasses.*

The MILKMAID *enters from round the corner carrying her bottles in a wire basket; she is dressed in summer clothes, with brown shoes, black stockings, and a white beret.*

The MILKMAID *takes off her beret and hangs it on the fountain; wipes the sweat from her forehead; takes a drink from the scoop which is*

*attached for this purpose to the fountain; washes her hands and tidies her
hair, using the water as a mirror.*

*A steamship bell can be heard, and now and then the silence is broken by
the bass notes of an organ in a nearby church.*

  After a couple of minutes' silence, when the MILKMAID *has finished her
toilet, the* STUDENT *enters from the left, sleepless and unshaven. He goes
directly to the fountain. Pause.*

STUDENT. May I borrow the scoop?

          The MILKMAID *hugs the scoop to her.*

STUDENT. Haven't you finished with it?

          The MILKMAID *looks at him in fear.*

OLD MAN [*to himself*]. Who is he talking to?—I can't see anyone!—
Is he mad?

          He continues to watch them in amazement.

STUDENT. What are you looking at? Do I look so terrible?—Oh, I've
    not slept a wink all night, so of course you think I've been out on
    the tiles— — —[*The* MILKMAID *as before*] Drinking punch,*
    eh?—Do I smell of punch? [*The* MILKMAID *as before*] I know I
    haven't shaved... Give me a drink of water, my girl, I've earned
    one! [*Pause*] Well then, I'd better tell you that I've spent all night
    binding up wounds and tending the injured. I was there, you see,
    yesterday evening, when the house collapsed... now you know.
    [*The* MILKMAID *rinses the scoop and gives him a drink*] Thanks!

          The MILKMAID *does not move.*

STUDENT [*slowly*]. Will you do me a big favour? [*Pause*] The thing
    is, my eyes are all swollen, as you can see, but I've been handling
    the injured and the dead therefore it's dangerous for me to touch
    them... Will you take my clean handkerchief, moisten it in some
    fresh water, and bathe my poor eyes?—Will you?—Will you be my
    good Samaritan?*

          The MILKMAID *hesitates, but does as he has asked.*

STUDENT. Thank you, my friend! [*He takes out his purse. The* MILK-
    MAID *makes a dismissive gesture*] Forgive me for being so thought-
    less, I'm not really awake...

                                        [*The* MILKMAID *leaves*

*

OLD MAN [*to the* STUDENT]. Excuse me asking, but I couldn't help hearing you were caught up in the accident yesterday evening... I've just been reading about it in the paper...

STUDENT. Have they already got hold of it?

OLD MAN. Yes, the whole story; and your picture as well, though they regret not having got the name of the brave young student...

STUDENT [*looks at the paper*]. Really? It is me, too! Oh dear!

OLD MAN. Who were you talking to just now?

STUDENT. Didn't you see?

Pause.

OLD MAN. Would it be impertinent to ask—to be allowed to know—your now-illustrious name?

STUDENT. What's the point? I don't like publicity—no sooner do they praise you than they find fault with you—these days cutting people down to size is one of the fine arts—besides, I'm not looking for a reward...

OLD MAN. Rich, I take it?

STUDENT. Not at all... quite the contrary! I'm extremely poor.

OLD MAN. One moment— — — I seem to have heard that voice before— — —when I was young I had a friend who couldn't say 'window' but always said 'winder'*—he's the only person I've ever heard speak like that; and now you—are you related to Arkenholz, the merchant, by any chance?

STUDENT. He was my father.

OLD MAN. Fate's a strange thing... I saw you as a little child, in particularly difficult circumstances...

STUDENT. Yes, I am supposed to have come into the world in the midst of a bankruptcy...

OLD MAN. Precisely!

STUDENT. Might I ask your name?

OLD MAN. My name is Hummel, Company Director...

STUDENT. Are you...? Then I do remember...

OLD MAN. You've often heard my name mentioned in your family?

STUDENT. Yes!

OLD MAN. And with a certain animosity, perhaps? [*The* STUDENT *remains silent*] Yes, I can imagine!—I suppose they said I ruined your father?—People who've ruined themselves with idiotic speculations always put their ruin down to the one person they couldn't fool. [*Pause*] The fact is, your father swindled me out of 17,000 crowns, all my savings at the time.

STUDENT. It's strange how a story can be told in two such different ways.

OLD MAN. You surely don't think I'm lying, do you?

STUDENT. What am I to think? My father didn't tell lies!

OLD MAN. That's true, a father never lies... I'm a father, too, though, so...

STUDENT. What are you driving at?

OLD MAN. I saved your father from destitution, and he rewarded me with all the terrible hatred that a debt of gratitude breeds... he taught his family to speak ill of me.

STUDENT. Perhaps you made him ungrateful by poisoning your help with needless humiliations.

OLD MAN. All help is humiliating, young man.

STUDENT. What do you want of me?

OLD MAN. I'm not after the money; if you would just do me some small favours, though, I'd be well paid. As you see, I'm a cripple. Some say it's my own fault, others blame my parents. To my mind, life itself's to blame, with all its snares; if you avoid one trap you walk straight into another. All the same, I can't run up and down stairs or ring doorbells, so I'm asking you: help me!

STUDENT. What can I do?

OLD MAN. First of all, push my chair over there so I can read those posters, I want to see what's on tonight...

STUDENT [*pushes the wheelchair*]. Don't you have a man to help you?

OLD MAN. Yes, but he's running an errand... he'll be back soon... Are you a medical student?

STUDENT. No, I'm studying languages, but I don't yet know what I'm going to do...

OLD MAN. Aha! Any good at maths?

STUDENT. Yes, not bad.

OLD MAN. Excellent!—Perhaps you'd like a job?

STUDENT. Yes, why not?

OLD MAN. Good! [*Reads one of the posters*] They're doing *The Valkyrie** this afternoon... The Colonel will be there with his daughter; he always has the end seats in row six, so I'll put you next to them... Go into that telephone kiosk, will you, and book a ticket for row six, number 82?

STUDENT. You want me to go to the opera this afternoon?

OLD MAN. Yes. Just do as I say, and you won't regret it. I want you to be happy, rich and renowned. Your debut yesterday as the brave rescuer will bring you fame tomorrow, and then your name will be worth a great deal.

STUDENT [*goes to the telephone kiosk*]. What a strange adventure...

OLD MAN. Are you a sportsman?

STUDENT. Yes, that's been my misfortune...

OLD MAN. Well, it shall be your fortune!*—Now do your telephoning!

He reads his newspaper. The DARK LADY *has come out onto the pavement and is talking with the* CARETAKER'S WIFE; *the* OLD MAN *listens, but the audience hears nothing. The* STUDENT *returns.*

OLD MAN. Done?

STUDENT. Yes.

OLD MAN. Do you see that house?

STUDENT. Yes, I've seen it before... I walked past here yesterday, when the sun was shining on the windows—and imagining all the beauty and luxury inside, I said to my companion: 'Fancy having an apartment there, on the fourth floor, a beautiful young wife, two pretty little children, and a private income of 20,000 a year...'

OLD MAN. Did you indeed? Did you, now? Well, there you are. I also love this house...

STUDENT. Do you speculate in houses?

OLD MAN. Mm—yes. But not the way you mean...

STUDENT. Do you know the people who live there?

OLD MAN. All of them. At my age you know everybody, their fathers and forefathers, you're always related to them in some way or other, too—I was eighty not long ago—but no one knows me, not properly—I take an interest in people's destinies...

The blind is raised in the round drawing-room. The COLONEL *can be seen, dressed in civilian clothes. After looking at the thermometer, he goes farther back into the room and stops before the marble statue.*

OLD MAN. Look, there's the Colonel. You'll be sitting next to him this afternoon...

STUDENT. Is that—the Colonel? I don't understand any of this, it's like a fairy tale...

OLD MAN. My whole life is like a book of fairy tales, young man; and though all the tales are different, they hang together on a single thread, with a leitmotif that recurs over and over again.

STUDENT. What's that marble statue in there?

OLD MAN. His wife, of course...

STUDENT. Was she really that lovely?

OLD MAN. Mmnn. Yes!—

STUDENT. Well, go on, tell me.

OLD MAN. My dear boy, we can't really judge a fellow human being!—And if I were to tell you that she left him, that he beat her, that she came back and married him again, and that *she* now sits in there like a mummy, worshipping her own statue, then you'd think I was crazy.

STUDENT. I don't understand!

OLD MAN. I don't suppose you do.—Then there's the hyacinth window. That's where his daughter lives— — —she's out riding, but she'll soon be home...

STUDENT. Who's the dark lady, the one talking to the Caretaker's wife?

OLD MAN. Now that's a bit complicated, but it has to do with the dead man, up there where you can see the white sheets...

STUDENT. Who was he then?

OLD MAN. A man, just like the rest of us, but what stuck out most was his vanity... If you were a Sunday child* you'd soon see him come out of that door to look at the consulate's flag at half-mast— he was a consul, you see, and liked crowns, lions, plumed hats, and coloured ribbons—

STUDENT. A Sunday child, you said—I was born on a Sunday, or so they say...

OLD MAN. No! Were you...? I almost knew... it was the colour of your eyes... but in that case you can see what others can't, have you noticed?

STUDENT. I don't know what other people can or can't see, but sometimes... well, one doesn't talk about things like that!

OLD MAN. I was almost sure of it! But you can tell me... because I— understand such things...

STUDENT. Yesterday, for example... I was drawn to that obscure little back street where the house then collapsed... the moment I got there I stopped in front of this building, which I'd never seen before... Then I noticed a crack in the wall and heard the joists snapping; I sprang forward and grabbed hold of a child who was walking close by the wall... The next second the house collapsed— — —I was safe, but in my arms, where I thought I had the child, there was nothing...

OLD MAN. Well, I must say... I thought as much... Tell me one thing, though: why were you gesticulating like that just now by the fountain? And why were you talking to yourself?

STUDENT. Didn't you see the milkmaid I was talking to?

OLD MAN [*recoils*]. Milkmaid?

STUDENT. Of course, the one who handed me the scoop.

OLD MAN. Really? So that's how it is?— — —Well, I may not be able to see, but I can do other things...

A white haired lady is now seen sitting down in the window by the gossip mirror.

OLD MAN. Look at that old woman in the window. Can you see her?—Good! That was my fiancée, once, sixty years ago!— — —I was twenty!—Don't worry, she doesn't recognize me. We see each other every day, but I don't mind that, not in the least, even though we did once vow to be eternally true to each other; eternally!

STUDENT. How foolish you were, in those days! We don't say things like that to our girlfriends, not nowadays.

OLD MAN. Forgive us, young man, we knew no better!—But can you see that this old woman was once young and beautiful?

STUDENT. No, I can't. Although yes, there's something about her expression, but I can't see her eyes!

The CARETAKER'S WIFE *comes out with a basket and scatters the ground with spruce twigs.**

OLD MAN. Ah yes, the Caretaker's wife.—The dark lady over there is her daughter, by the Dead Man, that's why her husband got the job as caretaker... but the dark lady has a suitor, who's very superior and has expectations of becoming rich; he's in the process of divorcing his wife, who's giving him a big house, all in stone, to get rid of him. This posh suitor is the dead man's son-in-law, you can see his bedclothes airing up there on the balcony... Complicated, isn't it?

STUDENT. Extremely!

OLD MAN. That's how it is, inside and out, even though it looks so simple.

STUDENT. But who was the Dead Man then?

OLD MAN. You just asked, and I just told you; but if you could see round the corner where the service entrance is, you'd see a crowd of poor people that he used to help... when he felt like it...

STUDENT. He was a kind man, then?

OLD MAN. Yes— — —sometimes.

STUDENT. Not always?

OLD MAN. No!— — —People are like that! Now, young man, just move my chair a little so it's in the sun, I'm so dreadfully cold. When you can't move about, your blood congeals—I'm going to die soon, I know, but there are one or two things I've got to do before I go—take my hand and you can feel how cold I am—

STUDENT. That's extraordinary!   [*Shrinks back*

OLD MAN. Don't leave me, I'm tired, I'm alone, but I haven't always been like this, you know; I've an endlessly long life behind me—endless—I've made people unhappy, and people have made me unhappy, the one cancels out the other—but before I die I want to see you happy... Our destines are entwined through your father—and other things...

STUDENT. But let go of my hand, you're taking all my strength away, you're freezing my blood, what do you want of me?

OLD MAN. Be patient, and you'll both see and understand— — — Here comes the young lady...

STUDENT. The Colonel's daughter?

OLD MAN. Yes, daughter! Look at her!—Have you ever seen such a masterpiece?

STUDENT. She's like the marble statue in there...

OLD MAN. That's her mother!

STUDENT. You're right—I've never seen such a woman of woman born—Happy the man who leads her to the altar and his home!—

OLD MAN. You can see it!—Not everyone sees her beauty... Well, so it is written!*

*

The YOUNG LADY *enters from the left in a fashionable English riding habit, with breeches, and walks slowly, without looking at anyone, to the door, where she pauses and says a few words to the* CARETAKER'S WIFE; *then enters the house. The* STUDENT *puts his hand over his eyes.*

OLD MAN. Are you crying?

STUDENT. When there is no hope, nothing remains but despair!

OLD MAN. I can open doors and hearts, if only I find an arm to do my will... Serve me, and you shall have power...

STUDENT. Is this some kind of pact? Must I sell my soul?*

OLD MAN. Sell nothing!—Listen, all my life, I've *taken*; now I've a longing to give! But no one will accept what I have— — —I'm rich, very rich, but I have no heirs except for one scoundrel, who plagues the life out of me— — —become my son, inherit me while I'm still alive, enjoy life and let me look on, at least from a distance.

STUDENT. What do I have to do?

OLD MAN. First, go and hear *The Valkyrie*.

STUDENT. That's already agreed—what else?

OLD MAN. This evening you'll be sitting in there, in the round room!

STUDENT. How am I to get in there?

OLD MAN. By way of *The Valkyrie*!

STUDENT. Why have you chosen me of all people as your medium? Did you know me before?

OLD MAN. Yes, of course! I've had my eye on you for a long time... But look now, up there on the balcony, the maid's hoisting the flag to half-mast for the Consul... and now she's turning the bed-clothes... Do you see that blue quilt?—That was meant for two to sleep under, now it's for one... [*The* YOUNG LADY, *who has changed her clothes, is now seen watering the hyacinths in the window*] There's my little girl, look at her, look!—She's talking to the flowers. Isn't she like a blue hyacinth herself?... She's giving them a drink, only pure water, which they transform into colours and fragrance... Here comes the Colonel with the paper.—He's showing her the accident... now he's pointing to your pic-ture! She's not exactly indifferent... she's reading about your bravery... I think it's clouding over, what if it should rain, then I'll be in a pretty pickle here, unless Johansson gets back soon...

It clouds over and grows dark; the OLD LADY *at the gossip mirror closes her window.*

OLD MAN. Now my fiancée's closing her window... seventy-nine, she is... that gossip mirror's the only one she uses, because she doesn't see herself in it, only the outside world, and from two directions, but the world can see her, she hasn't thought of that... A fine old lady, all the same...

Now the DEAD MAN *is seen coming out of the door in his winding-sheet.*

STUDENT. Good God, what's that?

OLD MAN. What can you see?

STUDENT. Don't *you* see, over there in the doorway, the Dead Man?

OLD MAN. I see nothing, but it's what I was expecting! Go on...

STUDENT. He's going out into the street... [*Pause*] Now he's turning his head, and looking at the flag.

OLD MAN. What did I say? You may be sure he'll count the wreaths as well, and read the cards... Woe to anyone who's missing!

STUDENT. Now he's turning the corner...

OLD MAN. He's going to count the beggars by the back door... the poor always make for a good show: 'Accompanied by the blessings of the many', yes, but he won't get my blessing!—Between you and me, he was a real rogue...

STUDENT. But charitable...

OLD MAN. A charitable rogue, who'd set his heart on a fine funeral... When he felt the end approaching, he cheated the state of 50,000 crowns... now his daughter's running around with another woman's husband, wondering about the inheritance... he can hear everything we say, the rogue, and serve him right!— There's Johansson.

> JOHANSSON *enters from the left.*

OLD MAN. Report!

> JOHANSSON *speaks inaudibly.*

OLD MAN. Not at home? You're a fool!—And the telegraph?— Nothing?— — —Go on!— — —Six o'clock this evening? That's good!—Special edition?—With his full name! Arkenholz, a student, born... parents... excellent... I think it's beginning to rain... What did he say?— — —Really, I see!—He didn't want to?—Well, he must!—Here comes that posh type!—Push me round the corner, Johansson, so I can hear what the poor are saying... And Arkenholz, you wait for me here... understand!— Hurry up, hurry up!

> *Johansson pushes the chair round the corner.*

*

The STUDENT *remains behind and looks at the* YOUNG LADY, *who is now raking the earth in the flowerpots.*

*

THE POSH MAN [*enters in mourning, speaks to the* DARK LADY, *who has been walking up and down on to the pavement*]. Well, what can we do about it?—We'll have to wait.

LADY. I can't wait!

THE POSH MAN. Really? Then go to the country.

LADY. I don't want to.

THE POSH MAN. Come over here, or people will hear what we're saying.

They go over to the advertising column and continue their conversation inaudibly.

∗

JOHANSSON [*enters from the right, to the* STUDENT]. My master asked you not to forget about that other matter.

STUDENT [*slowly*]. Listen—Tell me first, who is your master?

JOHANSSON. Ah! He's so many things, and has been everything—

STUDENT. Is he sane?

JOHANSSON. What does *that* mean?—All his life he's been looking for a Sunday child, or so he says, but that might not be true...

STUDENT. What does he want? Is he a miser?

JOHANSSON. He wants power.... All day long he rides around in his chariot like the god Thor∗... he looks at houses, pulls them down, founds new streets, and builds over squares; but he breaks into houses, too, creeps in through the window, ravages people's lives, kills his enemies and never forgives.—Would you believe it, sir, that limping little thing∗ has been a Don Juan, although he always lost his women?

STUDENT. How do you account for that?

JOHANSSON. Oh, he's so sly he gets the women to leave him when he's tired of them.— — —Now, though, he's like a horse thief at a human fair; he steals people, in all manner of ways... He's literally stolen me out of the hands of justice... I'd committed a little blunder, you see, which only he knew about. Instead of putting me away, he made me his slave; I slave for my food, nothing else, and that's none of the best...

STUDENT. What's he after here in this house?

JOHANSSON. I'd really rather not say. It's so complicated.

STUDENT. I think it would be as well to go...

JOHANSSON. Look at the Young Lady, she's dropped her bracelet out of the window...

The YOUNG LADY *has dropped her bracelet out of the open window. The* STUDENT *goes slowly forward, picks it up, and hands it to the* YOUNG LADY, *who thanks him stiffly. The* STUDENT *goes back over to* JOHANSSON.

JOHANSSON. So, you were thinking of going... It's not as easy as you think once *he's* got his net over your head... And there's nothing he's afraid of in this world... well, one thing, or person, rather ...

STUDENT. Wait a moment, maybe I know!

JOHANSSON. How can you?

STUDENT. I'm guessing.—Is it... a little milkmaid he's afraid of?

JOHANSSON. He always turns away when he meets a milk cart... and then he talks in his sleep, it seems he was in Hamburg once...

STUDENT. Can you believe this man?

JOHANSSON. You can believe anything and everything of him!

STUDENT. What's he doing round the corner now?

JOHANSSON. He's listening to the poor... Sowing a little word here, removing a stone at a time there, until the house collapses... figuratively speaking, of course. I'm an educated man, you know, used to be a bookseller... You going now?

STUDENT. I don't want to be ungrateful... This man once saved my father, and now he's only asking a small favour in return...

JOHANSSON. What's that?

STUDENT. I'm to go and see *The Valkyrie*...

JOHANSSON. It's beyond me... But he's always up to something... Look, now he's talking to that policeman... he always keeps in with the police, makes use of them, gets them fully involved, binds them with false hopes and promises, and all the while he's really pumping them.—You'll see, come nightfall and he'll have found his way into the round room.

STUDENT. What does he want there? What is there between him and the Colonel?

JOHANSSON. Well— — —I've a pretty good idea, but I'm not absolutely sure. You'll no doubt see when you get there!— — —

STUDENT. I'll never get in there...

JOHANSSON. That's up to you.—Go to *The Valkyrie*...

STUDENT. Is that the way?

JOHANSSON. Yes, if that's what he said.—Look, just look at him now in his battle waggon, drawn in triumph by the beggars, who'll not get a penny for their pains, just the hint of something nice at his funeral!

OLD MAN [*enters, standing in his wheelchair, drawn by one beggar and followed by all the others*]. Hail to the noble youth, who risked his own life to save so many in yesterday's disaster! Hail, Arkenholz!

The BEGGARS *bare their heads, but without cheering. The* YOUNG LADY *at the window waves her handkerchief. The* COLONEL *stares out through his window. The* OLD LADY *stands up at her window. The* MAID *on the balcony hoists the flag to the top of the mast.*

OLD MAN. Clap your hands, citizens, it may be Sunday but the ass in the pit and the ear in the field will absolve us,* and although I'm not a Sunday child, I possess both the spirit of prophecy and the gift of healing for I once summoned a drowned person back to life... it was in Hamburg one Sunday morning just like today...

*

The MILKMAID *enters, seen only by the* STUDENT *and the* OLD MAN; *she raises her arms as if she were drowning, and stares at the* OLD MAN.

OLD MAN [*sits down and shrinks back in horror*]. Johansson! Take me away!—Quickly!—Arkenholz, don't forget *The Valkyrie*!

STUDENT. What is all this?

JOHANSSON. We shall see! We shall see!

Curtain.

SCENE 2

*In the round drawing-room. At the back a white tiled stove with a
mirror,* pendulum clock, and candelabra. To the right an entrance hall
with a perspective of a green room with mahogany furniture. To the left
stands the statue, shadowed by palms. It can be concealed by curtains.
Upstage left a door to the hyacinth room, where the* YOUNG LADY *sits
reading. The* COLONEL*'s back can be seen as he sits writing in the
green room.*

    BENGTSSON, *the manservant, in livery, comes in from the hall with*
JOHANSSON, *in tails and white tie.*

BENGTSSON. You're to wait at table while I take their coats. Ever
done this kind of thing before?

JOHANSSON. Well, I may spend the day pushing a battle
waggon around, but in the evenings I wait at parties, and it's
always been my dream to get into this house... queer bunch,
aren't they?

BENGTSSON. Oh, ay, a bit out of the ordinary, you might say.

JOHANSSON. Is it a musical evening, or what?

BENGTSSON. Just the usual ghost supper, as we call it. They drink
tea and never say a word, or the Colonel talks all by himself; and
then they nibble their biscuits, all of them at the same time, so it
sounds like rats in an attic.

JOHANSSON. Why is it called a ghost supper?

BENGTSSON. They look like ghosts... And they've kept this up for
twenty years, always the same lot saying the same things, or else
keeping quiet so as not to be shown up.

JOHANSSON. Isn't there a wife here, too?

BENGTSSON. Oh yes, but she's crazy; she sits in a closet because her
eyes can't stand the light... She's in here...

                                       [Indicates a jib-door* in the wall

JOHANSSON. In there?

BENGTSSON. Yes, I said they were a bit out of the ordinary...

JOHANSSON. What does she look like?

BENGTSSON. Like a mummy... do you want to see her? [*Opens the jib-door*] Look, there she is!

JOHANSSON. Jesus Chr...

MUMMY [*like a baby*]. Why are you opening the dawer; didn't I twell you to keep it cwosed?...

BENGTSSON [*also babbling like a baby*]. Ta, ta, ta, ta! Ittle lolly must be nice now, then she'll get a sweetie!— Pretty Polly!

MUMMY [*like a parrot*]. Pretty Polly! Is Jacob there?* Currrrre!

BENGTSSON. She thinks she's a parrot. Maybe she is... [*To the* MUMMY] Come on, Polly, give us a whistle!

The MUMMY *whistles.*

JOHANSSON. I've seen a thing or two, but never anything like this!

BENGTSSON. You see, when a house gets old, it goes mouldy, and when people spend years tormenting each other, they go crazy. This little lady now—quiet, Polly!—this mummy's been sitting here for forty years—same husband, same furniture, same relations, same friends... [*He shuts the door on the* MUMMY *again*] And what's gone on in this house—I hardly know... Look at that statue... that's her when she was young!

JOHANSSON. Oh my God!—Is that the mummy?

BENGTSSON. Yes!—It's enough to make you weep, isn't it!—But somehow or other, imagination or whatever, this lady's got to be a bit like that loquacious bird—she can't stand cripples, for example, or the sick... She can't even stand her own daughter, because she's ill...

JOHANSSON. Is the young lady ill?

BENGTSSON. Didn't you know?

JOHANSSON. No!— — —And the Colonel, who is he?

BENGTSSON. You'll see!—

JOHANSSON [*looking at the statue*]. It's horrible to think... How old is she now?

BENGTSSON. No one knows— — —but they say that when she was thirty-five, she looked nineteen, and made the Colonel believe she was, too... Here in this very house... Do you know what that black screen's for, the Japanese one beside the chaise longue?—It's called the death screen. They put it up every time someone's going to die, just like in hospital...

JOHANSSON. What a horrible house!... And the Student was longing to find his way in here, as if it were paradise...

BENGTSSON. What student? Oh, him! The one who's coming here tonight... the Colonel and the young lady met him at the opera, they were both very taken with him... Hm!— — — But now it's my turn to ask you a question. Who's his master? The big boss in the wheelchair?

JOHANSSON. Oh, well—Is he coming too?

BENGTSSON. He hasn't been invited.

JOHANSSON. He'll come uninvited, if need be!— — —

*

The OLD MAN *appears in the hall, on crutches, wearing a frock coat, and top hat; he creeps forward, listening.*

BENGTSSON. He's a regular old robber, eh?

JOHANSSON. Fully fledged!

BENGTSSON. He looks like Old Nick* himself.

JOHANSSON. He's a bit of a magician, too.—He can pass through locked doors...

*

OLD MAN [*forward, takes* JOHANSSON *by the ear*]. Villain!—Watch out! [*To* BENGTSSON.] Announce me to the Colonel!

BENGTSSON. But we're expecting company...

OLD MAN. I know! But I'm half-expected, if not exactly with pleasure...

BENGTSSON. I see. What was the name? Mr Hummel?

OLD MAN. Correct!—

BENGTSSON *goes through the hall to the green room, closing its door behind him.*

*

OLD MAN [*to* JOHANSSON]. Beat it!—[JOHANSSON *hesitates*] Beat it!

[JOHANSSON *disappears into the hall*

*

OLD MAN [*scrutinizes the room; he pauses before the statue in amazement*]. Amalia!— — —It's her!— — —Her!

He wanders round the room, fingering things; arranges his wig in front of the mirror; returns to the statue.

MUMMY [*from the cupboard*]. Pret-ttty Polly!

OLD MAN [*startled*]. What was that? Is there a parrot in the room? I don't see one.

MUMMY. Is Jacob there?

OLD MAN. The place is haunted!

MUMMY. Jacob!

OLD MAN. Scarey!— — —So that's the kind of secrets they have in this house! [*He looks at a picture with his back to the closet*] It's him!— — —Him!

*

MUMMY [*appears behind the* OLD MAN *and pulls his wig*]. Currrrr-e! Is it Currrrre?

OLD MAN [*gives a jump*]. Dear God in heaven!—Who is it?

MUMMY [*in a normal voice*]. Is it Jacob?

OLD MAN. My name is Jacob, yes— — —

MUMMY [*with emotion*]. And mine's Amalia!

OLD MAN. No, no, no... Oh, Lord Jesus Chr—

MUMMY. How I look now! Yes!—And that's how I used to look. You live and learn—I live in the closet mostly, both to avoid seeing and being seen... But what are you looking for here, Jacob?

OLD MAN. My child! Our child— — —

MUMMY. She's sitting in there.

OLD MAN. Where?

MUMMY. There, in the hyacinth room!

OLD MAN [*looking at the* YOUNG LADY]. Yes, it's her! [*Pause*] What does her father say?—I mean the Colonel. Your husband?

MUMMY. I got angry with him once, and told him everything...

OLD MAN. And?

MUMMY. He didn't believe me, he said: 'that's what all wives say when they want to murder their husband.'—All the same it was a terrible crime. His whole life's been a lie though, his family name, too; reading through the Peerage sometimes I think to myself: 'she's got a false birth certificate like some servant girl; people get sent to prison for things like that.'

OLD MAN. Many do it; I seem to remember yours was also false...

MUMMY. My mother taught me that... I couldn't help it.— — — All the same, you were most to blame for our crime...

OLD MAN. No, it was your husband's fault for taking my fiancée away from me!—It's not in my nature to forgive before I've punished—I regarded it as a duty... I still do!

MUMMY. What are you after in this house? What do you want? How did you get in?—Is it my daughter? If you touch her, you'll die!

OLD MAN. I only want what's best for her.

MUMMY. But you must spare her father!

OLD MAN. No!

MUMMY. Then you must die, in this room; behind this screen...

OLD MAN. Maybe... but once I've got my teeth into someone, I can't let go...

MUMMY. You want to marry her off to the Student; why? He's nothing. He's got nothing.

OLD MAN. He'll be rich, I'll see to that!

MUMMY. Were you invited this evening?

OLD MAN. No, but I'm going to get myself an invitation to this ghost supper.

MUMMY. Do you know who's coming?

OLD MAN. Not exactly.

MUMMY. The Baron... who lives upstairs, whose father-in-law was buried this afternoon...

OLD MAN. The one who's getting divorced so as to marry the Caretaker's daughter... The one who was once your—lover!

MUMMY. And then there's your former fiancée, whom my husband seduced...

OLD MAN. A fine bunch...

MUMMY. Oh God, if we could die! *If* we could only die!

OLD MAN. Why do you get together then?

MUMMY. Crimes and secrets and guilt bind us together!—We've broken with one another and gone our ways so many times, but we're always drawn back together again...

OLD MAN. I think the Colonel's coming...

MUMMY. Then I'll go in to Adèle... [*Pause*] Jacob, think what you're doing! Spare him... [*Pause. She leaves*

*

COLONEL [*enters, cold, reserved*]. Won't you sit down?

The OLD MAN *sits slowly.*

COLONEL [*staring hard at him*]. You're the gentleman who wrote this letter?

OLD MAN. Yes!

COLONEL. Your name is Hummel?

OLD MAN. Yes!

Pause.

COLONEL. Since I now know you've bought up all my outstanding notes of hand, it follows that I'm entirely in your power. What is it you want?

OLD MAN. To be paid, one way or another!

COLONEL. In what way?

OLD MAN. Very simply—let's not talk about money—simply bear with me in your house, as a guest.

COLONEL. If you'll be satisfied with so little...

OLD MAN. Thank you!

COLONEL. What else?

OLD MAN. Dismiss Bengtsson!

COLONEL. Why should I? My trusted servant, who's been with me all his life?—Who's been decorated for loyal and faithful service?*—Why should I do that?

OLD MAN. Those virtues, that's only how you see him. He's not what he seems to be.

COLONEL. Who is?

OLD MAN [*recoils*]. True! But Bengtsson must go!

COLONEL. Are you running my house?

OLD MAN. Yes! Since I own everything here—furniture, curtains, china, linen... other things, too!

COLONEL. What other things?

OLD MAN. Everything! Everything you see, it's all mine!

COLONEL. Very well, it's yours! But my coat of arms and my good name, they're still mine!

OLD MAN. Not even those! [*Pause*] You're no nobleman!

COLONEL. How dare you!

OLD MAN [*taking out a piece of paper*]. Read what the College of Arms has to say here and you'll see that the family whose name you bear has been extinct for a hundred years.

COLONEL [*reads*]. I've heard rumours to that effect, yes, but I inherited the name from my father. [*Reads*] It's true; you're right... I'm not a nobleman!—Not even that!—Then I'll take off my signet ring.—It's true, it belongs to you— — —Here you are!

OLD MAN [*puts the ring on*]. Now we'll continue.—You're not a colonel either!

COLONEL. Aren't I?

OLD MAN. No! You were once an acting colonel in the American volunteer force, but after the Cuban war* and the reorganization of the army, all such titles were withdrawn...

COLONEL. Is that true?

OLD MAN [*gesturing to his pocket*]. Do you want to see?

COLONEL. No, there's no need!— — —But what gives you the right to strip me like this? Who are you?

OLD MAN. Time will tell. But talking of stripping— — —do you know who you are?

COLONEL. Have you no shame?

OLD MAN. Take off your wig and look in the mirror, but take out your teeth first and shave off your moustache, get Bengtsson to unlace your corset,* and then we'll see if a certain footman, Mr XYZ, doesn't recognize himself; the one who used to scrounge food in a certain kitchen...

The COLONEL *reaches for the bell on the table. The* OLD MAN *stops him.*

OLD MAN. Don't touch that bell, and don't send for Bengtsson, or I'll have him arrested— — —Here come the guests—keep calm, now, and we'll go on playing our old roles.

COLONEL. Who are you? I seem to recognize those eyes and that voice...

OLD MAN. Don't ask, just keep quiet, and do what I say!—

*

STUDENT [*enters, bows to the* COLONEL]. Colonel!

COLONEL. Welcome to my house, young man; following your noble conduct in this great disaster your name is on everyone's lips, I count it an honour to receive you in my home...

STUDENT. Colonel, my humble origins... Your illustrious name and noble birth...

COLONEL. Let me introduce you: Mr Arkenholz, Mr Hummel. — — —Would you be so good as to join the ladies, there's something else I need to discuss with Mr Hummel...

*

The STUDENT *is shown into the hyacinth room, where he remains visible, engaged in a shy conversation with the* YOUNG LADY.

COLONEL. A splendid young man, musical, sings, writes poetry... If he were a nobleman and our equal I'd have nothing against... well...

OLD MAN. What?

COLONEL. My daughter...

OLD MAN. *Your* daughter!—By the way, why does she always sit in there?

COLONEL. She insists on sitting in the hyacinth room when she's not out and about. It's a peculiarity of hers... Ah, here comes Miss Beate von Holsteinkrona... a charming woman... she's a secular canoness,* you know, with an income appropriate to her rank and circumstances...

OLD MAN [*to himself*]. My fiancée!

*

The FIANCÉE *enters, white haired; she appears mad.*

COLONEL. Miss Holsteinkrona, Mr Hummel— — —

The FIANCÉE *curtsies and sits down. The* POSH MAN *enters, secretive, dressed in mourning and sits down.*

*

COLONEL. Baron Skanskorg...

OLD MAN [*aside, without getting up*]. I do believe it's the jewel thief... [*To the* COLONEL] Bring in the Mummy, and the party's complete...

COLONEL [*in the door to the hyacinth room*]. Polly!

*

MUMMY [*enters*]. Currrrr-e!

COLONEL. The young people, too?

OLD MAN. No! Not them! They're to be spared...

They all sit silently in a circle.

COLONEL. May we serve tea?

OLD MAN. What for? No one likes tea, so there's no point sitting here pretending we do.

Pause.

COLONEL. Shall we converse, then?

OLD MAN [*slowly and with pauses*]. Talk about the weather, which we know all about? Ask how we are, which we already know? I prefer silence, then you can hear thoughts and see the past; silence cannot conceal anything... unlike words; I read the other day that the different languages really arose among primitive peoples in order to conceal the secrets of one tribe from the others; languages are thus codes, and he who finds the key will understand all the languages of the world; but this doesn't prevent secrets coming to light without a key, especially in those cases where paternity needs to be proved, but proof in a Court of Law is another matter; two false witnesses will do provided they agree,* but in the kind of errand I have in mind there are no witnesses, nature herself has endowed man with a sense of shame, which seeks to conceal what should be concealed; without wanting to, however, we still find ourselves in situations where opportunities sometimes arise to reveal what is most secret, when the mask is torn from the deceiver, when the villain is exposed... [*Pause. All look at each other in silence*] How quiet it's gone! [*Long silence*] Here, for example, in this respectable house, in this lovely home, where beauty, culture, and wealth have been united— — —[*Long silence*] All of us sitting here, we know who we are... isn't that so?... I don't have to tell you... and you know me, although you pretend you don't... In there sits my daughter, *mine*, you know that, too... Without knowing why, she'd lost the will to live... she simply withered in this air that reeks of crime, deception, and every kind of falsehood... that's why I sought a friend for her, someone with whom she might experience the light and warmth of a noble deed... [*Long silence*] That was my mission in this house: to root out the weeds, expose the crimes, settle past accounts, so that these young people may make a fresh start in this home, which I have given them! [*Long silence*] Now I grant you leave to go, each of you in turn and order; whoever stays will be arrested! [*Long silence*] Listen to the ticking of the clock, like a death-watch beetle in the wall. Do you hear what it says? 'Time's up! Time's up!' When it strikes, in a little while, your time will be up. Then you can go, but not before. But it raises its arm before it strikes!—Listen! It's warning you: 'The clock can strike.'— — —I, too, can strike... [*He strikes the table with his crutch*] Do you hear?

Silence.

*

MUMMY [*goes up to the clock and stops it; then lucidly and seriously*]. But I can stop time in its course—I can wipe out the past and undo what's been done, not with bribes, not with threats, but through suffering and repentance!— — —[*Goes up to the* OLD MAN] We are poor miserable creatures, all of us; we have erred and we have sinned, like everyone else; we are not what we seem, for at heart we are better than ourselves, since we hate our faults; but that you, Jacob Hummel with your false name, can sit here in judgement on us proves how much worse you are than us! You are also not who you seem to be!—You're a stealer of souls—you stole me once with your false promises; you murdered the Consul who was buried here today, you strangled him with notes of hand; and you've stolen the student by binding him with an imaginary debt of his father's, who never owed you a penny...

The OLD MAN *has tried to get up and interrupt her, but has crumpled over and fallen back in his chair; he shrinks more and more during what follows.*

MUMMY. But there's a black spot in your life, which I'm not sure about, though I have my suspicions... I believe Bengtsson knows!

[*Rings the bell on the table*

OLD MAN. No, not Bengtsson! Not him!

MUMMY. So, he *does* know! [*Rings again*

The MILKMAID *appears in the hall door, unseen by anyone except the* OLD MAN, *who recoils in fear; the* MILKMAID *disappears when* BENGTSSON *enters.*

MUMMY. Do you know this man?

BENGTSSON. Yes, I know him and he knows me. You know how it is, life has its ups and downs; I've served him, as he has me. He hung around my kitchen for two whole years—since he had to be gone by three, dinner was always ready at two, and the family had to make do with that brute's warmed up leftovers—but he also drank the juice from the meat, which then had to be eked out with water—he sat there like a vampire sucking all the goodness out of the house, and turned us all to skeletons—and he nearly got us put in prison for calling the cook a thief! Later I came across this man in Hamburg, under another name. He was now a usurer, a bloodsucker; besides which he was accused of having lured a young girl out on to the ice to drown her, all because she'd witnessed a crime he feared would be discovered...

MUMMY [*passes her hand over the* OLD MAN*'s face*]. This is you! Now let's have those notes of hand and the will!

JOHANSSON *appears in the hall door and watches the scene with great interest, since he is about to be liberated from slavery. The* OLD MAN *takes out a bundle of papers and throws it on the table.*

MUMMY [*strokes the* OLD MAN*'s back*]. Polly! Is Jacob there?

OLD MAN [*like a parrot*]. Jacob's there! Cacadora! Dora!

MUMMY. Can the clock strike?

OLD MAN [*clucks*]. The clock can strike! [*Imitates a cuckoo clock*] Cuck-oo! Cuck-oo! Cuck-oo!— — —

MUMMY [*opens the closet door*]. Now the clock has struck!—Get up and go into the closet where I've been sitting mourning our misdeed for twenty years—You'll find a rope in there like the one with which you strangled the Consul upstairs, and with which you thought to strangle your benefactor... Go!

[*The* OLD MAN *goes into the closet*

MUMMY [*closing the door*]. Bengtsson! Put up the screen! The death screen! [BENGTSSON *places the screen in front of the cupboard door*

MUMMY. It is finished!*—God have mercy on his soul!

ALL. Amen!

Long silence.

*

In the hyacinth room the YOUNG LADY *can be seen accompanying the* STUDENT *on a harp as he recites the following song.*

SONG [*preceded by a prelude*]

The sun I saw, and so it seemed
As if I saw the Hidden One;
Man must reap what he has sown,
Blest be he whose deeds are good.
For deeds you have done in anger

No penance do with evil;
Comfort him you have distressed
With your goodness, solace bring.
None need fear who did no ill;
Good it is to be innocent.*

Curtain.

SCENE 3

A room decorated in a somewhat bizarre style, with oriental motifs. Hyacinths in all kinds of colours everywhere. On the tiled stove the figure of a large seated Buddha with a bulb in its lap,* from which there rises the stalk of a shallot,* bearing its globe-shaped inflorescence of white, star-shaped flowers!

Upstage right a door leads to the round drawing-room where the COLONEL *and the* MUMMY *can be seen sitting in silence, doing nothing. Part of the death screen is also visible. To the left, a door to the kitchen and pantry.*

The STUDENT *and the* YOUNG LADY *(Adèle) are by the table. She sits at her harp; he is standing.*

YOUNG LADY. Sing now, sing for my flowers!

STUDENT. Is this your soul's flower?

YOUNG LADY. The one and only! Do you love the hyacinth?

STUDENT. I love it above all others, its virginal form rising straight and slender from the bulb as it rests upon the water and sinks its pure white root into the colourless liquid; I love its colours; the innocent and pure snow-white, the honey-sweet yellow, the rose of youth, the scarlet of maturity, but above all the blue—the deep-eyed, dewy-blue of fidelity— —I love them all, more than gold and pearls, I've loved them ever since I was a child, I've adored them because they possess all the fine qualities I lack... And yet...

YOUNG LADY. What?

STUDENT. My love is unrequited, for these beautiful flowers hate me...

YOUNG LADY. How is that?

STUDENT. Their fragrance, strong and pure from the first winds of spring that sweep across the melting snow, confuses my senses, deafens me, blinds me, drives me from the room, assails me with poisoned arrows that sadden my heart and set my head on fire! This flower—don't you know its story?

YOUNG LADY. Tell me.

STUDENT. But first its meaning. Resting on the water or buried in the soil, the bulb is the earth; here the stalk shoots up, straight as the axis on which the world turns, and here at the top the star flowers with their six-pointed petals*—

YOUNG LADY. Above the earth—the stars! Oh, it's magnificent! Where did you discover that? How did you see it?

STUDENT. Let me think!—In your eyes!—Then it's an image of the cosmos... That's why the Buddha sits there cradling the earth in his lap, with his eyes fixed upon it so he can watch it grow, outward and upward, as it transforms itself into a heaven—that's what the Buddha is waiting for—that one day this poor earth will become heaven.

YOUNG LADY. Now I understand—don't snowflakes also have six-pointed petals like the hyacinth lily?

STUDENT. You said it!—Then snowflakes are falling stars...

YOUNG LADY. And the snowdrop is a snow star... growing out of the snow.

STUDENT. But Sirius,* the biggest and most beautiful star in the firmament, all yellow and red, that's the narcissus with its red and yellow cup* and its six white rays...

YOUNG LADY. Have you ever seen the shallot in flower?

STUDENT. Of course I have!—It cradles its flowers in a ball, a globe resembling the sphere of heaven, strewn with white stars...

YOUNG LADY. How magnificent! Whose thought was that?

STUDENT. Yours!

YOUNG LADY. Yours!*

STUDENT. Ours!—We've given birth to it together, we're married...

YOUNG LADY. Not yet...

STUDENT. What else remains?

YOUNG LADY. The waiting, the trials, the patience!

STUDENT. Good! Try me! [*Pause*] Tell me. Why do your parents sit in there so silently, without saying a word?

YOUNG LADY. Because they've nothing to say to each other, because neither believes what the other says. My father once said:

'What's the point of talking, we can't pull the wool over each other's eyes?'

STUDENT. That's horrible...

YOUNG LADY. Here comes the Cook... Look at her, how big and fat she is...

STUDENT. What does she want?

YOUNG LADY. She wants to ask me about dinner, I'm looking after the house, you see, while mother's ill...

STUDENT. Is the kitchen our concern?

YOUNG LADY. We have to eat———Look at the Cook, I can't bear to...

STUDENT. Who is that monstrous woman?

YOUNG LADY. One of the Hummels—a vampire; she's devouring us...

STUDENT. Why not dismiss her?

YOUNG LADY. She won't go! We've no control over her. We've got her for our sins... Can't you see we're wasting and pining away...

STUDENT. Don't you get anything to eat then?

YOUNG LADY. Oh yes, one course after another, but all the goodness is gone... She boils the meat until there's nothing left but sinews and water while she drinks the stock herself, and when there's a roast, she cooks all the juice out of it, eats the sauce, and drinks the broth; everything she touches loses its strength; it's as if she sucked it out with her eyes, we get the dregs after she's drunk the coffee; she drinks the wine and fills the bottles with water...

STUDENT. Get rid of her!

YOUNG LADY. We can't!

STUDENT. Why not?

YOUNG LADY. We don't know! She won't go! No one can control her—she's taken our strength away!

STUDENT. Can I get rid of her for you?

YOUNG LADY. No! I think it's meant to be like this!—Here she is now. She'll ask what we want for dinner; I'll tell her this or that; she'll object, then go and do just as she likes.

STUDENT. Let her decide for herself, then.

YOUNG LADY. She won't!

STUDENT. What a strange house. It's bewitched!

YOUNG LADY. Yes.—But look, she turned away when she saw you!

*

COOK [*in the doorway*]. No, that wasn't why!

[*Grins, showing her teeth*

STUDENT. Get out, woman!

COOK. When I feel like it. [*Pause*] Now I feel like it!

[*She disappears*

YOUNG LADY. Don't get upset!—Practise patience; she's one of the trials we have to endure here in this house. There's also a maid whom we have to clean up after.

STUDENT. This is more than I can bear! *Cor in aethere!* * A song!

YOUNG LADY: Wait!

STUDENT. A song!

YOUNG LADY. Patience!—This is called the room of trial—it's beautiful to look at but full of imperfections— — —

STUDENT. Unbelievable; but we'll just have to overlook them. It is beautiful, but a bit cold. Why don't you light a fire?

YOUNG LADY. Because it smokes.

STUDENT. Can't you get the chimney swept?

YOUNG LADY. That doesn't help!— — —Do you see that desk over there?

STUDENT. It's very beautiful.

YOUNG LADY. But it wobbles; every day I put a piece of cork under one of its legs, but the maid removes it when she sweeps the floor, and I have to cut out a new one. Every morning there's ink on the penholder, on the inkstand, too; I have to clean up after her, every waking day.— — —[*Pause*] What do you most hate doing?

STUDENT. Counting the washing! Ugh!

YOUNG LADY. That's my job! Ugh!

STUDENT. What else?

YOUNG LADY. Being woken up in the middle of the night, and having to get up and fasten the catch on the window... the one the maid's forgotten.

STUDENT. What else?

YOUNG LADY. Climbing a ladder and mending the cord on the damper, when the maid has pulled it off.

STUDENT. What else?

YOUNG LADY. Sweeping up after her, dusting after her, lighting a fire in the stove after her—she only puts the logs in the grate. Checking the damper, polishing the glasses, relaying the table, uncorking the bottles, opening the windows and airing the rooms, remaking my bed, rinsing out the carafe of water when it's green with algae, buying the matches and soap that we always seem to have run out of, drying the lamps and trimming the wicks, so they won't smoke, and to make sure the lamps don't go out when we've got company, I have to fill them myself...

STUDENT. A song!

YOUNG LADY. Wait!—First the drudgery, the drudgery that keeps the dirt of life at bay.

STUDENT. But you're wealthy, why not have two servants?

YOUNG LADY. It wouldn't help, even if we had three! Life's hard, I get so tired sometimes... Imagine having a nursery as well!

STUDENT. The greatest of joys...

YOUNG LADY. And the dearest— — —Is life worth that much trouble?

STUDENT. It all depends on the reward you expect for your drudgery... I'd stop at nothing to win your hand.

YOUNG LADY. Don't talk like that!—I can never be yours!

STUDENT. Why?

YOUNG LADY. You mustn't ask.

Pause.

STUDENT. You dropped your bracelet from the window...

YOUNG LADY. Because my hand has grown so thin...

The COOK *enters, carrying a Japanese soya bottle in her hand.*

YOUNG LADY. She's the one who's devouring us all!

STUDENT. What's she got in her hand?

COOK. The colouring bottle, the devil's elixir* with the scorpion-like lettering.* Soya, the witch, who turns water into bouillon; we use it to replace the gravy, to cook cabbage in, and to make mock turtle soup.

STUDENT. Get out!

COOK. You suck the life out of us, and we out of you, we take the blood, and give you back the water—with colouring. This is the colouring!—I'm going now, but all the same I'll stay as long as I want!   [*Exits*

Pause.

STUDENT. Why does Bengtsson have a medal?

YOUNG LADY. Because of his great merits.

STUDENT. Has he no faults?

YOUNG LADY. Yes, big ones, but you don't get a medal for them.

They smile.

*

STUDENT. You have many secrets in this house...

YOUNG LADY. Like everyone else... let us keep ours!

Pause.

STUDENT. Do you love frankness?

YOUNG LADY. Yes, in moderation.

STUDENT. Sometimes I'm seized by a passionate desire to say exactly what I'm thinking; but I know that if people were absolutely frank the world would come to an end. [*Pause*] I went to a funeral the other day... in church—it was very solemn and beautiful.

YOUNG LADY. Was it Mr Hummel's?

STUDENT. My false benefactor's, yes!—At the head of the coffin stood an old friend of the deceased, carrying the funeral mace; the minister impressed me deeply with his dignified bearing and his moving words.—I wept, we all did.—Afterwards we went to a restaurant... There I learnt that the man with the mace had loved the dead man's son... [*The* YOUNG LADY *stares at him, to catch his meaning*] And the dead man had borrowed money from his son's admirer... [*Pause*] The next day the minister was arrested for embezzling church funds! A pretty story, isn't it?

YOUNG LADY. Ugh!

Pause.

STUDENT. Do you know what I'm thinking now about you?

YOUNG LADY. Don't tell me, or I'll die!

STUDENT. I must, or I shall die!— — —

YOUNG LADY. In asylums people say exactly what they think...

STUDENT. Precisely!—My father ended up in a madhouse...

YOUNG LADY. Was he ill?

STUDENT. No, he was quite well, just mad! Anyway, just the once, this is what happened... Like all of us he was surrounded by a circle of acquaintances, whom he called friends for short; like most people, of course, they were a sorry bunch of good-for-nothings. But he had to have someone to talk to; he couldn't just sit there all by himself. Now, you don't normally tell people what you think of them, and nor did he. He knew how false they were; he knew the depths of their deceit... but he was a wise man and well brought up, so he was always polite. One day though, he gave a big party— it was in the evening and he was tired, what with working all day and the strain of keeping quiet on the one hand and talking shit with his guests on the other...

The YOUNG LADY *shudders.*

STUDENT. Well, at table he called for silence and raised his glass to make a speech ... Then the safety-catch slipped and he spoke on and on, stripping the whole company bare, one after another, telling each and every one of them just how false they were. Then he sat down exhausted in the middle of the table, and told them all to go to hell!

YOUNG LADY. Oh!

STUDENT. I was there, and will never forget what happened next!... Father and mother came to blows, the guests ran for the door...

and father was taken away to the madhouse, where he died!
[*Pause*] Keeping silent for too long creates a pool of stagnant
water, which rots. There's something very rotten here.* And yet,
when I first saw you come in, I thought it was paradise... That
Sunday morning when I stood out there gazing in I saw a colonel
who was not a colonel, I had a noble benefactor who was a crook
and had to hang himself, I saw a mummy who wasn't one, and a
virgin who— speaking of which, where is virginity to be found?
And beauty? In nature and in my mind when it's in its Sunday
best. Where are faith and honour? In fairy tales and children's
plays. Where does anything fulfil its promise?... In my imagination!—Now your flowers have poisoned me, and I've poisoned you
in return—I begged you to be my wife and share my home, we
wrote poetry and sang and played music together, and then the
Cook appeared... *Sursum Corda!** Try once more to strike fire and
purple from your golden harp... try, I beg you. I implore you, on
my knees... Come, I'll do it myself! [*He takes the harp but no sound
comes from the strings*] It's deaf and dumb. To think that the most
beautiful flowers are so poisonous, are the most poisonous; all
creation, all of life is cursed... Why wouldn't you be my bride?
Because the very source of life in you is sick*... That vampire in
the kitchen, I can feel it now, beginning to suck my blood, it's like a
Lamia,* giving suck to children. The kitchen, that's where
children's hearts are nipped in the bud, unless it's the bedroom,
of course... There are poisons that blind and poisons that open the
eyes. I must have been born with the latter, for I can't see the ugly
as beautiful, or call what's evil good, I just can't! Christ descended
into hell, that was his pilgrimage on earth—to this madhouse, this
prison, this charnel-house the earth; and the madmen killed him
when he wanted to set them free; and let the robber go,* the robber
who always gets our sympathy!—Alas for us all, alas! Saviour of
the World, save us, or we perish!

YOUNG LADY [*has collapsed and appears to be dying. She rings.*
BENGTSSON *enters*]. Bring the screen! Quickly—I'm dying!

BENGTSSON *returns with the screen which he unfolds and places in front
of the* YOUNG LADY.

STUDENT. The deliverer is coming! Welcome, you pale and gentle
one!—And you,* you beautiful, unhappy, innocent creature who

bear no blame for your suffering, sleep, sleep without dreams, and when you awake again. . . may you be greeted by a sun that does not burn, in a house without dust, by friends without faults, by a love without flaw.— — —You wise and gentle Buddha, sitting there waiting for a heaven to grow up out of the earth, grant us patience in our time of trial, make pure our will that this hope may not maketh ashamed!*

The harp's strings begin to rustle; the room is filled with a white light.

> The sun I saw, and so it seemed
> As if I saw the Hidden One;
> Man must reap what he has sown,
> Blest be he whose deeds are good.
> For deeds you have done in anger
> No penance do with evil;
> Comfort him you have distressed
> With your goodness, solace bring.
> None need fear who did no ill;
> Good it is to be innocent.

A whimpering sound can be heard from behind the screen.

STUDENT. Poor little child, child of this world of illusion, guilt, suffering and death; this world of endless change, disappointment and pain. May the Lord of Heaven have mercy on you on your journey. . .

The room disappears. Böcklin's painting The Isle of the Dead* appears as the background.* Music, soft, tranquil, and pleasantly melancholy is heard from the island.

EXPLANATORY NOTES

THE FATHER

2 *Nöjd*: pronounced 'Noyd'; ironically, this typically monosyllabic Swedish soldier's name of the type given to families who received small plots of land in exchange for military service, means 'satisfied' or 'content'. Unable to retain the precise meaning of this charactonym in his own French translation of *The Father*, Strindberg called him 'Pierre', or 'stone'.

3 *jib-door*: a door standing flush with the surrounding wall and usually painted or papered over to appear indistinguishable from its surroundings.

5 *the girl's only . . . berth there*: if an unmarried mother was engaged as a wet-nurse in a public orphanage which cared for children born out of wedlock by women without means, her own child might be adopted by the orphanage so long as she relinquished part of her wages.

10 *as the law stands . . . father's faith*: according to a law dating back to 1734, as his child's guardian a father was responsible for bringing up her (or him) 'in the true evangelical faith, fear of God, virtue and honour'. Since the Captain is an atheist, this would bring him into conflict with this law, to which he refers.

she's sold her birthright . . . None whatever!: refers to ch. 9, s. 1 of the Act of Marriage in force at the time. Not until 1949 did Swedish law accord a wife equal rights with her husband over their children. The paragraph stipulating a wife's loss of rights on marriage was abolished earlier, in 1920.

15 *spectral analysis*: the chemical analysis of substances by means of their spectra, i.e. the pattern of absorbtion or emission of any electromagnetic radiation over a range of wavelengths characteristic of a body or substance.

spectroscope: an instrument for the production and examination of spectra, developed by the chemist Robert Bunsen and the physicist G. R. Kirchoff in 1859. This led rapidly to the discovery of new elements such as rubidium and thallium, and to the identification in 1868 of some unknown solar lines as an element apparently not present on earth, which Norman Lockyer named Helium. The Captain is thus working at the cutting edge of contemporary science.

19 *Stagnelius*: Erik Johan Stagnelius (1793–1823), Swedish Romantic poet in whose work erotic and religious themes are closely intertwined. Since Stagnelius is little known outside Sweden, Strindberg replaced him in his own French translation with the French poet and politician Alphonse de Lamartine (1790–1869).

20 *spring morning*: referring to the inner windows that used to be inserted in Swedish houses in autumn and removed again in the spring, Bertha actually says: 'but when you come, father, it's like taking out the inner window on a spring morning!'

23 *Svärd*: another soldier's name (see note to p. 2), meaning 'sword'. Thus, the the Captain's exit is a metaphorical call to arms. In Swedish the name is also integral to the imagery of the play in which Strindberg stresses the battle of the sexes and describes how, like Hercules (see note to p. 50), the Captain is caught in the net that Laura weaves about him. However, as Barry Jacobs points out, a literal translation of Svärd's name would accomplish nothing: 'What have been traditionally called the "spear side" and the "distaff side" of the family in English are designated *svärdsida* and *spinnsida* in Swedish. The Captain first calls Svärd by name near the end of Act I—at the moment when he decides to exercise his male prerogative and take action against the women who, he says are "spinning a net" around him; but despite his efforts, the "spinning side" (Omphale) triumphs over the "sword side" (Hercules). Since "spear side" is unfamiliar to most English-speakers and "sword side" is meaningless, there is really nothing the translator can do to salvage this name'; 'Strindberg's *Fadren* (The Father) in English Translation', *Yearbook of Comparative and General Literature*, 35 (1986), 112–21.

28 *A sorrowful and wretched thing . . . All is vanity*: hymn 391 in J. O. Wallin's Swedish hymnal of 1819.

Oh, what is this . . . trial and test: hymn 457 in the 1819 hymnal.

Christmas Eve: in Sweden gifts are traditionally exchanged on Christmas Eve, not Christmas Day.

30 *is it true . . . striped foals*: behind the Captain's questions lies the now discredited, but during the nineteenth century widely entertained, theory of telegony, in which it was supposed to be possible for the characteristics of one species to be inherited 'at a distance' from another. Referred to by Darwin as 'the direct action of the male element on the female form', the most famous instance, often quoted in the scientific literature of the period, had to do with the attempt of the Earl of Morton to cross a male quagga (a now extinct zebra-like member of the horse family that once flourished in South Africa) with a chestnut mare of seven-eighths Arabian blood. See Richard W. Burckhardt, 'Closing the Door on Lord Morton's Mare: The Rise and Fall of Telegony', *Studies in the History of Biology*, 3 (1979), 1–22.

a man must . . . Goethe says: Strindberg may be thinking of Faust's response to his servant, Wagner: 'Ja, was man so erkennen heißt! | Wer darf das Kind beim rechten Namen nennen?' (The things people call 'knowing'! Who dares to call a child by its proper name?), *Faust* I, 588–9.

31 *Lysekil*: a resort on the Swedish west coast, north of Gothenburg. In his translation of *The Father* into French Strindberg removed this local reference along with all the other Swedish names or culturally specific allusions to Sweden.

31 *their instinct for villainy is quite unconscious*: the notion of woman's instinctive villainy is taken from Schopenhauer's essay 'On Women' (Über die Weiber) from his *Parerga und Paralipomena*, which Strindberg quotes as one of the epigraphs to the second volume of his stories entitled *Getting Married* (written 1885–6): 'Women's original sin is injustice. It stems from their lack of common sense, and their inability to pause and think. This fault is aggravated by the fact that nature, which has denied them strength, has compensated for this by making them cunning. Hence their instinctive villainy, and their unquenchable taste for telling lies.' See *Getting Married*, trans. Mary Sandbach (London, 1977), 193.

32 *Mrs Alving . . . dead husband*: the protagonist of Ibsen's drama *Ghosts* (1881), in which she tells Pastor Manders, the spokesman of conventional morality, about her dead husband's dissolute life.

34 *you've dropped them into my ear like henbane*: cf. *Hamlet*, I, v. 61ff, where the Ghost of Hamlet's father describes how 'the uncle stole, | With juice of cursèd hebenon [henbane] in a vial, | And in the porches of my ears did pour | The leperous distilment'.

36 *But has not a man . . . a soldier weep?*: a close paraphrase of Shylock's words in *The Merchant of Venice*, III. i. 50–61, which Strindberg knew in Carl August Hagberg's Swedish translation.

37 *the one who awoke us was himself a sleepwalker*: Henrik Ibsen (1828–1906), whose plays (e.g. *Brand*, *A Doll's House*, and *Ghosts*) inspired the new, radical literature of Scandinavia in the 1880s; they were at the centre of an ongoing debate about the relationship between the sexes and the place of women in society.

38 *Those who . . . spayed hens*: a reference to the group of writers known as 'Det Unga Sverige' (Young Sweden), whose literary radicalism looked to Ibsen for inspiration, especially in the Woman Question. Once their natural leader, Strindberg and Young Sweden had parted company following publication of *Getting Married* (1884), for which he was charged with blasphemy. Although they rallied round him in court, these writers subsequently distanced themselves from Strindberg for his increasingly vehement attacks on Ibsen and on women's emancipation in general.

the court: Laura threatens him with *förmyndarkammaren*, a now-defunct (1667–1956) organization, based in Stockholm, from where it administered the property of minors as well as those declared incapable of managing their own affairs.

42 *a tare among our wheat*: the Pastor is quoting from the Sermon on the Mount; see Matthew 13: 25, 'But while men slept, his enemy came and sowed tares among the wheat.'

Not one spot of blood: an echo of *Macbeth*, v. i. 33, 'Out, damned spot! out, I say!', where Lady Macbeth walks in her sleep and rubs her hands to remove the stain left by the murder of the old king, Duncan.

45 *Look here, the 'Odyssey' . . . virtuous of women*: the Captain quotes from Johan Fredrik Johansson's revised translation of Homer's *Odyssey* (Uppsala, 1870).

Here's the prophet Ezekiel . . . begotten him?: the quotation is presumably a fabrication; at least it is not to be found in the Old Testament Book of Ezekiel.

Mersljakov's History of Russian Literature: this reference is also presumably a fabrication; the literary historian F. J. Mersljakov (1778–1830) died seven years before Pushkin.

Alexander Pushkin: Russian poet and prose writer (1799–1837), author of *Evgeny Onegin*. Incensed by widespread rumours about his wife he challenged a French émigré officer in the Horse Guards to a duel; Pushkin was shot in the stomach and died shortly afterwards.

48 *Saturn . . . eat him*: a Roman god of whom it was foretold that he would be overthrown by one of his sons; in order to forestall his fate he therefore ate up his children as soon as they were born.

To eat or be eaten! That is the question: cf. *Hamlet*, III. i. 56: 'To be, or not to be, that is the question.'

49 *Caught, clipped, and double-crossed*: an allusion to Samson, shorn of his hair (and hence of his strength) by Delilah; see Judges 16: 19.

Today shalt thou be with me in paradise: the Nurse quotes from Luke 23: 43.

50 *Omphale . . . Hercules spins your wool*: in one of the most famous accounts of gender reversal in Greek mythology Hercules, the epitome of male heroism, spent three years in slavery at the court of the Lydian queen, Omphale, where he was dressed in women's clothes and forced to sit at a spinning-wheel doing women's tasks while she wore his lion pelt and wielded his mighty club. Omphale's name also evokes the Omphalos, a conical block of stone at Delphi, which the Greeks regarded as the earth's navel, and which was thus associated with the earth as a primal mother.

51 *takes her shawl and spreads it over him*: like the straitjacket, this shawl is a reminiscence of the *Agamemnon* of Aeschylus, in which the scheming Clytemnestra ensnares her heroic husband in a net, and then kills him. Shortly before writing *The Father* Strindberg had been much taken by an article entitled 'Le Matriarcat' by Karl Marx's son-in-law, Paul Lafargue (1842–1911), in *La Nouvelle Revue*, 15 March 1886. Basing his argument heavily on Aeschylus' *Oresteia*, of which the *Agamemnon* is the first part, Lafargue argued that society was originally a matriarchy and only became a patriarchy after a long and violent war between the sexes.

53 *Once to die, but after this the judgement*: the Pastor quotes from Hymn 499 in the Swedish hymnal of 1819, which promises God's lasting judgement on the newly departed soul.

MISS JULIE

56 *Biblia pauperum*: a 'poor man's Bible', a medieval work of edification richly illustrated with pictures from the Bible, aimed at those with little or no education.

57 *real incident*: see the Introduction, pp. xv–xvii.

recently, my tragedy . . . merry: Strindberg claimed that Ernst Lundqvist, the dramaturge of the Stockholm Royal Theatre, had found the play 'too gloomy and painful' (ASB VI, 315).

pretentious talk about the joy of life: a dig at Ibsen, in whose sombre drama *Ghosts* (1881) the notion of the joy of life (*livsglæde*) is a central theme.

theatre managers commission farces . . . congenital idiocy: St Vitus's dance is a non-technical term for chorea, a word derived from the Greek *khoros* (dance) to describe a disorder of the central nervous system characterized by uncontrollable, irregular, brief, and jerky movements. However, Strindberg is also alluding to the hysterical tarantella danced by Nora at the end of Act 2 of Ibsen's *A Doll's House* (1879), thus associating his rival's play with 'congenital idiocy'.

59 *'That's capital'*: 'det var galant', an often repeated phrase in *Det skadar inte!* (*No Harm Done*, 1870) by the Swedish dramatist Frans Hedberg (1828–1908).

'Barkis is willin'': the Yarmouth carrier Barkis's recurring phrase in *David Copperfield* (1850) by Charles Dickens (1812–70). The tone of this remark should not conceal the fact that Strindberg was otherwise an enthusiastic admirer of Dickens's novels.

Harpagon: the protagonist of Molière's comedy *L'Avare* (*The Miser*, 1668). Strindberg is in fact echoing Zola who, in *La Naturalisme au théâtre*, had compared Molière's miser with Balzac's Grandet in *Eugénie Grandet* (1833), to Molière's disadvantage, because in *L'Avare* there is no description of the milieu that forms Harpagon's character.

Darwinism: Darwin's *Origin of Species* appeared in 1859 and had been translated into Swedish (by A. M. Selling) in 1871. Although he draws attention to the contemporaneity of his play here, and deploys Darwinian terminology in this Preface, Strindberg was always wary of, and ultimately deeply hostile to, Darwin's ideas.

Giordano Bruno: Italian philosopher (1548–1600). During the 1580s several of his major works were published in Latin in Elizabethan England. He was burnt at the stake by the Inquisition.

Bacon: the English statesman and philosopher Francis Bacon (1561–1626). The theory that Bacon wrote Shakespeare's plays was one to which Strindberg sometimes subscribed.

60 *Gedankenübertragung*: thought-transference, telepathy (German).

waking suggestion: Strindberg derives the idea, which accounts for the power that Laura assumes over the Captain in *The Father* and Jean's ascendency over Julie in the final scene of *Miss Julie*, from the theories of Hippolyte Bernheim (1840–1919) concerning 'suggestion à l'état de veille' (suggestion in a waking state), in *De la suggestion dans l'état de veille* (1884) and *De la suggestion et de ses applications à la thérapeutique* (1886). Bernheim defined suggestibility as 'the aptitude to transform an idea into an act' without the need fully to hypnotize a subject, which was a far more promising prospect for a dramatist like Strindberg than the insistence of his more celebrated rival, Jean-Martin Charcot (1825–93), that the subject be rendered entirely comatose. See ASE 25 ff. and a letter to Edvard Brandes, where Strindberg congratulates himself on having written a 'completely modern play, with waking hypnotism (battle of the brains)' (ASB VII, 130).

60 *Mesmer's time*: the German doctor and practitioner of hypnotism, Fr. Anton Mesmer (1734–1815), who was mainly active in Vienna and Paris.

[and the child]: inserted by the translator to make sense of a passage that closely echoes similar arguments in Strindberg's essays and letters on women. This paragraph has not been included in previous translations of the Preface.

61 *Aryan home*: essentially the construction of philologists, who posited an originating source for all Indo-European languages among the so-called Aryan peoples whose primordial homeland was usually traced to Persia or India, the idea of a pure Aryan race became a central notion in nineteenth-century racial theory. Thus, Arthur de Gobineau (1816–82) believed that the purest Aryans were to be found in Scandinavia, and by the 1880s the idea of the Aryan as the quintessential fair-haired, white, north-European male was widely disseminated.

Don Quixote: the eponymous hero of Miguel de Cervantes's (1547–1616) novel.

poor tied-worker's son: Strindberg describes Jean as a *statbarn*, i.e. the child (*barn*) of an agricultural labourer hired annually by a large estate and paid principally in kind (*stat*). Such labourers were at the very bottom of the social scale.

63 *if some people have found my minor characters abstract*: a reference to the misgivings that Émile Zola entertained about Strindberg's characterization in *The Father*. In a letter to Strindberg, dated 14 December 1887, Zola wrote: 'You perhaps know that I am not much for abstraction. I like it when characters are given a proper context, that we may elbow them and feel they are steeped in our air. And your Captain who has not even a name, your other characters who are almost creatures of reason, do not give me the complete sense of life which I require' (SV 27, 290–1).

64 *Goncourt brothers*: Edmond (1822–96) and Jules (1830–70) de Goncourt who together wrote several novels of psychological realism focusing closely on a central female character, e.g. *Sœur Philomène* (1861) and *Germinie Lacerteux* (1864). Strindberg may also have in mind *La Fille Elisa* (1877), the story of a prostitute imprisoned for murder, and espe-

cially *La Faustin* (1882), a study of an actress, which Edmond wrote alone. The Goncourts argued fervently for literature to become a kind of case history, of the kind that Strindberg claims he is writing here. Their novel *Charles Demailly* (1860), in which a wife drives her husband insane by arousing his jealousy, may also have been in Strindberg's mind when writing *The Father*.

64 *as long ago as 1872 . . . The Outlaw*: in fact this early play had received its first performance at the old Royal Theatre in Stockholm in 1871.

mime: Strindberg uses the French word 'pantomime'. He may well have been responding to the recent revival of interest in 'pantomime' plays in France during the 1880s, where they were currently being promoted by the Cercle Funambulesque.

monody: in Greek tragedy an ode sung by a single actor; subsequently a style of musical composition for a single voice, originally without accompaniment, later (*c*.1600) with the support of a figured bass or continuo.

65 *Italian theatres have returned to improvisation*: i.e. to the traditions and practice of the *commedia dell'arte*, which originally flourished in the sixteenth century.

singing game: Ollén (SV 27, 346) points out that there are some 200 variants of this singing game in the Swedish Song Archive in Stockholm, recorded from Skåne in the south to Lapland in the north.

impressionist painting: the movement in French painting, developed in the 1870s chiefly by Monet, Renoir, Pissarro, and Sisley, with the aim of objectively recording experience by a system of fleeting impressions, especially of natural light effects. Its name derives from Claude Monet's painting *Impression*, exhibited in 1874.

66 *painted saucepans*: the use of real props was already standard practice at the court theatre of the Duke of Saxe-Meiningen (1826–1914), as was the kind of asymmetrical set design that Strindberg is advocating here.

Aida: Verdi's opera (1871), commissioned for the opening of the Suez Canal, and set in ancient Egypt. It had been in the repertoire of the Stockholm Royal Theatre since 16 February 1880.

67 *the full back of an actor*: the acting style associated with the newly opened Théâtre Libre in Paris; Strindberg was hoping this Preface would help sell the play to its director, André Antoine (1858–1943).

dispense with the visible orchestra: as Strindberg probably knew, Richard Wagner had covered over the orchestra pit at the Festival Theatre in Bayreuth, which opened in 1876.

complete darkness in the auditorium: in fact Sir Henry Irving had already introduced this practice at the Lyceum in London.

69 *Miss Julie*: the Swedish title, *Fröken Julie*, is sometimes translated as 'Lady Julie'. This takes into account the fact that during the nineteenth

century the title 'Fröken' (Miss) was given only to unmarried daughters of the aristocracy. In the Swedish text Jean and Kristin frequently refer to Julie as 'Fröken' rather than 'you', even when she is present, thus highlighting her status, and the distance separating them from her in class terms, as well as the breadth of the divide she subsequently crosses in coupling with Jean. However, to translate the title as 'Countess Julie', as has been done, is incorrect; though she is the daughter of a Count, that does not make her a Countess.

71 *birch leaves*: traditional Swedish decorations on Midsummer Eve.

crazy: the word Strindberg employs here, *galen*, carries the association that Julie is on heat, like an animal.

are you: in speaking to Jean (as well as about him), Kristin uses the third person singular (*han*) rather than the intimate form of you, *du*; literally, 'Oh, so he's back then, is he?' This now old-fashioned form of address confers a demotic flavour on her speech not readily recoverable in translation.

72 *broke it into a thousand pieces*: nowadays, in performance, directors (e.g. Ingmar Bergman) sometimes choose to substitute Strindberg's original words, 'and drew a weal across her left cheek', in place of this phrase, thus rendering visible the humiliation that is one of the factors determining Julie's behaviour.

you don't say !: responding to Jean's original speech, Kristin then concluded this speech by remarking, 'So that's why she's painting herself all white now !'

délice: pleasure (French).

yellow seal, see: a yellow seal denoted a quality wine from Burgundy.

pur: wine without water; *du vin pur* (French).

chambré: the French term for wine at room temperature.

73 *Diana*: given the way she conducts herself with the gatekeeper's mutt, the fact that Miss Julie's thoroughbred dog shares her name with the virginal Roman goddess of chastity and the hunt is presumably ironic. It is also noteworthy that in searching for a mythological correlative for Siri von Essen in his account of his first marriage in *A Madman's Defence* (1888), Strindberg settles for 'Diana! The pale goddess of the night . . . too much the boy, too little the girl', which the Preface maintains is one of Julie's problems. *En dåres försvarstal* (Stockholm, 1976), 53.

74 *some magic potion*: or 'troll soup' (*trollsoppa*); an allusion to the custom of cooking *drömgröt* on Midsummer Eve in order to see in one's dreams (*drömmar*) who one's future husband or wife will be.

like those cards . . . marry: if playing-cards were laid in the shape of a star it was supposed to be possible to foresee the future in their suits, values, and placing.

schottische: a dance resembling a slow polka.

75 *Pantomime*: i.e. mime. Strindberg employs the standard French term, whose meaning has shifted in English.

76 *Très gentil . . . français*: 'Most elegant, Jean. Most elegant.' | 'You're disposed to joke, madame.' | 'And you to speak French.'

sommelier: restaurant-keeper, wine-waiter; but also simply a waiter (French).

Lucerne: the lakeside resort in German-speaking Switzerland.

Charmant !: delightful, charming (French).

77 *labourer*: a *statkarl*, i.e. the lowest form of agricultural labourer, hired annually and paid largely in kind.

79 *verliebt*: in love (German).

80 *if we sleep . . . come true*: in folklore a young, unmarried woman would see her husband-to-be if she picked nine different kinds of flowers on Mid-summer Night and placed them beneath her pillow.

Attention ! Je ne suis qu'un homme: 'Take care! I'm only a man!' (French).

81 *a Joseph*: see Genesis 39 where Joseph eludes the attempt of Potiphar's wife to seduce him. A 'Joseph' is thus someone who is not to be seduced from his (generally sexual) continency by the severest temptations. It is noteworthy that in the autobiographical fiction devoted to his first marriage Strindberg writes, of the protagonist's partner: 'There's no doubt about it. She had intended to seduce me. It was she who kissed me first, who made the first advance. But from now on it is I who am going to assume the seducer's role, in earnest, for I am no Joseph, in spite of my firm principles where honour is concerned.' *En dåres försvarstal*, 112.

82 *tree of life*: the tree in the middle of the garden of Eden, which gave eternal life to those who ate its fruit. Elsewhere in this speech, however, Jean's account of his forays into the Count's park evokes the neighbouring tree of the knowledge of good and evil, which is more in keeping with the action of the play.

Turkish pavilion: a euphemistic building of wood decorated with crescent moons and stars in the Turkish style; in fact an earth closet, or toilet.

enfin: in short, in a word (French).

85 *There came two women from out the wood . . . Tridiridi-ralla-la*: see note to p. 65.

87 *Como*: a lakeside town in Northern Italy, near the border with Switzerland.

Gotthard Pass: the alpine road and rail pass connecting Switzerland and Italy, built between 1872 and 1880, and opened for rail traffic in 1882.

But Jean—you . . . Call me Julie: here, in a crucial shift of register, Julie switches to the intimate Swedish form of 'you', *du*, and tries to get Jean to do likewise. However, he persists in addressing her formally as *ni*. In fact the original reads 'Ni! [You!]—Säg du! [Say you!], but this obviously doesn't work in English. Hence the need to play upon the formal and direct ways of using her first name.

88 *Have you no feelings?*: Julie reverts to *ni* here, and retains the formal, plural form for the remainder of the play.

90 *Merde !*: shit! (French).

91 *among animals and prostitutes*: originally Jean continued, 'But I know it's normal among your class; it's called being free, of course; emancipated, or something else well-bred; yes, I've seen high-born ladies run off with cadets and waiters'; but this was cut on publication by Strindberg or his publisher, Seligmann, perhaps because the closing allusion appeared too transparent.

94 *or was there a settlement*: before 1920 in Sweden a husband had all the rights not only to any property held jointly with his wife, but also to any property she brought with her to the marriage, unless the latter had been specifically excluded by mutual consent in a premarital settlement.

95 *how he broke off the engagement*: referring back to his earlier account of this scene (see note to p. 72), Jean originally continued: 'You can still see it, there on your cheek.'

The offender . . . is killed: Strindberg was originally more explicit and the passage in inverted commas, which refers to the penalty imposed by law for bestiality, began 'The sodomist is condemned. . .'

96 *mésalliance*: misalliance, bad match (French).

Peerage book: *adelskalender*, the Swedish equivalent of *Burke's Peerage* or the *Almanach de Gotha*.

97 *pietism*: a movement originated by P. J. Spener (1635–1705) in Frankfurt for the revival of piety in the Lutheran Church. It became a force in Swedish life in the early eighteenth century, but by the mid-nineteenth century it had become identified with other nonconformist sects which emphasized simple puritanical virtues and, like Methodism, exerted a powerful appeal upon the poor. The Swedish term for pietist, *läsare*, indicates the stress these sects placed on an assiduous reading of the Bible, but followers of the movement were sometimes given to more emotional display. Strindberg's mother had been converted to pietism by the charismatic revivalist minister Carl Olof Rosenius (1816–68), who taught a contempt for worldly problems, a longing for the world to come, and the conviction that in an irremediably sinful world the individual could only be redeemed by the grace of God. Strindberg himself embraced pietist ideas briefly but strongly during his adolescence.

98 *crazy*: see note to p. 71.

99 *The beheading of John the Baptist, I suppose*: until 1942 the biblical text for 24 June was indeed Mark 6: 14–29, the beheading of John the Baptist, but the image of John's beheading also anticipates both the death of Julie's siskin and her suicide.

100 *the 24th of October*: since 1833 the day on which servants moved out if notice had been given by either side between 26 July and 24 August.

101 *which breaks the troll's spell*: in Scandinavian folklore trolls, which normally dwell in caves and mountains, shatter into pieces if caught abroad by the sun at dawn.

103 *I'd like to see your sex*: the resonance of the original, where the word *kön* can mean both a person's gender and his or her sexual organ, is lost in translation.

our coat of arms will be broken upon the coffin: when a Swedish nobleman died his coat of arms was normally installed as a memorial tablet in the church where he was buried; however, if he was the last of his line it was broken over the coffin.

105 *Rubens and Raphael*: Sir Peter Paul Rubens (1577–1640), Flemish painter. Raffaello Santi or Sanzio (1483–1520), Italian painter and architect.

King Ludwig: Ludwig II of Bavaria (1854–86); Wagner's patron, who helped finance the Festival Theatre at Bayreuth; he also built and furnished castles, e.g. Neuschwanstein, on a lavish scale. Mentally unstable, he had recently drowned himself in the Starnbergersee, near Munich.

107 *even the groceries?*: this line was deleted from the original manuscript, and from the first published edition, possibly on the grounds that it might be thought blasphemous.

the last shall be first: cf. Matthew 19: 30, 'But many that are first shall be last; and the last shall be first.'

it's easier . . . the Kingdom of Heaven: cf. Matthew 19: 24.

109 *he says to his subject . . . sweeps*: this example of hypnotic suggestion is taken from Hippolyte Bernheim's *De la suggestion* (1884—see note to p. 60), but throughout this final scene, the way in which Miss Julie needs Jean's encouragement in order to act owes much to Théodule Ribot's account of abulia, or impairment of will, in *Les Maladies de la volonté* (1883).

THE DANCE OF DEATH I

111 *[title]*: with its evocation of the many, often macabre, medieval paintings, engravings, and woodcuts as well as poems, sermons, and plays in which Death, usually personified as a skeleton, invites a wide range of citizens up to dance, and hence to their inevitable death, the title aligns one of the most modern of Strindberg's plays with other works of the period (*To Damascus*, *Advent*, *Easter*) in which reminiscences of the medieval morality plays are more immediately obvious than they are here. As with *To Damascus*, Strindberg wrote a second part to what was originally conceived of as an independent drama almost as soon as he had completed the first play. In both cases he recognized the achievement of the recently written first part, and had material to hand which had not found a place

there; also in both cases, however, the second part is generally inferior to its predecessor, and is not essential to its understanding or performance.

117 *Is there to be a quarantine here?*: in Sweden the practice of imposing a quarantine upon incoming travellers suspected of having been in contact with infectious disease, especially cholera, continued into the nineteenth century. Quarantine stations were established at the Swedish border, often on islands offshore. Ships suspected of infection with cholera were held outside Stockholm for forty-eight hours; if suspicions proved well grounded they were disinfected for five days before being allowed to proceed.

118 *Nimb's*: a well-known restaurant in nineteenth-century Copenhagen.

navarin aux pommes: mutton stew with potatoes (French).

Tivoli: the entertainment park created in 1843 by G. Carstensen. Situated in central Copenhagen, it is designed for concerts, ballet, and stage-plays as well as all the fun of the fair.

Alcazar waltz: the 'Alcazar, Spanischer Walzer' by Otto Roeder. That 'Alcazar' is Spanish for 'fortress' is germane to the imagery of the play.

120 *rentier*: someone who lives off the income of property or investment.

122 *The Champagne Galop*: a short work for orchestra (1845) by the Danish composer H. C. Lumbye (1810–74), often called 'the Danish Strauss'.

126 *Have you become . . . American?*: i.e. a teetotaler. The growing temperance movement originated in the United States, where it enjoyed widespread support.

129 *my own cheque account*: a status symbol at the turn of the century in Sweden.

130 *the walls smell of poison*: literally, 'it smells like poisonous wallpaper'. Lindström (SV 44, 258) points out that around the turn of the century a green pigment was sometimes used in decorating and wallpapering; it included arsenic which could, and did, lead to cases of poisoning. It was subsequently banned.

133 *'Entry of the Boyars'*: a triumphal march (1895) by the Norwegian composer Johan Halvorsen (1864–1935).

135 *Baron Bluebeard*: the story of Bluebeard, 'La Barbe bleue', was recorded by Perrault in his *Histoires ou contes du temps passé* (1697). It tells the tale of a rich man who murdered his wives when curiosity drove them to open a door to a closet he had forbidden them to enter. His last wife's brothers succeeded in rescuing their sister and killing Bluebeard at the very moment he was about to kill her.

Meli-tam-tam-ta, meli-ta-lia-ley: the refrain in the Swedish version of the once internationally known 'Marlborough Song', called 'Mellbomvisan' in Swedish.

sword dance: the collective name for a group of folk dances for men, danced either over crossed swords on the floor or ground, or with sword in hand.

140 *Stony heart*: cf. Ezekiel 11: 19, 'And I will give them one heart, and I will put a new spirit within you; and I will take the stony heart out of their flesh, and will give them an heart of flesh.'

146 *Judith*: the name is not gratuitous. As an exchange in *The Dance of Death II* makes clear (ALICE: Judith! Judith! CAPTAIN: And Holofernes?—Is that supposed to be me?'), Strindberg is recalling the story told in the apocryphal Book of Judith, in which the young and beautiful Hebrew heroine, Judith, saves her city by gaining entry to the tent of the besieging Assyrian commander, Holofernes, and cutting off his head. With the rise of 'the New Woman', Strindberg was not the only male author or painter to find renewed resonance in this narrative at the end of the nineteenth century.

152 *vampire*: as, for example, in *The Ghost Sonata*, Strindberg was drawn to explore the theme of the vampire in several of his later works. In one set of notes for *The Dance of Death*, entitled 'Allt går igen' (everything repeats itself), he describes the Captain's 'vampire stage': 'When life runs out of him he begins to fasten upon other people and identify with them; [he] lives their lives, tries to eat their souls', SgNM 4: 23, 8. Part II of *The Dance of Death* may have been written because Strindberg felt he had not exhausted this theme in the first play; in a letter to his German translator, Emil Schering, he called this second part 'The Vampire', and considered extending that title to cover both plays (ASB XIV, 8).

166 *Tout beau !*: 'careful'; 'don't go too far' (French).

174 *best man*: literally, 'guardian' (*giftoman*), someone whose permission had to be obtained before a minor could be married.

A DREAM PLAY

176 *his former dream play, 'To Damascus'*: the first part of *To Damascus*, which Strindberg wrote in 1898. While it clearly broke with the naturalism of *Miss Julie* and launched his later experimental dramatic style, he did not initially call *To Damascus* a dream play but (in a letter to the writer and editor, Gustaf af Geijerstam) 'a fiction . . . with a terrifying half-reality behind it' (ASB XII, 279).

the torment of the dream: presumably in order to help orientate the first-night audience in the complexities of his new dramatic style, Strindberg sent the director, Victor Castegren, an addition to this note, in which he stressed both the play's theatrical antecedents and its affinity with music:

'Until recently the notion that life is a dream seemed to us only a poetic figure of Calderon's. But when Shakespeare in *The Tempest* has Prospero say "We are such stuff as dreams are made on" and on another occasion employs Macbeth to comment on life as "a tale, told by an idiot", we ought surely to give the matter some further thought.

'Whoever accompanies the author for these brief hours along the path of his sleepwalking will possibly discover a certain similarity between the apparent medley of the dream and the motley canvas of our disorderly life, woven by "The World Weaver" who sets up the "warp" of human destinies and then elaborates "the weft" of our conflicting interests and changing passions.

'Anyone who sees the similarity will be justified in saying to himself: "maybe it is like that".

'As far as the loose, disconnected form of the play is concerned, that, too, is only apparent. For on closer examination, the composition emerges as quite coherent—a symphony, polyphonic, now and then in the manner of a fugue with a constantly recurring main theme, which is repeated and varied by the thirty odd parts in every key.

'There are no solos with accompaniments, that is, no bravura roles, no characters, or rather, no caricatures, no intrigues, no curtain lines that invite applause. The vocal parts are strictly arranged, and in the sacrificial scene of the finale, everything that has happened passes in review, with the themes repeated once again, just as a man's life with all its incidents, is said to do at the moment of death. Yet another similarity!

'Now it is time to see the play itself—and to hear it! With a little goodwill on your part, the battle is almost won. That is all we ask of you.

'Curtain up!'

177 *Characters*: presumably in order to emphasize the dreamlike nature of a play in which the characters frequently 'appear from nowhere', Strindberg deliberately omitted to include a list of dramatis personae in the original.

178 *Prologue*: on first publication the play had no prologue. As a letter to Emil Schering makes clear—'*The Dream Play* opens in a week . . . I have written a Prologue in verse; among the clouds Indra's Daughter talks with her invisible father about going down to see what life is like for mankind' (ASB XV, 355)—it was composed several years after the play itself, in 1906, in anticipation of its first performance. Like the extension to the Prefatory Note, it also helps situate an audience in relation to the drama that follows.

The Constellations Leo . . . brightly among them: in his translation of the play (University of Minnesota Press, 1986) Evert Sprinchorn notes that 'Leo, the Lion, is associated with Hercules and stands for man; Virgo, the Virgin, represents woman; Libra is the balance; and Jupiter is God' (p. 649), but all these figures admit multiple interpretations (astrologically, for example, Jupiter is considered the bringer of good fortune), and Strindberg's precise intention with this configuration is not self-evident. As signs of the zodiac, and three of the twelve divisions of the ecliptic through which the sun passes, Leo, Virgo, and Libra form a sequence: the sun enters Leo on 23 July and reaches Libra via Virgo on 23 September, the autumnal equinox to which Indra refers in his third speech.

Indra's Daughter: in Indian mythology Indra is one of the eight gods keeping watch over the world. The god of thunder and of the air and clouds, he is arguably the most popular of the Vedic gods, but there is no record of him having a daughter, something that Strindberg, who was well versed in oriental religions, would surely have known.

178 *You have left the second world and entered the third*: according to Indian mythology there were three worlds: heaven, the air, and the earth. Having descended from the first of these, Indra's Daughter is approaching the earth by way of the air.

Sukra: the name given to the planet Venus in Indian mythology.

the Morning Star: the name given to the planet Venus when it is visible in the East before sunrise.

Libra: the Scales or balance, the seventh sign of the zodiac.

day star: the sun.

the autumn balance . . . equal: the autumn equinox (23 September).

179 *Brahma*: in Hinduism Brahma was originally conceived as an abstract, entirely impersonal creative principle; he was later endowed with personality, and became the creator of the universe, the first in the divine Triad, of which the others are Vishnu, the maintainer, and Siva (or Shiva), the destroyer.

181 *the gilded roof . . . resembling a crown*: as his diary makes clear, Strindberg has in mind the cavalry barracks on Sturevägen (nowadays Lidingövägen), built in 1897, which was topped by a curious golden, bud-like baldachin and visible from his window when he lived at 40 Karlavägen. The barracks forms the basis of a sketch he made, probably in 1909, for a planned performance of the play at the Intimate Theatre (SV 46, 154), and in an article entitled 'Stockholm at Seven O'Clock in the Morning' he described it as 'Stockholm's "most beautiful building" . . . with its crowned roof and four wings above the tops of the trees' (SS 54, 44).

At the base . . . stable manure: stable litter placed next to the foundations of buildings was used as an early form of insulation.

The castle keeps on growing out of the earth: the growing castle ('Det Vexande Slottet') was both Strindberg's name for the cavalry barracks visible from 40 Karlavägen and an alternative title for *A Dream Play*, which he continued to employ even after the play was finished.

182 *Agnes*: of Greek origin, the name means 'chaste'. St Agnes, who was martyred at the age of 12 in *c*.303, is the patron saint of young virgins. She is frequently depicted with a lamb (Latin: *agnus*) at her side and sometimes standing on a flaming pyre with a sword in her hand. The name may also have been associated by Strindberg with 'Agni', the Vedic god of fire and a mediator between the gods and men.

184 *'The Swiss Family Robinson'*: Der Schweizerische Robinson (1813) by the Swiss priest, Johann David Wyss (1743–1818); a popular nineteenth-century children's book inspired by Daniel Defoe's *Robinson Crusoe* (1719).

185 *to be pitied!*: as Egil Törnqvist points out in *Strindbergian Drama* (Stockholm, 1982), this recurring statement, which has assumed almost proverbial status in Swedish, can also mean 'Human beings are sinful' or 'rooted in sin' (p. 150).

186 *love conquers all*: a translation of the Latin adage, 'Amor omnia vincit'.

  four-leaved clover: a clover with four leaves rather than three is supposed to bring good luck, but Strindberg also has in mind the opening in the door of a corridor in the old Royal Theatre in Stockholm where he had frequently had occasion to wait for two of his wives, Siri von Essen and Harriet Bosse, who were both actresses. The eminent Strindberg scholar Martin Lamm recalls that '[Harriet] Bosse told me that Strindberg always used to puzzle over where it led, when he waited for her there' (*Strindbergs dramer*, vol. 2 (1926), 326). An early working title for these scenes outside the theatre was 'The Corridor Drama'.

  green: traditionally signifies hope.

189 *two doves . . . under that hood*: the uppermost leaf of the perianth of a monkshood, or *Aconitum*, is shaped like a helmet enclosing two long-stemmed leaves that serve as nectary; the variety *Aconitum napellus* has hooded dark blue flowers, sometimes called 'blue doves'. Flowers of this genus are poisonous.

194 *Whoever heard of a glazier without a diamond?*: with its unusual hardness, which enabled it to cut glass, a diamond belonged to a glazier's traditional equipment.

  'Die Meistersinger': Wagner's opera *Die Meistersinger von Nürnberg* (1868) was first performed in Stockholm in 1887.

  'Aida': according to the *Occult Diary*, Strindberg had seen a further performance of Verdi's opera (see note to p. 66) on 6 October 1901, together with Harriet Bosse.

196 *He who feeds the birds*: cf. Matthew 6: 26: 'Behold the fowls of the air: for they sow not, neither do they reap, nor gather into barns; yet your heavenly Father feedeth them.'

197 *the four faculties of Philosophy, Theology, Medicine, and Law*: the four faculties of the Swedish university system. (Philosophy comprises both the arts and the sciences.) The ceremony that follows, in which successful candidates are crowned with a laurel wreath, accords with the traditional ceremony in a Swedish university when Doctors' degrees are conferred.

  crowned with laurels: a Doctor of Law would normally be crowned with a doctor's hat rather than a wreath.

198 *what the original images were like*: an allusion to the Platonic notion that the sensible world is an imperfect reflection of the world of ideas.

  bits of the devil's mirror in my eye: cf. Hans Christian Andersen's story 'The Snow Queen', about the devil's magic mirror 'which had the strange power of being able to make anything good or beautiful that it reflected appear horrid; and all that was evil and worthless seem attractive'. When it fell to earth and broke the splinters fastened in people's eyes so that they could only see the faults, and not the virtues, of everyone around them.

198 *crown of thorns on his head*: a symbol of vicarious suffering. See also Matthew 27: 29 and John 19: 5.

199 *Kyrie*: or 'Kyrie eleison'; 'Lord, have mercy upon us', a formal invocation in the liturgy of the Roman Catholic, Greek Orthodox, and Anglican churches. Also a musical setting of these words.

Mercy, oh Eternal One . . . Hear us!: cf. Psalm 130: 1: 'Out of the depths have I cried unto thee, O Lord.'

Fingal's Cave: a cave, *c*.35 metres high, 12 metres broad, and 70 metres deep on the island of Staffa in the inner Hebrides, off the west coast of Scotland. Its roof and the six-sided pillars for which it is famous are made of basalt. In Gaelic the cave is called *Uiamh Binn*, the Musical Cave, from the melodious tones created by the waves as they flow into it. Well known in the nineteenth century through the poetry of James MacPherson (1736–96), e.g. *Fingal* (1762), and Felix Mendelssohn's 'Fingal's Cave Overture' (1832), the cave features frequently in Strindberg's later writings as one of the natural phenomena in which he sought to find evidence for the shaping hand of a divine architect in nature.

201 *Kristin is busy . . . inner windows*: it was customary in Scandinavia to insert an inner window in winter and to seal the cracks by pasting over them with strips of paper, which were removed again, along with the window, in the spring.

202 *heliotrope*: any one of the genus *Heliotropium*, named after the Greek *helios* (sun) and *trepein* (turn) because, when placed in a window, they naturally reach towards the incoming light.

205 *Parnassus*: the mountain near Delphi in Greece, sacred to Apollo and the Muses. From its association with the latter, 'to climb Parnassus' traditionally meant 'to write poetry'; however, Strindberg uses it more loosely to indicate great achievement generally.

206 *machines that resemble instruments of torture*: for these central scenes of *A Dream Play* Strindberg drew on the landscape on and around the island of Furusund in the Stockholm archipelago, where he had spent the summer of 1899 and part of 1900. The baths at Furusund were equipped by their intendent, Dr Gustaf Zander, with various types of mechanical apparatus designed for physiotherapy and other medical purposes.

quarantine building: during the cholera epidemics of the nineteenth century a quarantine station was established on the island of Isola Bella at Furusund.

207 *Italian-style villas*: the blind jeweller and art collector Christian Hammer, who acquired the island of Furusund in the 1880s, had given Italian names to many of the summer-houses there.

207 *Ordström*: literally, 'stream of words', although he is not unduly loquacious.

Fairhaven . . . Foulstrand: originally 'Fagervik' (Fair or Beautiful Bay) and 'Skamsund' (Shame Sound), which Strindberg derives from Fagervik, a bay on Furusund, and 'Skarmsund' on nearby Köpmanholm, which is situated opposite Fagervik, on the sea lane into Stockholm. In several notes for material that he utilized in *A Dream Play*, Strindberg called Skamsund and Fagervik 'Ebal' and 'Garizim', from Deuteronomy 11: 29: 'And it shall come to pass, when the Lord thy God hath brought thee in unto the land whither thou goest to possess it, that thou shalt put the blessing upon mount Gerizim, and the curse upon mount Ebal.'

Varuna: the ancient Hindu sky god, later the god of the waters and rain-giver. In earlier traditions he was also the all-seeing divine judge and Indra's predecessor as the king of the gods.

208 *Hennessy*: a high-quality brand of French cognac.

corridor: another echo of the corridor in the theatre where Strindberg had also waited for his actress wives.

209 *mudbath*: a massage with mud followed by a bath was one of the remedies for rheumatism available at the baths in Furusund.

Ptah: in ancient Egypt the god who was believed to have created the world; a patron of artists and craftsmen.

C'est mon affaire: normally, 'it is my own concern', but here, 'It's my speciality' (French).

210 *they're killing the fatted calf*: cf. the parable of the prodigal son in Luke 15.

Haroun the Just: the historical Harun ar-Rashid (?763–809), was the fifth caliph of the Abbasid dynasty and caliph of Islam from 786 to 809. He ruled over an empire that extended from the western Mediterranean to India, excluding only Byzantium. His court at Baghdad was idealized in the *Arabian Nights*, where he frequently disguises himself and passes through the city at night in order, like Indra's Daughter, to determine his people's circumstances.

211 *Eros*: in Greek mythology, the God of love and son of Aphrodite.

212 *Forty days and forty nights*: alludes both to the period Moses spent fasting in the desert (Exodus 34: 28) and Jesus's fast there for a similar period (Matthew 4:2), but also to the derivation of the word quarantine (*quarante* = forty); the original quarantine, introduced in medieval Venice, isolated ships outside the city for forty days.

the fumes of sulphur and carbolic acid: disinfectants in use at the end of the nineteenth century.

213 *many are called, but few are chosen*: cf. Matthew 20: 16.

215 *Bach's Toccata and Fugue, No. 10*: the Toccata and Fugue, BWV 913 by Johann Sebastian Bach (1685–1750). The passage quoted occurs approximately midway through the toccata.

217 *Ergo*: therefore; hence (Latin).

posterius prius: the later earlier (Latin), i.e. a departure from logical order in a syllogism; a term in classical logic.

219 *he owns these hundred Italian villas . . . game in the woods*: see note to p. 207.

220 *the lieutenant's 'Yes' in red . . . blue veins . . .*: 'yes' and 'no' according to the International Code of Signals, introduced in 1900.

the angel's greeting on Christmas night . . .: an allusion to the angel's words to the shepherds, Luke 2: 10–11, 'And the angel said unto them, Fear not: for, behold, I bring you good tidings of great joy, which shall be to all people. For unto you is born this day in the city of David a Saviour, which is Christ the Lord.'

221 *Repetition*: Strindberg uses the Danish word *Gentagelsen*, a deliberate echo of the book of that name (1843) by the Danish philosopher, Søren Kierkegaard (1813–55). Strindberg read widely, if idiosyncratically, in Kierkegaard's major works, and the idea of repetition features prominently in his later plays both as a concept (cf. the idea in *The Dance of Death* that everything repeats itself) and in their circular structure; see e.g. the first parts of *To Damascus* and *The Dance of Death*, *Crimes and Crimes*, and even *A Dream Play* itself.

each stage in turn, one, two, three: the process of obtaining a divorce entailed (1) a warning before a parson; (2) a warning before a church council; and (3) proceedings before a lower court with the power to institute a divorce between husband and wife.

223 *A beach by the Mediterranean*: the following scene, which draws on impressions from Strindberg's short visit to the Mediterranean coast of Italy in 1884, was written some time after the rest of the play, probably in 1902. Ollén (SV 46, 146) conjectures a link between this scene, with its social pathos, and the political riots and strikes that took place in Sweden in April and May that year; certainly, it sounds a different tone to the remainder of the play, and is the least dreamlike section.

228 *To dust they return*: cf. Genesis 2: 7, 'And the Lord God formed man of the dust of the ground', and God's words to Adam in Genesis 3: 19, 'for dust thou *art*, and unto dust shalt thou return'.

233 *The Flying Dutchman*: the legend of the Flying Dutchman, condemned, because of his godlessness, to sail the seas on a phantom ship until Judgement Day, dates back to the sixteenth century. Wagner wrote his opera on this theme in 1843 and Strindberg his own, unfinished play, *Holländarn*, with the Dutchman as protagonist, in which he once again explored the irreconcilable contradictions of man's relation to woman, in July 1902.

234 *One who walks on water*: cf. Matthew 14: 25, where Jesus 'went unto them [his disciples], walking on the sea'.

234 *Peter, the rock, for he sank like stone*: in Matthew 16: 18, Jesus calls Peter 'this rock [upon which] I will build my church'; in Matthew 14: 28–30, Peter sinks when he tries to emulate Jesus in walking on the sea.

a telephone tower: Strindberg has in mind the 50 metres-high rectangular tower of the Public Telephone Company on Malmskillnadsgatan 30 in Stockholm, erected in 1887, which was visible across the city. Festooned with innumerable telephone wires which shone with hoar-frost in winter, it was described by Claes Lundin in *Nya Stockholm* (1890) as the city's 'most distinctive building'.

Tower of Babel: see Genesis 11: 1–9 for the biblical account of how the original Adamic language common to all men was 'confounded' by God into a multitude of tongues, 'that they may not understand one another's speech'. Strindberg devoted much time during his later years to comparative philology and the search for this original, unfissured primal language.

235 *riddle of existence*: a common enough phrase, perhaps, but Strindberg would have been aware of the recently published *Die Welträtsel* (*The Riddle of the Universe*) by the German biologist and Darwinist Ernst Haeckel (1834–1919). Strindberg had once proclaimed himself a follower of Haeckel, and sent him his most extended scientific tract, *Antibarbarus* (1893), for approval (Haeckel responded diplomatically, with evasive praise), but he was now deeply hostile to Darwinism and to all such attempts to explain 'the riddle of existence'.

236 *Credo*: I believe (Latin).

237 *What is truth?*: The question addressed to Jesus by Pontius Pilate, John 18:38.

Anything can be proved with two witnesses: according to the prevailing Swedish Code of Judicial Procedure, ch. 17, para. 29: 'Two witnesses entail complete proof, in that they agree.'

238 *I am the truth and the life*: cf. Jesus's words to Thomas, John 14: 6: 'I am the way, the truth, and the life: no man cometh unto the Father, but by me.'

Now go in peace with your gain: these exchanges between the Daughter and the Dean of Law echo the words of Paul in 1 Timothy 6: 1–6.

239 *Nothing will come of nothing*: from the Latin 'de nihilo nihil'; see Lucretius, *De rerum natura*, i. 156. It also echoes *King Lear*, 1. i. 92.

242 *if God has spoken why do people not believe?*: cf. John 8: 46, 'And if I say the truth, why do ye not believe me?'

243 *In the dawn of time . . .*: this account of the origin of the world is derived almost entirely from the chapter on Indian literature in Volume 1 of Arvid Ahnfelt's *Verldslitteraturens historia* (1875, p. 36 ff.). 'Am reading about the teachings of Indian religion', Strindberg notes, in the *Occult Diary* (18 November 1901), and goes on to paraphrase Ahnfelt as he does in the play: 'The whole world is only a semblance (= Humbug or relative emptiness). The divine primordial force (Maham–Atma, Tad, Aum, Brahma) allowed

itself to be seduced by Maya, or the impulse of Procreation. Thus the divine primordial element sinned against itself. (Love is sin; therefore the pangs of love are the greatest of all hells.) The world has therefore only come into existence through Sin—for it is only a dream or image [*bild*]. (Consequently my *Dream Play* is an image of life), a phantom which it is the task of the ascetics to destroy. But this task conflicts with the impulse to love, and the sum total of it all is a ceaseless wavering between sensual orgies and the agonies of penitence. This appears to be the key to the riddle of the world!'

243 *Maya*: Hindu goddess of illusion and in Hindu and Buddhist philosophy the power by which the universe becomes manifest; the illusion or appearance of the phenomenal world. The idea informs many of Strindberg's later works, where his early reading of Schopenhauer's *The World as Will and Idea* (1819) is combined with his interest in oriental religion, on which Schopenhauer had also drawn. Thus, in the opening sections of his treatise Schopenhauer quotes from an Indian source ('it is Maya, the veil of deception, which covers the eyes of mortals, and causes them to see a world of which one cannot say either that it is or that it is not; for it is like a dream'), and draws attention to both Prospero's observation that 'We are such stuff as dreams are made on' and Calderón's play *La Vida es Sueño* (Life is a Dream), to which Strindberg also refers in his extended Prefatory Note to *A Dream Play*. See note to p. 176.

244 *white sheets . . . spruce-twigs lie in the doorway*: after someone had died it was a Swedish custom to hang white sheets over the windows and spread spruce twigs across the path which the coffin would take.

245 *A report . . . sources of the Ganges*: traditionally, two futile subjects of investigation: since 1700 popes have not been allowed to wear a beard, and speculating on which popes wore one before that date does not get one very far; the Ganges has so many sources that pursuing the question makes little sense.

247 *As the castle burns . . . chrysanthemum*: as has sometimes been noticed, the final image of the bud on the roof of the illuminated castle bursting into brilliant bloom is, on one level, clearly phallic, but the burning castle is also captured in a note in Strindberg's diary made (18 November 1901) 'just as I was completing *The* [sic] *Dream Play*, "The Growing Castle" . . . that same morning I saw the Castle (= the cavalry barracks) illuminated, as it were, by the morning sun'.

THE GHOST SONATA

249 *[title-page] Opus 3*: to stress their affinity with music and their nature as a cycle on associated themes, each of the four chamber plays of 1907 is given an opus number. Commenting on Max Reinhardt's recently opened Kammerspiele in Berlin, Strindberg defined its programme as 'the concept of chamber music transferred to drama' (SS 50, 11).

249 *[title]*: not the 'Spook Sonata', which might have been an alternative of the Swedish *Spöksonaten*. Strindberg experimented with several different titles for the play, but having settled upon *The Ghost Sonata* he sought to maintain this distinction wherever the language admits it. Thus, on 1 April 1907 he tells Emil Schering: 'It was a great and novel pleasure for me in my Easter suffering to find you so quickly taken by *The Ghost Sonata* [*GespensterSonaten*] (that's what it should be called, after Beethoven's Ghost Sonata in D minor and his Ghost Trio, not 'Spook' [*Spuk*] therefore' (ASB XV, 355). Beethoven's Piano Trio No. 4 in D Major (Opus 70, No. 1) is commonly known as the 'Geister-Trio' because of its spectral slow movement, but Strindberg's reference to 'Beethoven's Ghost Sonata in D minor' is more confusing. In fact he has in mind the Piano Sonata No. 17 (Op. 31, No. 2), which is commonly known as 'The Tempest'. However, the piano sonata held a personal resonance for Strindberg, who specified that bars 96–107 of the Finale should be played over and over again to accompany part of Act II, Scene 1 of *Crimes and Crimes* (1899). 'These notes always act like a centre bit drill upon my conscience', he told his friend Leopold Littmansson, who was translating the play into French, adding: 'Did you notice that [the structure of] my play is based upon this sonata; fugal?' (ASB XIII, 115). See the essays by Järvi and Sondrup listed in the Select Bibliography for accounts of *The Ghost Sonata* in terms of musical structure.

250 *Beggars*: like the Maid and the Cook included here, Strindberg omitted the Beggars of the opening scene from his original list of dramatis personae; just as carelessly, he did include 'The Caretaker', although the latter never appears in the play.

251 *covered in white sheets*: the custom of the period when someone died; see note to *A Dream Play*, p. 244.

gossip mirror: a mirror attached to the outside of the window, which enables someone sitting inside to see what is going on in the street, in both directions.

252 *punch*: rum punch, the traditional alcoholic drink among Swedish students at the turn of the century.

Will you be my good Samaritan?: apparently an allusion to the Samaritan who goes to the assistance of the man who has fallen among thieves in Luke 10: 30–7. In both the Swedish Bible and Strindberg's text the Samaritan is referred to as 'compassionate' rather than 'good'. But see also John 4: 7–16 and the woman of Samaria who comes to Jacob's well 'to draw water', and of whom Jesus requests a drink, adding: 'Whosoever drinketh of this water shall thirst again: But whosoever drinketh of the water that I shall give him shall never thirst; but the water that I shall give him shall be in him a well of water springing up into everlasting life.'

253 *couldn't say 'window' but always said 'winder'*: this is a celebrated crux in the play. The Student has not said this (in Swedish *fönster* and *funster*), or

anything like it; however, it is likely that Strindberg intended the remark, which adds significantly to the hallucinatory quality of the scene.

255 *'The Valkyrie'*: music drama by Richard Wagner (1813–83), first staged in Munich in 1870 and premièred at the Stockholm Royal Opera in November 1906. Precisely why Strindberg should have chosen a performance of the second part of the *Ring* cycle as the setting for the Student's introduction to the Young Lady remains unclear. Wagner's libretti interested him as possible models for the kind of monodrama that sometimes attracted him as a dramatist during the 1900s, and as an alchemist he was intrigued by the gold motif at the heart of the tetralogy—in *Legends* (1898), for example, he maintained that *Das Rheingold* had been written especially for him (SS 28, 313). But otherwise he detested Wagner's music, and criticized it savagely both in the novel *Black Banners* (written 1904, published 1907) and in *A Blue Book*, a collection of prose pieces in progress at the time he wrote *The Ghost Sonata*, where Wagner is described as 'the musical representative of evil' (SS 46, 213).

Are you a sportsman . . . it shall be your fortune?: another enigma. Even if the idea of a sportsman is associated with the Student's apparent good health and willingness to take risks, there is no indication why it should have been his misfortune.

257 *Sunday child*: according to popular belief, a child born on a Sunday had supernatural powers and could, for example, see the dead as the Student does here. A Sunday child was also likely to enjoy good fortune in life.

258 *spruce twigs*: see note to *A Dream Play*, p. 244.

259 *so it is written*: cf. Matthew 4: 4.

Must I sell my soul?: the implication is that, like Faust in, for example, Goethe's treatment of the legend, the Student is to enter a pact with the Devil and sell his soul, thus gaining access to the Young Lady in the process. Hummel's icy handshake is another of his infernal qualities.

262 *Thor*: the old Scandinavian god of war and of thunder, often depicted wielding a hammer, emblematic of a thunderbolt, and riding in a chariot.

limping little thing: another allusion to Hummel's infernal aspect (Strindberg was originally more explicit and wrote 'little limping devil'). Johansson's speech as a whole suggests a more specific intertextual association between Hummel and Asmodeus, a demonic figure in Alain-René Lesage's novel *Le Diable boiteux* (*The Lame Devil*, 1707), translated into Swedish in 1878 as *Asmodeus. A Young Student's Adventure*. Set in Madrid, Lesage's novel relates how the lame Asmodeus conducts a young student behind the façades of the city's houses and reveals to him the secrets of those who live there in apparent virtue and prosperity. Asmodeus also features in Strindberg's dramatic fragment *The Flying Dutchman* (1902), where the protagonist contemplates a sleeping town and remarks: 'If only I had an Asmodeus to draw aside the curtains I'd like to see into these houses and look beneath the floorboards to see if there

isn't the odd corpse buried beneath the soft Brussels carpet of happiness.'
Samlade otryckta skrifter, vol. 1 (Stockholm, 1918), 217.

264　*the ass in the pit and the ear in the field will absolve us*: a dual allusion to (1)
Luke 14: 5 ('Which of you shall have an ass or an ox fallen into a pit, and
will not straightway pull him out on the sabbath day?'), and (2) Mark
2: 23–8, where Jesus is likewise drawn by the Pharisees' attack upon his
disciples who 'began, as they went, to pluck the ears of corn', to clarify
permitted exceptions to the rule of keeping the Sabbath.

265　*mirror*: the mirror would be set in the tiles of the stove.

　　　jib-door: see note to *The Father*, p. 3.

266　*Is Jacob there?*: according to Egil Törnqvist (*Strindbergian Drama: Themes
and Structure*, Stockholm, 1982), 'There is an old Swedish game known as
"Jacob where are you?", in which a blinded person (the master) has to
catch the other (the servant Jacob), assisted by the sounds he receives in
answer to his question: "Jacob, where are you?" When the servant has
been caught, the roles are reversed' (p. 194). The play's second scene is
structured around this game of hide-and-seek and the subsequent reversal
of roles.

267　*Old Nick*: the Devil.

271　*decorated for loyal and faithful service*: it was common practice to honour
servants with the Royal Patriotic Society's medal for long and faithful
service.

　　　Cuban war: the Spanish–American war of 1898 in which Spain lost the
final remnants of its empire (Cuba, Puerto Rico, and the Philippines) to
the United States.

272　*corset*: a *järnliv*, or corset made of leather and framed with iron (*järn*).

273　*secular canoness*: untranslatably, the Colonel describes Hummel's former
fiancée as a *stiftsjungfru*, i.e. an unmarried noblewoman registered in a
diocese (*stift*) as a virgin (*jungfru*) and in receipt of a small pension from
Riddarhuset, the Swedish House of the Nobility.

274　*two false witnesses . . . agree*: see note to *A Dream Play*, p. 237.

276　*It is finished*: an echo of Christ's last words in John 19: 30: 'When Jesus
therefore had received the vinegar, he said, It is finished: and he bowed his
head, and gave up the ghost.'

277　*The sun I saw . . . to be innocent*: a paraphrase of various lines from stanzas 4
and 5 in the medieval Icelandic 'Song of the Sun', the *Sólarljóð*, in Arvid
August Afzelius's translation, *Swenska folkets sagohäfder* (1841), iii. 8 ff.
Strindberg had utilized 'The Song of the Sun' before, in two earlier
plays, *The Saga of the Folkungs* (1899) and *The Crown Bride* (1901). In
the Prelude to the unfinished play *Starkodder the Skald*, written in
Spring 1906, Strindberg also quotes this poem and provides the
music to accompany several of these lines. See *Samlade otryckta skrifter*,
i. 269–70.

278 *On the tiled stove . . . a bulb in its lap*: although Strindberg was familiar with some of the ideas informing Buddhism ('Spent all day reading Buddhism', he notes in the *Occult Diary*, for example, 18 November 1901), and described *The Ghost Sonata* as 'A Buddhist Drama' on one of its alternative title pages, the setting here also has more mundane origins. Among the preparatory notes for the play there is an advertising flier for the Stockholm import firm of Paul Peters which depicts 'a splendid, original ornament', namely, a 16-centimetre-high ivory statue of a seated Buddha at whose feet, on an extension to its base, there is a flowering bulb.

shallot: the reverse of the flier from Paul Peters carries an advertisement for 'one of nature's wonders in the world of flowers', a *Sauromatum venosum*. According to the blurb, this bulb from the Himalayas produces its flower 'without either water or soil', and Buddha and bulb may be acquired for 3 crowns 75. For the play, however, Strindberg specifies not a *Sauromatum venosum* but an *Askalonlök*, or *Allium ascalonicum*, named after the ancient city of Askalon, once situated to the North of Gaza.

279 *the star flowers with their six-pointed petals*: star flowers (*sjärnblommor*) are normally stitchworts, or starworts, thus named because of their starlike flowers or stellately arranged leaves, like the *Stellaria holostea*, or greater stichwort. But as well as botanical accuracy Strindberg is also concerned here with other possible signifiers. Prominent among these is Swedenborg's theory of correspondences, in which there is a normally hidden relationship between material objects in this world, and most particularly the world of nature, and their prototype in the spiritual world, to which they correspond in the manner of a shadowy image. Everything in the natural world is thus an emblem or symbol of a prototype in the spiritual world, although this analogy or correspondence is normally occluded in daily life. However, with the second sight of a Sunday child and the heightened sensibility of his infatuation, the Student is able to perceive these correspondences, and briefly to endow the Young Lady with similar powers of association.

Sirius: the brightest star in the night sky, lying in the constellation Canis Major. Its varying yellow or red hue is accounted for by its low position in the sky, where observation is effected by the density of the earth's atmosphere.

cup: i.e. the perianth or outer part of the flower, consisting of the calyx and corolla.

Yours: up to this point, the Student and the Young Lady have addressed each other in the formal, plural pronoun, *ni*. Here, the affinity of their thoughts encourages them to switch briefly to the intimate form of 'yours', *din*. But they return immediately to the formal *ni* for the rest of the scene, until the Student addresses the dying Young Lady as *du*.

281 *Cor in aethere*: a Latin supplication to 'a heart in the heavens'; an appeal to higher powers.

283 *devil's elixir*: probably an allusion to E. T. A. Hoffmann's novel *Die Elixiere des Teufels* (*The Devil's Elixirs*, 1815). That Strindberg was pre-occupied by Hoffmann at this time is suggested by a letter to Victor Castegren, who had recently directed the première of *A Dream Play*. Writing to him in October 1907, Strindberg observed: 'I was waiting to hear your impression of *The Ghost Sonata*, which you nevertheless ought to see is "theatre", that it looks good, holds together [and] . . . has both action and characters . . . A contemporary fairy-tale or fantasia [*fantasie-stycke*] with modern houses was what I intended (ASB XVII, 150–1). *Fantasiestücke in Callots Manier* (*Fantasias in the Manner of Callot*, 1814–15) was the title of a collection of Hoffmann's short stories much admired by Strindberg.

scorpion-like lettering: refers both to the Japanese lettering on the bottle and to the fact that its contents poison the lives of those who eat the food they adulterate. Strindberg, who attributed some of his own problems at the time of writing *The Ghost Sonata* to the neglect of a series of cooks and maids, was concerned that the passage should make its point in transla-tion. As he reminded Emil Schering: 'Don't forget the Soya-bottle, the colouring, which I've been suffering for thirty days now; eaten coloured water!' (ASB XV, 360).

285 *something very rotten here*: an echo of *Hamlet*, I. iv. 90: 'Something is rotten in the state of Denmark.'

Sursum Corda !: 'Lift up your hearts!'; the introductory words to the Roman Catholic Mass.

the very source of life in you is sick: in his notes for the play Strindberg identifies this sickness as cancer of the womb, but there are indications in the completed text that she may, as Hummel's daughter, be suffering from inherited syphilis. See Hummel's remark to the Student: 'As you see, I'm a cripple. Some say it's my own fault, others blame my parents. To my mind, life itself's to blame, with all its snares . . .'

Lamia: in Greek mythology a woman above the waist and a snake below. She sought to rob mothers of their children, to kill them, or to lure young men away to suck their blood.

and let the robber go: an allusion to Barrabas, though Mark (15: 7) identifies him as a murderer and a rebel rather than a thief.

you: from this point the Student addresses the Young Lady in the intimate, singular prounoun, *du*, rather than the formal, plural *ni*.

286 *that this hope may not maketh ashamed*: cf. Romans 5: 5, 'And hope maketh not ashamed; because the Love of God is shed abroad in our hearts by the Holy Ghost which is given unto us.'

Böcklin's . . . 'The Isle of the Dead': inspired by the volcanic island of Ischia in the Bay of Naples, the Swiss painter Arnold Böcklin (1827–1901) painted five versions of *Toten-Insel* (*The Isle of the Dead*) between 1880 and 1886. Strindberg is referring to the one in the National Gallery in

Berlin, which he had seen during his stay there in 1893. At Strindberg's insistence a copy of this painting was hung on one side of the proscenium in the Intimate Theatre for which *The Ghost Sonata* was written, along with a copy of Böcklin's pendant painting, *The Isle of Life*, on the other. Strindberg envisaged this island on the lines of one of the play's alternative titles, 'Kama Loka', which was, for theosophists, the first resting-place of the soul after death. *Toten-Insel* is also the title of an unfinished chamber play, written shortly after *The Ghost Sonata*.

286 *background*: in a letter to Emil Schering (7 April 1907) Strindberg wondered: 'Don't you think the following could be inserted into the last scene of *The Ghost Sonata*, or made visible in letters of fire above *Toten-Insel*: "And God shall wipe away all tears from their eyes; and there shall be no more death, neither sorrow, nor crying, neither shall there be any more pain (*Leiden*): for the former things have passed away." (*Revelation*, 21: 4)' (SL 2, 738). Although Schering incorporated the direction into his German translation at this point, Strindberg finally reserved the passage for the aborted play *Toten-Insel*.

Six French Poets of the Nineteenth
   Century

HONORÉ DE BALZAC   **Cousin Bette**
Eugénie Grandet
Père Goriot

CHARLES BAUDELAIRE   **The Flowers of Evil**
The Prose Poems and Fanfarlo

BENJAMIN CONSTANT   **Adolphe**

DENIS DIDEROT   **Jacques the Fatalist**
The Nun

ALEXANDRE DUMAS (PÈRE)   **The Black Tulip**
The Count of Monte Cristo
Louise de la Vallière
The Man in the Iron Mask
La Reine Margot
The Three Musketeers
Twenty Years After
The Vicomte de Bragelonne

ALEXANDRE DUMAS (FILS)   **La Dame aux Camélias**

GUSTAVE FLAUBERT   **Madame Bovary**
A Sentimental Education
Three Tales

VICTOR HUGO   **The Essential Victor Hugo**
Notre-Dame de Paris

J.-K. HUYSMANS   **Against Nature**

PIERRE CHODERLOS   **Les Liaisons dangereuses**
DE LACLOS

MME DE LAFAYETTE   **The Princesse de Clèves**

GUILLAUME DU LORRIS   **The Romance of the Rose**
and JEAN DE MEUN

GUY DE MAUPASSANT   A Day in the Country and Other Stories
   A Life
   Bel-Ami
   Mademoiselle Fifi and Other Stories
   Pierre et Jean

PROSPER MÉRIMÉE   Carmen and Other Stories

MOLIÈRE   Don Juan and Other Plays
   The Misanthrope, Tartuffe, and Other
     Plays

BLAISE PASCAL   Pensées and Other Writings

ABBÉ PRÉVOST   Manon Lescaut

JEAN RACINE   Britannicus, Phaedra, and Athaliah

ARTHUR RIMBAUD   Collected Poems

EDMOND ROSTAND   Cyrano de Bergerac

MARQUIS DE SADE   The Crimes of Love
   The Misfortunes of Virtue and Other Early
     Tales

GEORGE SAND   Indiana

MME DE STAËL   Corinne

STENDHAL   The Red and the Black
   The Charterhouse of Parma

PAUL VERLAINE   Selected Poems

JULES VERNE   Around the World in Eighty Days
   Captain Hatteras
   Journey to the Centre of the Earth
   Twenty Thousand Leagues under the Seas

VOLTAIRE   Candide and Other Stories
   Letters concerning the English Nation

Émile Zola

L'Assommoir
The Attack on the Mill
La Bête humaine
La Débâcle
Germinal
The Kill
The Ladies' Paradise
The Masterpiece
Nana
Pot Luck
Thérèse Raquin

The Oxford World's Classics Website

www.worldsclassics.co.uk

- Information about new titles
- Explore the full range of Oxford World's Classics
- Links to other literary sites and the main OUP webpage
- Imaginative competitions, with bookish prizes
- Peruse the Oxford World's Classics Magazine
- Articles by editors
- Extracts from Introductions
- A forum for discussion and feedback on the series
- Special information for teachers and lecturers

www.worldsclassics.co.uk

American Literature

British and Irish Literature

Children's Literature

Classics and Ancient Literature

Colonial Literature

Eastern Literature

European Literature

History

Medieval Literature

Oxford English Drama

Poetry

Philosophy

Politics

Religion

The Oxford Shakespeare

A complete list of Oxford Paperbacks, including Oxford World's Classics, Oxford Shakespeare, Oxford Drama, and Oxford Paperback Reference, is available in the UK from the Academic Division Publicity Department, Oxford University Press, Great Clarendon Street, Oxford OX2 6DP.

In the USA, complete lists are available from the Paperbacks Marketing Manager, Oxford University Press, 198 Madison Avenue, New York, NY 10016.

Oxford Paperbacks are available from all good bookshops. In case of difficulty, customers in the UK can order direct from Oxford University Press Bookshop, Freepost, 116 High Street, Oxford OX1 4BR, enclosing full payment. Please add 10 per cent of published price for postage and packing.